# NICOLEHOLLIS

## CURATED INTERIORS

# NICOLEHOLLIS
## CURATED INTERIORS

By Nicole Hollis
Introduction by Pilar Viladas
Photography by Douglas Friedman and Laure Joliet

**RIZZOLI** NEW YORK

New York · Paris · London · Milan

hold on hold on
on hold hold on
hold on on hold
on hold on hold
hold on hold on
on hold on hold
on hold
on hold on hold
hold on on
hold on on
hold on on hold on
on

off hand
off hand
off hand
off hand
off hand
off hand
off hand
off hand
off hand
off hand
off hand
off hand

*for Lewis, Poppy, and Beckett*

# CONTENTS

# INTRODUCTION

*by Pilar Viladas*

In the years since she founded her design firm in 2003, Nicole Hollis has become known for residential interiors that combine comfort and understated luxury. Her focus is an architectural one: there is no cozy clutter, no riot of color, and no rush to embrace the latest trends. Her preferred color palette is neutral; the tones and textures of furnishings and materials provide a subtle, tactile backdrop for paintings, objects, and pieces, like screens or chandeliers, by the contemporary artists, designers, and artisans with whom Hollis and her office collaborate. Hollis notes that she has "no single style," because her work responds to the architectural context, and for a new house, she is often involved with the architect on decisions regarding the layout and materials. "For us," Hollis says, "the architecture and the interior flow seamlessly," whether the house is contemporary or historic.

On Hawaii's Kona Coast, for example, Hollis worked with Walker Warner Architects to create a serene, contemporary vacation house, the centerpiece of which is a minimalist pavilion—containing living, dining, and kitchen areas—with a spectacular ocean view. The tone of architectural materials is deliberately limited: the wall panels and ceilings are cedar; the floors, both inside and on the terrace beyond, are made of basaltina, a honed-finish basalt; and a single block of Calacatta marble was used for both the kitchen and the master bathroom. Hollis notes that "nothing is precious—it's beautifully made but not fragile." For the master bedroom, the artist Michele Oka Doner designed bronze door handles that are shaped like branches, and a delicate bronze screen in the powder room.

Hollis encountered an entirely different context when the owners of a 1916 Italianate house in San Francisco by the pioneering architect Julia Morgan—who designed William Randolph Hearst's famous castle at San Simeon—asked Hollis to create elegant but comfortable, family-friendly spaces that left the original architecture intact. Hollis says, "We thought of it as an intervention." In the living room, a custom console conceals a television that pops up when in use, then lowers to preserve the view through the original windows. In the dining area, Hollis designed a brass bar cabinet that adds a glamorous, slightly retro touch, in contrast to the room's more minimalist custom table and classic modern chairs. In the master bedroom (originally the house's ballroom), Hollis designed a pair of freestanding brass-clad wardrobes—one for each end of the room—that create warm reflections while accentuating the dialogue between the historic architecture and its contemporary contents. Hollis loves the "challenges of honoring the architecture of a historic house, while making it function for a modern lifestyle," adding that "the house tells you what it wants to be. You have to study it."

Hollis is also adept at working with houses at widely varying scales. In the Marin County town of Tiburon, she designed the interiors of a spacious contemporary house—her first collaboration with Walker Warner Architects—that was commissioned by a couple who are avid collectors of contemporary art, and who wanted a house that could accommodate visits from their families. Hollis created spaces that feel welcoming and intimate, with a palette of warm-toned, natural materials that respect the house's sweeping views of San Francisco Bay. "A lot of my projects have amazing views, and I don't want to compete with them," she says. The interiors provide a backdrop for custom and designer furnishings, as well as dramatic touches like the glowing, silver-nitrate-treated brass panels surrounding the living room fireplace, or the lacy bronze screen, designed by Oka Doner, in the dining room.

At the other end of the scale spectrum, Hollis, in collaboration with the architect Cass Calder Smith, renovated the interiors of a "tiny" 1950s-modern house in Stinson Beach for another couple who collect contemporary art. "It's not about fancy furniture," Hollis says. "It's a comfortable family environment." The exterior facade of gray-painted shingles conceals a series of light-filled spaces, and Hollis painted the interior's cedar paneling white, to create a foil for the mostly colorful works by artists like Tara Donovan, Anne Collier, and Sheila Hicks.

Although Hollis is not a collector—"I'm a little more minimalist," she says—she has long been inspired by twentieth-century and contemporary art. Among her heroes, she names Helen Frankenthaler, Eva Hesse, Richard Serra, and Donald Judd. (Judd's influence can be seen in an elegantly austere wooden bed that Hollis designed for a house in Larkspur, California.) She admires the work of artists like Damien Hirst, Anish Kapoor, and Olafur Eliasson. And Hollis reveres the powerfully abstract sculpture of Constantin Brancusi, whose reconstructed studio she visited as a student, on her first trip to Paris.

In architecture, Hollis's inspiration comes from the work of twentieth-century Modernist masters like Mies van der Rohe, Le Corbusier, and Carlo Scarpa, as well as the furniture designs of Jean Prouvé and Jean Royère. The work of contemporary architects like John Pawson and Peter Bohlin informs Hollis's design approach.

One of Hollis's favorite aspects of her work is collaborating with artists like Michele Oka Doner, and with contemporary designers like Michael Anastassiades, Lindsey Adelman, Bec Brittain, David Wiseman, and Jeff Zimmerman, and the architect and artist Johanna Grawunder. Their work runs the gamut from minimalist to more naturalistic, but shares the power to inspire an "emotional response" in Hollis. "I love to give these people work," she says, "and to see what they do."

Hollis has been fascinated by design since her youth—even when she wasn't consciously aware of it. Growing up in Jupiter, Florida—a "kind of surfer town, with a lot of snowbirds," she says—she would rearrange the furniture in her friends' rooms. "I thought in three dimensions," she explains. But she had started reading fashion magazines as a girl, and always thought that fashion would be her calling. Even at age ten or eleven, Hollis was hoping that she would one day attend the Fashion Institute of Technology in New York, the renowned school that has produced designers like Calvin Klein, the late Isabel Toledo, and Ralph Rucci.

But by the time she was in high school, Hollis began to think seriously about interior design, and "the idea that people could hire someone to design their homes," she recalls. Her interest was further piqued by a job she had, at a fashion store in Palm Beach, that involved delivering clothing to clients at their houses, which helped her to "understand what they liked," she says. "I felt that I could understand and predict people's needs, something that serves me well as an interior designer." Another job, at an antiques store in Jupiter that had its own wood shop, taught Hollis about how furniture was designed and built, and she also learned about styling and how to arrange things in a room.

During this time, Hollis would spend summers in New Jersey with her family, and made frequent trips to New York City, where she visited the Museum of Modern Art, and studied the period rooms at the Metropolitan Museum of Art, which "made me appreciate the history of design. I didn't want to replicate them, but I was inspired by them," Hollis recalls. She did, as she had hoped, attend FIT, but with a focus beyond fashion. As part of a school-sponsored program, she spent a summer in Paris studying the history of architecture and interiors, as well as fashion.

Hollis visited the Centre Pompidou and the reconstructed studio of Constantin Brancusi, whose work she finds endlessly inspiring. She visited the workshops of Hermès and Lanvin, sketched historic furniture at the Louvre, saw the work of the Italian architect and designer Gio Ponti at the Musée des Arts Decoratifs, and admired the furniture and interiors of Jean-Michel Frank. His sense of "minimalist luxury," Hollis says, "formed my personal style." For Hollis, who is dyslexic, doing this "visual research" was a revelation. Multiple-choice test questions were daunting, but "when they said to draw the interior of a château, I could do it." These exercises served her well. "I was always the last one in the group to move along," she recalls. "I needed longer to take it in, study it, sketch it. But I'm fascinated by craft, and my job is to explain to the client the value of craft."

Ultimately, Hollis realized that her true interest was in a "minimalist, architectural" brand of interior design. She was more attracted to the notions of scale, symmetry, and detail than to the idea of decorating. While she was at FIT, she started working for James D'Auria, an architect known for designing retail stores and fashion showrooms in addition to his residential work. Learning about architecture, and having architects critique her work, proved invaluable.

In the late 1990s, Hollis moved to San Francisco. She worked for Starwood Hotels & Resorts' W Design Group for a year and a half, and admired the company's "overall cohesive brand design." After that, she went to work for the Napa Valley-based architect Howard Backen, a founding partner of the firm now called Backen & Gillam, who is known for designing some of the region's leading wineries and houses for a celebrity clientele. Hollis calls Backen "a great mentor; he had the ability to bring out the best in people." She stayed for five years, at which point her husband, Lewis Heathcote, suggested that she start her own firm.

"I had to start from the ground up," Hollis recalls. "I went from working with Robert Redford to doing house renovations. But one project led to another—it has just been a slow burn." Back then, along with some former Starwood colleagues, Hollis began working on hotels and resorts, which her firm continues to do—in places like Georgia, California, and Hawaii—with its in-house hospitality design studio, in addition to the firm's residential work, which makes up the bulk of its extensive portfolio.

"I never worried about making money or having a big office—it was important to maintain design integrity," Hollis says. But she has excelled at both. The office, which started out with twelve people, now numbers around ninety, and Heathcote, a software consultant, became its CEO in 2014, allowing Hollis to stay focused on the firm's clients. The fact that the firm also includes a studio devoted to interior architecture gives it a distinct advantage, Hollis says, by making it easier to coordinate with architects on a project. In addition to her residential work, Hollis has also designed a collection of seating and tables for McGuire Furniture, lighting for Phoenix Day, and a one-of-a-kind lounge chair for *The Chair,* a 2019 exhibition at The Future Perfect, which featured the work of more than forty designers and artists. According to Hollis's collaborative method of design, "The best idea wins—it doesn't matter if it comes from an intern," she says.

This collaborative approach, Hollis says, is also part of the reason that the firm has so many repeat clients, and returns periodically to their homes to make minor tweaks, especially as a family grows or changes. When meeting a client for the first time, Hollis says, "We talk about how they live—and not just about function, but about how a house feels." She believes that the amount of time spent with a client is crucial, especially in an age where so much communication is electronic. "Email and teleconferencing just don't create the same connection," she says. "I can tell if a client likes something I've shown them by their body language, even before they say it." If they don't like something, Hollis believes in knowing when to back down. "It's important not to be in love with your own design," she warns. But she also knows when to press for something she feels is important, because ultimately, she wants to exceed the client's expectations—and to persuade them to take risks. "I try to be a guiding force," she adds.

Given her years of experience working for and with architects, it's no surprise that Hollis approaches a project by looking at "flow, light, finishes, and materials," as she explains. "It gives me the ability not to 'cover up' the architecture, but to compliment it. I'm drawn to nature, texture, and craft. I like the imperfect, and I like working with artists and makers, and having personal conversations with them, so that there's a story behind every piece. We have things made more often than we buy them, so that we can create pieces that are specific to the house or client." Hollis describes her own style as "very restrained," but when a client's vision is not, she focuses on "communicating the client's dreams and aspirations," and helping them "identify and develop their style."

Hollis often starts by asking about a client's favorite artists or fashion designers, preferences that tell her a lot, for example, about whether they favor darker or lighter interiors. In her initial presentations, Hollis employs mood boards that are more conceptual, like the one that was based on the egg colors of a client's chickens. Later in the process, she shows boards with furniture, finishes, or details to get the client's feedback. "We educate clients about value and quality," Hollis says. The fact that her firm is knowledgeable about construction, schedules, and budgets, and "takes the business side seriously" makes it a hybrid, she says, "we can draw the lacquer room, and build the lacquer room."

A designer's own home usually offers the purest illustration of his or her philosophy, and Hollis's own house in San Francisco, which she shares with Heathcote and their two children, is no exception. Although many of her clients are extremely wealthy, Hollis, unlike some of her peers, does not aspire to live like them. Her house is a rather modest wood-frame Victorian building that was bought and remodeled in the 1920s by—in a happy coincidence—Julia Morgan, who lived there until her death in 1957. Hollis and Heathcote renovated the house to make it more family-friendly, adding a lower story that contains a garage and a master bedroom and bathroom, and restoring a stairway from the front door to the street, which Morgan had removed. They painted the exterior black.

The first floor has children's bedrooms at the front and back, and in between is an open, warm space that contains a living area with a black marble fireplace, a dining area with a hanging light fixture by Michael Anastassiades, and a kitchen with a black island opposite a wall of cabinets that can disappear behind white pocket doors. "We spend ninety-five percent of our time in this room," Hollis notes. While she honored the house's historic details, replicating its crown moldings and baseboards, keeping the original doors, and using reclaimed wood for the new floors, Hollis wanted a "relaxed-modern" feeling for the interiors. In addition to creating the open family space, she used both classic-modern designs and contemporary pieces by designers she admires. "The pieces I do want to own are very personal," she says, like the master bedroom's solid walnut headboard and bedside tables, which were carved by the artist Ido Yoshimoto. The second floor contains a guest suite, a family/media room, and a small gym.

Hollis enjoys this rather cozy domestic arrangement. "Living simply is good," she says. "It's not about 'bigger is better.' It's a modern way of life—not a style—and a state of mind." And whether the house she's designing is a cottage or a palace, Hollis's approach guarantees that it will always feel like home.

PROJECTS

# RUSSIAN HILL

*San Francisco*

Reimagining, reinventing, and reprogramming historic homes is not for the fainthearted. "Respecting the architecture" has become a cliché, but my studio's interior architects have gained exceptional experience working in classical architecture, which is a prerequisite to be able to both transform and restore the intent of an historic residence.

This wonderfully creative and well-traveled young family decided to leave a Los Angeles suburb to live an urban lifestyle in San Francisco. They purchased this architecturally significant three-bedroom family residence, which sits atop Russian Hill, in no small part for its central location, as well as its potential to be renovated into an enveloping family home with enough space for cooking, climbing, and cars—their three main interests.

The original John Bricknell Victorian was built in 1866 and, in 1916, transformed into a classic Italianate townhouse by famous San Francisco architect Julia Morgan for prominent art importer David Atkins. Once the home of designer Anthony Hail, the challenge lay in how to transform the elegant but small rooms into a home that felt spacious and current.

The project involved a three-year full remodel in which the building was seismically upgraded and carefully installed with twenty-first century amenities. The renovation preserved the home's myriad original details, including moldings and fireplaces, and emphasized the expansive windows, natural light, and large backyard. After removing a wall, the kitchen now opens into the living room, creating a multifunctional living area ideal for entertaining, as well as casual meals and homework. A new lower level comprises a new staircase, family room, guest room, guest bath, wine room, and a "gear room," which includes custom shelving for colorful mountaineering equipment and a reclaimed black steel cabinet by La Cornue.

The second floor's ballroom was transformed into the master bedroom, which preserved the original character of the space with herringbone flooring and Victorian moldings. We installed two tall custom-designed mirror-polished brass cabinets to house his-and-hers wardrobes floating on each side of the room. The master bath features a double vanity, brass fixtures, and custom wallpaper with an historical etching of Yosemite blown up to grand scale by artist Yedda Morrison.

I've spent many glorious hours before, during, and following the completion of this residence. Its juxtaposed beauty is reflective in the family's joyous ease of living in an elegant yet comfortable and intimate home.

# DIVISADERO
*San Francisco*

In 2012, while looking for a new home, my husband and I toured an Italianate-Victorian that had once been owned by renowned San Francisco architect Julia Morgan. Both thrilled and overwhelmed to purchase this special property, we knew this outdated two-story home was in need of a complete remodel.

We began by removing the front retaining wall and excavating a new garage and master bedroom suite on the lower level. We removed several walls, a small bathroom, and a brick fireplace located in the center of the living room to create a spacious floor plan. The new space allowed us to design an open kitchen with a large custom Nero Marquina marble island, a dining area with natural light, and a cozy sitting area positioned in front of a custom marble surround fireplace. The newly excavated master suite was designed with our beautifully landscaped garden in mind. I wanted to create a tranquil space that offered a view to the garden, whether enjoyed while soaking in the freestanding tub or relaxing on the reclaimed walnut bed.

We felt it was important to restore many of the original details. The mounding profiles, carved doors, and moldings still remain and often remind me of Morgan's imprint on the design world. For the flooring throughout the house, we selected a reclaimed oak sourced from an old barn in Tennessee. I love the way the rustic wood contrasts with the modern cabinetry and classical details, creating tension in the spaces.

We took a mindful approach when selecting furnishings and art, finding pieces with personal or special connections to us, slowly building our collection over time. I met Michael Anastassiades several years ago and have always admired his minimal yet commanding aesthetic. Using his lighting throughout the house has a calming sculptural effect. The master bedroom headboard and bedside tables were carved from California coast reclaimed walnut by Ido Yoshimoto, a self-taught woodworker who embodies organic minimalism. I have had the pleasure of working with David Wiseman on several custom commissions for my clients over the years. I was thrilled to add one of David's pieces in the form of an owl watching over us. I was introduced to Ralph Pucci when I started my career in interior design, and years later we selected a custom-sized Patrick Naggar sofa for the sitting room. Complementing the sofa is a sculptural brass table by Mauro Mori, whom I met through my friend Melanie Courbet, the owner of Les Ateliers Courbet, who has an exceptional eye for design and craft.

The artwork throughout was collected slowly through friends and artists with a focus in modern art by black artists. I worked with Andrew McClintock from Ever Gold [Projects] to source several pieces including *Troy Lee*, 2019, by Shaina McCoy, *Triple Samurai (Kuniyoshi)*, 2018, by Kour Pour, and *The Edge of Form: Projective Identifications,* 2019, by Zio Ziegler. My friend Jessica Silverman, owner of Jessica Silverman Gallery, helped me find an incredible Isaac Julien triptych, *Baltimore Series (Street Life/Still Life)*, 2003. My sister, Tanya Hollis, created a highly textural piece from her *PARCH Series, Untitled*, 2015, which hangs in the media room.

Never a day goes by when I don't stop to think about what went into making this house our home. As I watch my family grow up in a house that is perfectly suited to us, I am reminded of the reasons why I design uniquely personal homes for my clients.

# PRESIDIO

*San Francisco*

One of my first significant projects after founding NICOLEHOLLIS was a remodel in San Francisco for a young finance professional. Born in Tokyo to European parents, he formed a great appreciation for both Japanese and European design. He requested a minimal modern home where he could live comfortably as a bachelor, entertain guests, and accommodate the occasional large event.

The two-story California ranch-style home had been previously remodeled before the new owner acquired it. When we first spoke, he asked for design assistance in furnishing the house, but before long we were in the midst of a major remodel. We began to look closer at the function and flow of the house, along with the quality of the finishes. Incrementally we began to strip back the layers and reduced the number of materials in order to achieve the minimalism that he requested.

Relocating the master bedroom and bathroom to the lower level allowed for a more expansive main kitchen, with an added catering kitchen and connecting family room. The living room and dining room were initially divided by a fireplace that made the space feel confined. The original fireplace was removed, and a new eight-foot-long gas fireplace was installed on the west wall, allowing the dining and living rooms to become one large great room for entertaining. The existing bamboo flooring and wall-to-wall carpet were removed and replaced with European white oak boards to create a continuous floor throughout the entire house.

After several years in the house, his life changed; newly married and now with two young daughters, he wanted the home to be adapted for family living and gatherings. The recent addition of the girls' bedroom, home theater, and office have all remained within the original spirit of the design. Through many phases of their lives, I have been fortunate enough to witness the growth and evolution of this loving family and their home.

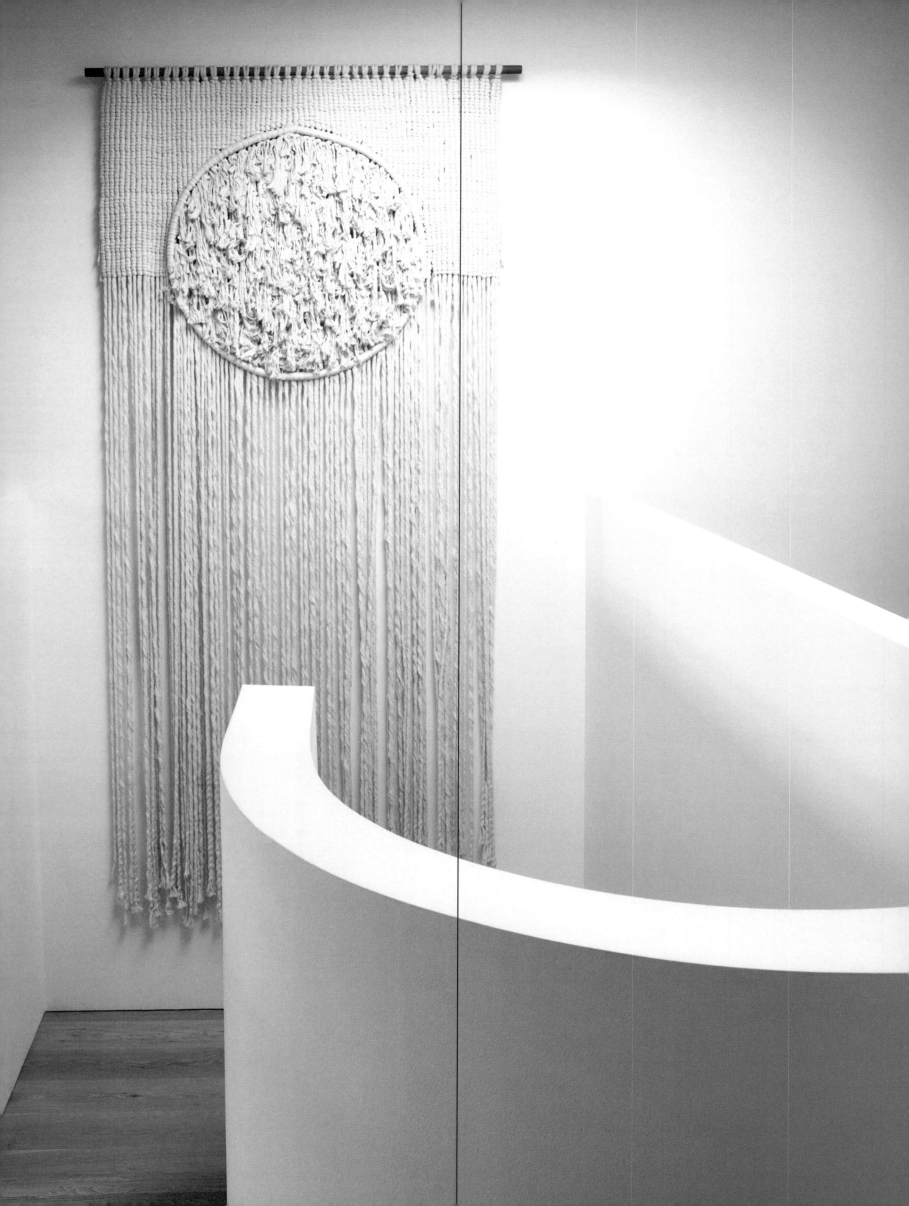

# PACIFIC HEIGHTS

*San Francisco*

I have been lucky enough to make many connections with young families who give deep thought to the value of design in their lives. Our clients with children, from babies to high schoolers, far outweigh any other demographic. I personally wade through parenthood together with certain clients trying to find balance and perspective. These relationships often evolve through the months and years it takes us to design their ideal home.

I instantly connected with a European entrepreneur and his Californian wife with a toddler and one-on-the-way who purchased this light-filled Queen Anne–style home in the Pacific Heights neighborhood with views of the San Francisco Bay. Just a block away from Alta Plaza Park, this traditional Victorian was built by architect Samuel Newsom in 1889. With its asymmetrical facade and curved bay windows, it embodies the quintessential San Francisco aesthetic, which has previously made it the perfect backdrop for a feature film and television pilot. It also caught the eye of Meg Ryan and Dennis Quaid, who owned the property during the 1990s.

Local architect Tim Murphy was brought in to breathe new life into all four stories to accommodate their entertaining and lifestyle needs. The redesign resulted in a gut renovation that continued for the next four years. Not a single surface was left untouched, but the clients made sure to retain many of the original details like the thick crown molding that hovers over each room. As part of its modern reinterpretation, the house acquired a new kitchen, family room, master bedroom, and upstairs lounge. The owners approached us to upgrade the house with custom furnishings and interior finishes that would sustain the wear and tear of toddlers, golden retrievers, and frequent visits from friends and family.

The result was a top-to-bottom transformation incorporating the client's youthful stylish aesthetic with functional materials and furniture layouts. In the formal living room a show-stopping Barnaby Barford mirror is perched above a custom black marble fireplace surround. The newly relocated dining room opens into a family room and an adjoining kitchen with stunning views just beyond the Vitrocsa sliding glass doors. The expansive master bedroom is an ode to the wife and mother's feminine sensibility with its dusty lavender palette and luxurious materials. A curved sofa by India Mahdavi and porcelain artwork by Fenella Elms contribute to the softness of the room. In contrast, an upstairs lounge embodies a much more masculine atmosphere with a vintage pair of Fritz Hansen chairs reupholstered in a deep green alpaca fabric and walls coated in a muted charcoal.

To accommodate the family's functional needs, we designed several custom pieces like the T. H. Robsjohn-Gibbings–inspired cabinet in the dining room, which opens into a full bar with glass shelving and pull-out drawers. A custom leather upholstered ottoman contains just enough padding at the corners to make it kid friendly, while the boy's bedroom features a custom full-size daybed with a pull-out trundle bed that's intended to be grown into. Unique artworks throughout the house were sourced from various San Francisco–based galleries, including a photograph by John Chiara and a painting by JMary from Almond & Co.

This home feels both ageless yet appropriate for the young family beginning their life's journey.

Peter
Lindbergh

A Different
Vision on Fashion
Photography

TASCHEN

KIEFER    RODIN

BORAGÓ    Rodolfo Guzmán

# NOB HILL
*San Francisco*

Designing a pied-à-terre is a challenge in creating something both personal and purposeful. As it is not a primary residence, many important decisions are required to design a temporary home that feels comfortable and unique, either for numerous guests or long stretches of quiet relaxation.

I met this recently retired tech executive with his young family several years ago, while they were relocating from the Bay Area to the mountains. To retain a connection to San Francisco, they chose to work with us to create a beautiful two-bedroom urban haven with classical plasterwork and dramatic bay views of the Palace of Fine Arts and the Golden Gate Bridge.

Looking to create a home that offers a careful balance of elegance and informality, we devised a neutral canvas to highlight the skyline while showcasing their love of mid-century modern design and contemporary artisanship.

Iconic mid-century pieces, including a Frank Gehry *Wiggle* chair, a Hans Wegner *Papa Bear* chair, and an Eero Saarinen table, anchor the space and mix with modern light fixtures and artwork by up-and-coming artists such as Christopher Badger, Robert Kingston, and Bernadette Jiyong Frank.

Creating a few areas to gather with family and friends, we installed a custom-designed breakfast nook in the kitchen and a hemlock dining table focused on the dramatic views. As the sun sets and the shadows lengthen, the mood changes, with lights dotting the slopes of Nob Hill, revealing a different view of this mysterious city.

# BROADWAY

*San Francisco*

We've built our studio to sustain the pressure of large-scale residential projects, which include complex renovations of historic buildings and ground-up construction with unique material selections. But sometimes we choose to work on rapid, smaller-scale projects that clients have an urgent need to move into but also a clear desire to live in a beautiful home.

In this instance, a young family, recently relocated from Asia, asked me to create a beautiful pied-à-terre in San Francisco's Pacific Heights neighborhood within a short time span. In 2013, they purchased this private co-op in a classic 1920s residential building with sweeping views of the San Francisco Bay. Over the next six months, we worked together to create a space that would effortlessly host guests and showcase their world-class collection of contemporary Asian art and digital photography.

When I first saw the apartment, I noticed its solid bones and ornate moldings, but the floor plan was jumbled and the rooms were dim, requiring clear thought on how to maximize space while retaining the building's integrity and respecting the architecture. To take advantage of the skyline views and highlight the client's art collection, we worked with Walker Warner Architects to open up the kitchen, dining, and living areas. A corner guestroom was converted into a study with glass doors, which now flows into the main living and dining room spaces.

To further unify the interior, a clean palette of off-white walls was paired with smoky, refinished original wood flooring. At the focal point of the newly expanded central living area is a luxurious new fireplace with a surround in black Nero Marquina marble. The renovated kitchen includes an expanded breakfast nook, Calacatta marble countertops, and glass-front custom cabinetry painted in Farrow & Ball's *All Black*. Adding to the owners original furniture collection we selected refined pieces, including a mirrored dresser by Luis Pons in the master bedroom, a custom dining banquette, and a custom dining table for formal entertaining.

# THOUSAND OAKS
## *California*

Occasionally, you meet people with whom you feel a special kinship. As you become acquainted, you realize you have so much in common that ideas simply roll back and forth, and it is easy to forget who actually came up with them in the first place. Sometimes design is a stream of consciousness in which we organically discover something unique and beautiful. This family, this home, and this moment embodied all these truths.

I had recently designed a beautiful new residence in Hawaii with this family of five—they so enjoyed the place that they extended their visits as long and as often as possible. They kept returning to their Los Angeles home reflecting on how they had outgrown it in many ways, and realized it was time to create a home in which they could raise teenagers and prepare their family for the next phase of life. They chose a site in Thousand Oaks, California, where they envisioned a home with the heart of a modern farmhouse. Collaborating with architects Rios Clementi Hale Studios, we designed a light-filled home to embrace indoor-outdoor living with soaring ceilings, steel-frame windows, and a series of interconnected patios with alfresco seating and entertaining areas.

We worked very closely with the clients to devise an integrated, layered, and refined design that supported their lifestyle and interest in entertaining. The dusty pale jade color of an egg from one of the family's Araucana chickens established the muted materials palette. The nuanced interiors highlight the clients' art collection with works by Richard Serra, Damien Hirst, and Ed Ruscha, as well as up-and-coming West Coast artists.

The great room is centered on the first floor and encompasses the kitchen, dining area, and living room. The large space was designed to bring family and friends together, but when a quiet moment is needed, adjoining wings offer different areas to wind down. One wing includes a bar and lounge for enjoying drinks and cigars, a home theater, and the children's bedrooms, which channel their distinct personalities. The serene master suite sits at the other end overlooking the backyard and the Santa Monica Mountains.

This home truly represents everything about the family and is constantly filled with warmth, laughter, and light.

# KUA BAY

*Hawaii*

George Orwell wrote that "the best books ... are those that tell you what you know already." Often the client, design team, or project truly inspires me to strive for the unimagined. However, at other times it is the environment that shapes the design, as if it had been there all along.

While searching for a stretch of rugged coastline north of Kona to build their ultimate getaway, this inspiring, California-based family discovered a site with a volcanic rock formation that had proven disconcerting to other potential buyers. Despite the site's incredible, dramatic views of Kua Bay, the lava flow would prove challenging when designing a modern, minimal six-bedroom residence for entertaining, extended getaways, and down-to-earth, easy living for kids. A clear statement of the clients' intent was to create a space versatile enough be able to sit anywhere in a wet bathing suit yet feel refined enough to host elegant chef-prepared events.

Fortunately, the clients had selected their team wisely. We worked with Walker Warner Architects and landscape architects Lutsko Associates to envision and create a beautiful home that would nestle perfectly into the landscape. With an eye toward refined lines and exquisite detailing, we created a holistic interior scheme inspired by the juxtaposed

tranquility and movement of the surroundings. The materials palette includes rustic jute and rope, lush linens, hand-carved marble, warm metals, and ebonized woods.

While the floor-to-ceiling sliding doors open to dramatic vistas, it is also clear that this home does not rely entirely on its incredible views. There are quiet moments such as the guest bedroom facing a calm water feature carved into the lava, which is a place of unexpected, serene beauty. The clients desired a curated environment anchored by special, highly personalized pieces such as the master bedroom's haute couture-inspired custom bed. The master bathroom contains a vanity and drawers that were hand-carved in Italy from a single piece of marble. Found throughout the property are bronze-cast, branch-shaped door handles by artist Michele Oka Doner, who also created a floor-to-ceiling cast-bronze hand-polished screen for the powder room.

During the project, I visited and collaborated with world-renowned artisans to create one-of-a-kind pieces, including custom light fixtures by Hervé Van der Straeten and Lindsey Adelman, furnishings by Christian Liaigre, Christian Astuguevieille, and numerous others, to complete a home that is comfortably luxurious.

LESLIE WILLIAMSON

# KAKAPA BAY
*Hawaii*

I reflect on this project—a turning point in my firm's growth—with pride, pleasure, and immense gratitude. I will always owe a great debt to these clients, who, during the Recession of 2008, took a chance on a plucky young design firm that had never worked in Hawaii. In the initial interview I stated that I wanted to veer away from the expected and collaborate on something that felt truly Hawaiian but also never before seen. After the interview, they left my studio and called minutes later to ask if I wanted to jump on this ride with them. I will never forget the trust they placed in me, and it has inspired me to offer others the opportunity to prove their potential.

An L.A.-based couple purchased a lot on the Kona Coast of Hawaii to build a new home for their family of five. Having explored the coast in his youth, the husband wanted to share his love of the island with his family, and his wife, an architect by training, was clear in her desire to build a house with a modern interpretation of Hawaiian design. They envisioned clean lines, an open layout, and furniture curated carefully according to specific needs and sense of purpose.

The home is set on a lava field, some yards back from the beach, a lot selected specifically for its incredible views as well as being shielded from the Pacific Ocean's potent force. This unique, custom-built residence reimagines a Hawaiian sanctuary with an unexpected, integrated, and completely modern design. A traditional Hawaiian open-plan hale (house) scheme, consisting of seven separate pavilions, is transformed into a contemporary amalgamation of rich texture, tone, and surface.

Embracing the site's context, the materials palette underscores deep elemental ties incorporating lava-basalt floor tiles and coral wall blocks. Collaborations include lighting by the artist Michele Oka Doner, who employs the shape of branches from the property's indigenous kiawe tree to explore the volcanic isles' verdant nature. This distinctive home encapsulates a poetic ode to the rugged Kona Coast and the beloved beach culture of its owners.

# KAHUWAI BAY

*Hawaii*

Through the years, I've been fortunate enough to work with clients who share my appreciation for the design process. Fortunate because it can be rare to find people willing to take the time to think and rethink key elements until they feel perfectly in place. This had certainly been the case for a dynamic California-based couple looking to create a unique getaway on the Kona Coast of the island of Hawaii.

In collaboration with Greg Warner of Walker Warner Architects, we created a serene four-bedroom family retreat located on black lava flow dating back to the 1801 eruption that flowed from the volcano Hualalai directly into the Pacific Ocean—paving the way for a site that is romantic and rugged. With expansive windows and doors that open directly to the ocean beyond, the main building, or hale, showcases a stunning view of the Pacific where one can hear the whales and dolphins passing. Walker Warner Architects took cues from the area's rugged, exposed landscape when selecting the materials palette. Textural coral wall blocks, rich cedar wood, and sandstone floors were the key elements used throughout the design of each hale and outdoor space.

With a focus on the endurance of craft, the interiors feature a highly curated array of refined furnishings, including numerous custom designed and fabricated pieces. Without unnecessary decoration or ornament, the rooms are minimally outfitted for guests, allowing a direct connection to the surroundings. Shade material was encased in the rolling doors to avoid the need for window treatments.

This beautifully restrained Hawaiian residence offers family and guests the most inspiring moments of raw Pacific power, with waves throwing white coral across the volcanic rock. The interiors are considered a backdrop to this incredible home on the eastern edge of the Big Island.

# TIBURON
## *California*

I knew when I met this young family relocating from Hong Kong that our creative relationship would be both rewarding and enduring. Having purchased an incredible lot on the Tiburon hillside with wide-ranging views of the San Francisco Bay, they were focused on creating a home with great balance between intimacy and the need for solitude and quiet. They wanted to present their exceptional Asian art collection, but they also wished for their home to feel relaxed and comfortable for large family gatherings. The house needed to feel the warmth of a smaller space but be expansive enough to include separate corners for grandparents and guests.

Working with Brooks Walker of Walker Warner Architects and landscape architect Todd Cole, we took cues from the clients' worldly sophistication, minimalist sensibilities, and the site's unique location to create an environment that embraces the essence of San Francisco—glimmering water views and the beauty of the Northern California landscape.

Collaborating with the clients on every detail, we crafted a wholly integrated, intensely personal interior environment that connected seamlessly with the stunning architecture and landscape. Basing our design approach on rigorous materials exploration, we devised an expressive vocabulary of rich finishes, custom touches, and unparalleled artisanship. Additionally, the highly edited interior spaces provide an essential showcase for the client's world-class art collection, including

works by Candida Höfer, Richard Misrach, Robert Rauschenberg, Li Songsong, and Zhang Huan.

Emphasizing the design goals of the project, we commissioned an extraordinary two-ton bronze interior screen from Michele Oka Doner. This immense structural artwork acts to anchor the space, making an ambitious creative statement and setting the tone for the compelling interior scheme. Crafting an environment that would emphasize artistic achievement, we worked in-depth with flow and a floor plan highlighting fifteen feature walls for artwork with an intense focus on space planning, curation, and functional necessity.

We relied on the juxtaposition of striking, innovative materials to weave the design narrative, including white oak flooring, laminated glass panels, limestone countertops, and stunning silver nitrate panels for the entry and fireplaces. An original gilded mural for the interior powder room was commissioned from artist Mariko Jesse. Due to the high degree of specialization within the design, we customized furnishings with the highest degree of artisanship, including fine cabinetry throughout the home as well as beds, desks, case goods, and shelving.

What I love most about this residence is that it reflects this family's incredible compassion. Every design decision has been considered in order to enrich the lives of the inhabitants, family, and visitors in a way that is personal and inspiring.

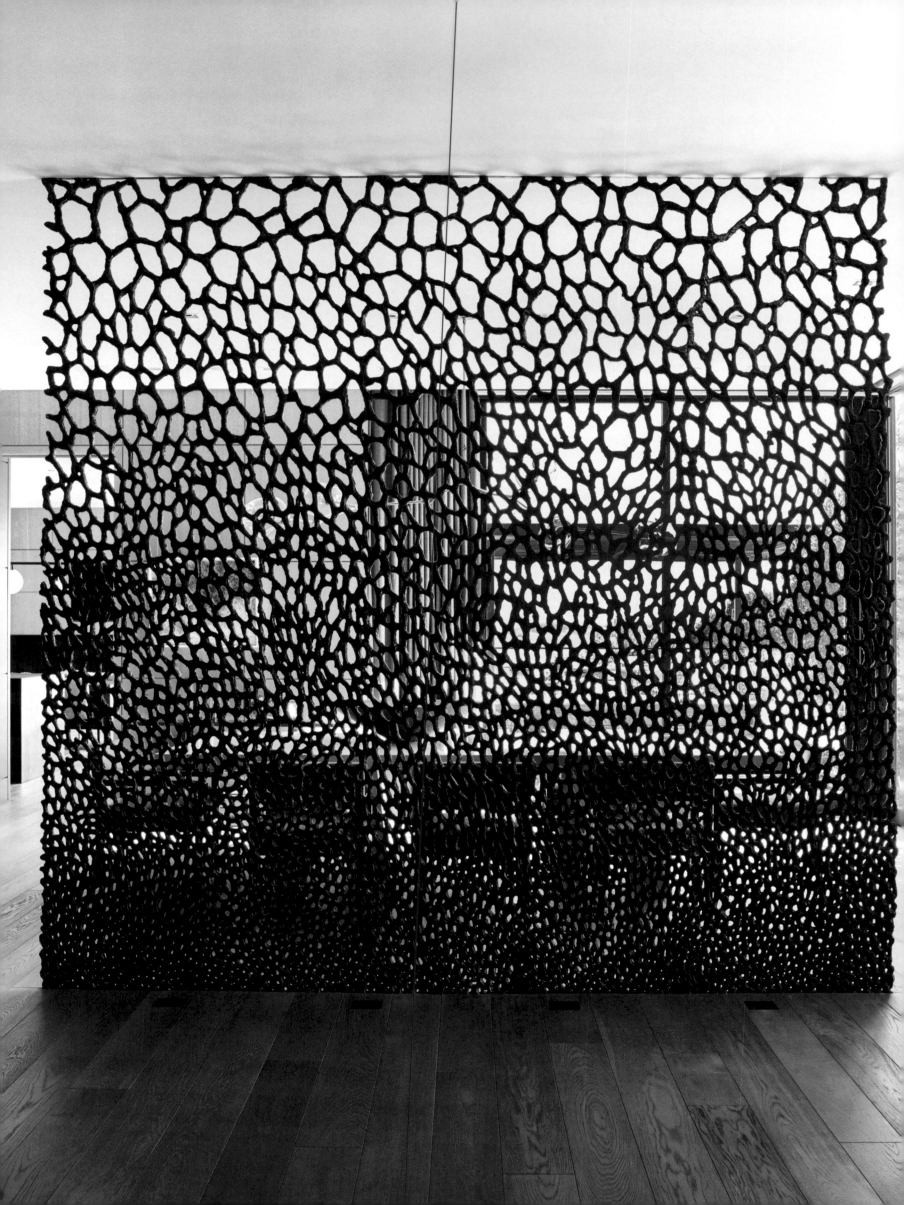

# LARKSPUR
*California*

A brilliant advertising executive, his creative wife, and their young family had been collaborating with Jensen Architects for five years to create a minimalist structure on a unique property when they asked us to help furnish the interiors of their new home. Nestled into the Marin hillside, with stunning views of Mount Tam and the San Francisco Bay, the remarkable residence consisted of a series of floating planes that opened to the landscape and blurred the lines between indoors and out.

Inspired by Jensen's beautifully clean structure, my focus was to curate a highly edited collection of furniture that would bring a sense of comfort and personal history to their residence. After learning the family was leaving a larger, more antiquated house for something minimal, I knew that paring down was to be an essential part of the design process. We designed two large-scale custom pieces to provide the anchors for the upstairs: a sofa banquette for the dining area and a large sectional sofa for the living space. Chaise longues and bright ceramic side tables punctuate the pool and deck. In the downstairs master bedroom, we designed a custom white oak master bed.

Moments of whimsy and beauty are found throughout the home, including a cobalt-blue rope chair by Christian Astuguevieille and an oversize coffee table made of recycled black rubber tire treads. Floor-to-ceiling sheer white linen curtains delineate the main living areas and open completely to the outside, creating a gossamer glow at sunset. Natural finishes, such as white oak and concrete, further emphasize indoor-outdoor living.

# STINSON BEACH
## *California*

Stinson Beach, California, is a small beach town located in Marin County about thirty-five minutes from the Golden Gate Bridge. Known for its scenic views of the headlands and its wide-open beaches, it is a community of surfers, artists, poets, and musicians. It has been a home to such creatives as Jerry Garcia, Steve Miller, and James Grant, as well as architect Joseph Esherick of Sea Ranch fame. It's been said that Janis Joplin's ashes were scattered there.

When I was asked by a family of notable art collectors with four sons to collaborate with them and the architect to renovate a small cottage on the lagoon into a family retreat, it was a unique opportunity to weave the modern with the nostalgic. I was instantly attracted to this project, which, at 2,200 square feet was small by our studio's typical standards. This family is both adventurous yet home-loving. They wanted a weekend getaway where they could launch kayaks and casually entertain friends while surrounded by great art and custom furnishings.

This particular location offers a range of microclimates in one day. The mornings can be moody and fog filled, but the fog burns off by midday to allow afternoons at the beach. Once the sun sets, the clear nights grow chilly, encouraging gatherings around the firepit.

The clients have filled the cottage with works by Tara Donovan, Sheila Hicks, and George Nakashima. A mix of modern and mid-century furnishings and lighting complement the art collection and give the cottage an approachable lived-in feel that reflects its surroundings.

The newly remodeled kitchen anchors the property with its connection to the interior courtyard with firepit seating and the lagoon-facing deck with a large dining table and matching benches. The master bedroom and guest bedroom are paired down with large windows showcasing expansive views outside. A double bunk room with built-in closets was designed to accommodate four growing, energetic boys.

This beautiful weekend home on the edge of a lagoon combines purpose, fun, and serenity and is ideally suited for this spirited and affable family.

*Thank you to the incredible architects, builders, artists,*
*and craftspeople who have collaborated on the projects featured in this book.*
*I also want to acknowledge the many talented professionals in my studio*
*who have dedicated their passion and skill to make these projects a reality.*
*Finally, I am deeply grateful to my clients for their trust and friendship.*

*Nicole Hollis*

**4** Custom media cabinet by NICOLEHOLLIS, fabricated by Miriam Dym and Chambers Art & Design
**6** Custom sconce by Kevin Reily
**12** *Untitled*, 2015, by Bernadette Jiyong Frank

## RUSSIAN HILL

**16 & 17** *Vauban Sofa* by Christian Liaigre; *Contour Low Back Lounge Chair* by Vladimir Kagan; *Joe Colombo 4801 Armchair* by Joe Colombo; *Chester Moon Pouf* by Paola Navone; *Monolith Side Table* by Kelly Wearstler; *Atollo Table Lamp* by Vico Magistretti for Oluce
**18** *SHY 18* by Bec Brittain; *Conche Wall Sconce* by Serge Mouille; *Tetragonn Construction* by Christopher Badger
**19** *Tall Stool* by Sawkille Co.; *SHY 17* by Bec Brittain
**20 & 21** Custom brass bar cabinet by NICOLEHOLLIS, fabricated by Custom Furniture Design; *Air Sofa* for Luteca; Custom dining table by NICOLEHOLLIS, fabricated by Custom Furniture Design; *CH24 Wishbone Chair* by Hans Wegner
**22** *Light Socket* by Commune; *Italian Modernist* mirror brass frame, circa 1960, from 1stdibs; *Hope* wallpaper by Damien Hirst
**23** *Sculpture Chairs* by Preben Fabricius & Jorgen Kastholm; Vintage *Spider Table Lamp* by Joe Colombo; *Boom Chandelier* by Stickbulb; *Head Trip* rug by Eddy Bogaert for Marc Phillips; *Manila Hemp* wallcovering by Phillip Jeffries; *Themes*, 2013, C-Print by Matt Lipps
**24** *Joe Colombo 4801 Armchair* by Joe Colombo; *Untitled*, 2005, by Lyla Trollope
**25** *Helix Hanging* pendant by Bec Brittain; *Guise Series*, 2007, by Deborah Oropallo
**26 & 27** Custom floating brass wardrobe cabinets by NICOLEHOLLIS; *Bergere Bed* by Autoban; Custom *Niguel Side Table* by Lawsen-Fenning; *Maxhedron* pendant by Bec Brittain
**28** *Stingray Stool* by Michael Boyd
**29** *The Serpentine Tub* by Drummonds; *Henry* tub filler by Waterworks; *Ball Light* by Michael Anastassiades; Custom wall covering from vintage engraving of Yosemite National Park by Yedda Morrison

## DIVISADERO

**32** *Hallway Table* by Arno Declercq; *Tube* chandelier by Michael Anastassiades; *Triple Samurai (Kuniyoshi)*, 2018, by Kour Pour
**33** *Mother Ann* table and custom bench by Paul Loebach for Mattermade; *Prouvé Standard Chair* by Jean Prouvé; *Mobile Chandelier 2* by Michael Anastassiades; *A Rock, Summer-Winter*, 2018 by Christopher Duncan;

*The Edge of Form: Projective Identifications*, 2019, by Zio Ziegler
**34** *Swivel Egg Chairs* by Jean Royère; *Unum Coffee Table* by Mauro Mori; *Curve Sofa* by Patrick Naggar; *Mardi Gras_mmmarvellous mmmufins NADA.COM*, 2018, by Petra Cortright
**35** Vintage cabinet restored by NICOLHOLLIS; *Into the Deepest Darkness*, 2015, by Sanaz Mazinani
**36 & 37** *Tall Stool* by Sawkille Co.; *Parsons Table* by Union Studio
**39** *Zellige* series by Clé Tile; *Belgian Reproduction Terracotta* by Clé Tile
**40** *Evia Lounge* and *Evia Chair* by Galanter & Jones
**41** *Groundpiece* sofa by Flexform; *Copper Coffee Table* by Lorenzo Burchiellaro; *Arca Single Tier Chandelier* by Philippe Malouin; *Atollo Table Lamp* by Vico Magistretti for Oluce; *Gospel Song*, 2016, by Serge Attukwei Clottey
**42 & 43** Custom headboard and bedside table by Ido Yoshimoto; *Puffball Table Lamp* by Faye Toogood; *Owl on Branch* by David Wiseman
**44** *Chandigarh*, circa 1955, chair by Pierre Jeanneret; *Ottocento* bathtub by Benedini Associati for Agape; *Chimney, Sca Fell, 5 August, 1802*, 2018, by Jason Leggiere
**45** *Ball Light* by Michael Anastassiades

## PRESIDIO

**47** *U Bench* by Christopher Stuart; Hand-knotted Moroccan wool runner by Woven; *Curtain Wall Vector Model – Elevation 03*, 2016, by Julian Hoeber
**48 & 49** *Toja Coffee Table* by Christian Liaigre for Holly Hunt; *Bruxelles Armchair* by Paola Navone; *Hamilton* sofa by Minotti; *Dew* floor pouf by Nendo for Moroso; *Sellette Rythme* marble table by Hervé Langlais; Custom jute rug by Mark Nelson Designs; *Mil Mi-26* by Peppi Bottrop; *Lisa Chic*, 2010, by Jean Philippe Piter
**50** *Originals Counter Stool* by Lucian Arcolani for Ercol; *Flower of Life* chandelier by Willowlamp
**52 & 53** *PLOT Cabinet* by Erjan Borren for Van Rossum; Custom table and bench by NICOLEHOLLIS, fabricated by Custom Furniture Design; *CH24 Wishbone Chair* by Hans Wegner; *Upright Wing Chair* by Coup D'etat
**54** *Valley of the Moon*, 2016, by Sally England
**55** Custom headboard by NICOLEHOLLIS, fabricated by Barry Serota and Kroll; *Chandigarh, India*, bench, 1955, by Pierre Jeanneret; Custom coverlet by C&C Milano
**56 & 57** *Resort* sofa by Flexform; *Tavola Basso 080* coffee table by Dimore Studio; *Versailles V, France, 2003*, by Massimo Listri

## PACIFIC HEIGHTS

**60** *Italian Club Chair* by Coup d'Etat; *Laurel* side table by De La Espada; *Gelule* sconce by Joseph Dirand for Ozone; *Hushmoney*, 2018, by Hunt Rettig

**61** *Groundpiece* sofa by Flexform; Custom *Plank Series* side table by Plane Furniture; *Beetle Counter Chair* by Gubi; *Branching Bubbles* chandelier by Lindsey Adelman

**62 & 63** *Canapé Dossier Droit* sofa by Jean Michel Frank for Ecart International; Custom shagreen drum side table by Bardeaux Mobilier; *Plano Side Table* by Holly Hunt; *Regis Botta* floor lamp for Ozone; *Elance #182* table lamp by Hervé Van der Straeten; Custom coffee table by NICOLEHOLLIS, fabricated by Fox Marble and Thomas Sellars Furniture; *Untitled*, 2001, painting by JMary

**64** *Madison* console by Tom Faulkner; *Tip of the Tongue* table lamp by Michael Anastassiades; *Untitled (Curtain)*, 2018, by Matt Lipps

**65** *Acqua* mirror by Barnaby Barford; *Oval Cumulus* pendant by Ted Abramczyk

**66** *Brass Cabinet* by Studioilse; *Spaces in Between*, 2018, by Bernadette Jiyong Frank

**67** Custom bar cabinet by NICOLEHOLLIS, fabricated by Custom Furniture Design; *Jewel Metal Framed Mirror* by Tom Faulkner; *Biedermeier* candelsticks by Ted Muehling for E. R. Butler & Co.

**68** Custom sofa by NICOLEHOLLIS, fabricated by Kroll Furniture; Custom handwoven area rug by Beauvais Carpets

**69** *Crown Armchair* by Massproductions; *Saarinen Round Dining Table* by Eero Saarinen

**70 & 71** *Canopy Bed* by Uhuru Design; Custom lacquer nightstands by NICOLEHOLLIS, fabricated by Bardeaux Mobilier with custom bronze drawer pulls by Rogan Gregory; *Soufflé Bench* by Kelly Wearstler; *Jelly Pea Sofa* by India Mahdavi; Custom coffee table by NICOLEHOLLIS, fabricated by Richter Fine Furniture and De La Marque Edouard; Vintage *Clam Chair* by Philip Arctander

**72** *Wu Side Table* by Egg Collective; *Stay Lounge Chair* by Gubi

**73** *Float Pendant* by Articolo

**74** Custom ottoman by NICOLEHOLLIS, fabricated by Hardesty Dwyer Co.; *Rudi Loop* pendants by Lukas Peet for Roll & Hill

**75** *Split Mirror Round* by Lee Broom; *Atlas 02 Table Lamp* by Karl Zahn for Roll & Hill; *Dark Floral* wallcovering by Ellie Cashman Design

**76 & 77** Custom daybed with trundle by NICOLEHOLLIS, fabricated by Hardesty Dwyer Co.; *Seeing Glass Big Round* mirror by Sabine Marcelis and Brit Van Nerven; *Kids Chair* and *Kids Table* by Tom Frencken; *Flynn 6-Drawer Dresser* by Room and Board; *Maison Wallmount* sconces by The Urban Electric Co.

## NOB HILL

**79** *Agathos Swivel Armchair* by B&B Italia; *Bridger Cast Bronze Tables* by Caste; *Totah Table* by ROOM

**80 & 81** *Solo Bar Stool* by Neri & Hu for De La Espada

**82** *Upright Wing Chair* by Coup D'etat; *CH24 Wishbone Chair* by Hans Wegner; *Minimo Light* table by Piero Lissoni for PORRO

**83** *Wiggle Chair*, 1972, by Frank Gehry

**84 & 85** *Wing* sectional by Flexform; *Zig Zag Chair* by Gerrit Rietveld

**86** Custom banquette by NICOLEHOLLIS, fabricated by Julian Giuntoli Custom Furniture; *CH24 Wishbone Chair* by Hans Wegner; *Saarinen Round Dining Table* by Eero Saarinen; *NA6 Mass Cluster of 9 Pendant Lights* by &Tradition

**87** *The Tate Bench* by Hudson Furniture; *Kopra Burst* chandelier by David Weeks; *Black Cherry Breezer*, 2014, by Conrad Ruiz

**88** *Mills Upholstered Bed* by BDDW; *One Arm Sconce No. 202* by David Weeks Studio

**89** *Papa Bear Chair* by Hans Wegner; *Bend Back the Bow in Dreams*, 2013, by Robert Kingston

## BROADWAY

**91** *Saarinen Round Dining Table* by Eero Saarinen; *Volt Stool* by Caste; *2097 Chandelier* by Gino Sarfatti for FLOS; *Secretive Three Graces*, 2008, by Debbie Han

**92** *The Stefan Cocktail Table* by Studio Van den Akker; *Infinity Sconce* by John Pomp; *One and Other XXV11*, 2009, by Antony Gormley

**93** *Break In The Clouds Table* by Atelier Gary Lee; *PH Artichoke* pendant by Louis Poulsen; *Square Word Calligraphy: After Apple Picking*, 2003, by Xu Bing

**94 & 95** *Mousson Sofa* by Christian Liaigre; *Nabab Chair* by Christian Liaigre; *Amsterdam Chair* by Magni Home Collection; *Artificial Rock No. 146*, 2011, by Zhan Wang; *I Love U*, 2004, by Tsang Kin-Wah

**96** Custom worktable by Union Studio for MARCH

**97** Custom banquette and table by NICOLEHOLLIS, fabricated by Julian Giuntoli Custom Furniture; *Nerve* chair by Piero Lissoni; *Honeycomb Pendant* by Tim Clark

**98** *Diamond Mirror* by Piet Houtenbas; *Beat Stout Pendant* by Tom Dixon; *Birdcage Superwide* wallcovering by Timorous Beasties

**100** *Illusion Dresser* by Luis Pons; *Paint the Posters of Hong Kong Museum of Art*, 1 of 24, 2009, by Wong Wai Yin

**101** Custom table by NICOLEHOLLIS, fabricated by Julian Giuntoli Custom Furniture; *Eve* dining chair by Polka for Wittmann; *Lumiere Chandelier* by Jean de Merry; *Japanese Sky I*, 1988, by Robert Rauschenberg

**102 & 103** Custom bed by Jacob May Design; Custom bench by Mark Albrecht Studio; *Untitled, 2012,* by Liu Wei

## THOUSAND OAKS

**105** Custom sofa by NICOLEHOLLIS, fabricated by Bespoke Furniture; Vintage *Sculptura Chairs,* circa 1950, by Russell Woodard; *Minimal Table* by Andrianna Shamaris; *Soho* pendant by Joan Gaspar for Marset

**106** *Manta Dining Chair 349* by Matthew Hilton; *Clay* table by Desalto; *21 Series* custom chandelier by BOCCI; *Listen if You Ever Tell,* 2007, by Ed Ruscha

**107** *PL80* series planters by Atelier Vierkant; *The End XXII,* 2015, by Luke Butler

**108 & 109** Custom sofa by NICOLEHOLLIS, fabricated by Bespoke Furniture; *Surface* coffee table by Vincent Van Duysen for B&B Italia; *Triple Burnt* side table by Andrianna Shamaris; *Elysia Lounge Chair* by Luca Nichetto for De La Espada; *Contour Chaise Lounge* by Vladamir Kagan; *Lampe élancée No. 182* by Hervé Van der Straeten

**112 & 113** *Plank Series* dining table and bench by Plane Furniture; *Siren Dining Arm Chair* by Holly Hunt; *Branching Bubble* chandelier by Lindsey Adelman; *Flumequine,* 2011, by Damien Hirst; *Double Rift I,* 2012, by Richard Serra

**114** *Elbow Chair* by Hans Wegner for Carl Hansen & Son; Custom table by NICOLEHOLLIS, fabricated by Bespoke Furniture; *Ball Light* by Michael Anastassiades; *Smoke Screen,* 2013, by Tammy Rae Carland

**115** *Barrel Chair* by Vladimir Kagan; *Tavolo Basso 062* cocktail table by Dimore Studio; *Biedermeier* candelsticks by Ted Muehling for E. R. Butler & Co.

**116** *Hepburn Fixed 3-Seat Sofa* by Matthew Hilton for De La Espada; Vintage Kofod-Larsen lounge chairs; *Totah Table* by ROOM; *Branching Floor Lamp* by Lindsay Adelman; *Carbon AP,* 2015, by Channing Hansen

**117** *Mills Canopy Bed* by BDDW; *Contour Chaise Lounge* by Vladimir Kagan; Custom nightstands by NICOLEHOLLIS, fabricated by Custom Furniture Design; *Bleach on Black Denim,* 2014, by Christopher Badger

**118** *Amazon Braid* runner by Woven Designs LLC; *Tube Chandelier* by Michael Anastassiades; *Sylvia* sconce by NICOLEHOLLIS for Phoenix Day

**120** Custom bench by NICOLEHOLLIS, fabricated by Julian Giuntoli Custom Furniture

**121** *Symi* sofa by CASAMIDY; Pendant by Grant Larkin

**122** *Locking Round Dining Table* by James De Wulf;

*HARP 759 Armchair* by Roda; *Altamura* sofa by CASAMIDY; Custom coffee table by NICOLEHOLLIS with Heath Ceramics tile inlay, fabricated by OHIO; *Bell 95* pendant by Gervasoni

**123** *LC Series* stone seating by Atelier Vierkant

## KUA BAY

**125** *Drum* table by AMMA Studio

**128** Custom bench by NICOLEHOLLIS, fabricated by Custom Furniture Design

**129** *Shell* pouf by Paola Lenti

**130** *Wave Candlestick* by AKMD

**131** *Vines #2* by Karl Zahn; *Fauteuil Bridge Metteur en Scène 1932* chair by Jean-Michel Frank and Adolphe Chanaux

**132 & 133** *Arctique Armchair* by Christian Liaigre; *Barrel Chair* by Vladimir Kagan; *Afritamu Coffee Table* by Christian Astuguevieille; Custom *Cherry Bomb* chandelier by Lindsey Adelman

**134** *Fauteuil Bridge Metteur en Scène 1932* chair by Jean-Michel Frank and Adolphe Chanaux; *Chiaroscuro Lamp* by Blackman Cruz Workshop; *Ridgeline,* 2015, by Michael Gaillard

**136 & 137** *Leather Cord Stool* by Thomas Hayes Studio; *Atollo Table Lamp* by Vico Magistretti for Oluce

**138** *Pavé* stool by Enzo Berti for Kreoo

**139** *Appique Anneau 295* sconce by Hervé Van der Straeten; *Starling Mirror* by KGBL

**140** Custom bronze door handle by Michele Oka Doner

**141** Custom bronze screen by Michele Oka Doner; *Lampada 079* sconce by Dimore Studio; Custom bronze mirror by Bardeaux

**142 & 143** Custom bed by NICOLEHOLLIS, fabricated by Julian Giuntoli Custom Furniture; Hand crocheted *GLUCK Pendant* by Naomi Paul; *Antony Sconce* by Serge Mouille; Custom desk by NICOLEHOLLIS, fabricated by Custom Furniture Design; *Kilo TL Table Lamp* by Kalmar Werkstatten; *Woven Leather Dining Chair* by Smilow Furniture; *Bazane I Stool* by Christian Liaigre; Custom tapestry by Boho by Lauren

**144** *HARP 768 Lounge Chair* by RODA; *Drum* table by AMMA Studio

**145** *Circuit 1* sconce by Apparatus

## KAKAPA BAY

**147** L-shape outdoor sofa by Urban Zen

**148 & 149** Custom table and benches by NICOLEHOLLIS, fabricated by Tree to Table;

Dining chairs by John Houshmand; Custom branch chandelier by Michele Oka Doner

**150** *Seal Chair* by Ib Kofod-Larsen; Custom mahogany root table by Jerome Abel Seguin; *T-Stool* by Pierre Chareau

**151** *Swing Chair* by Egg Designs

**152** Custom bed and nightstands by NICOLEHOLLIS, fabricated by Julian Giuntoli Custom Furniture; *Vitra Cork Stool C* by Jasper Morrison for Vitra; Surfboards from Mollusk Surfshop

**153** Custom surfboard table by NICOLEHOLLIS, fabricated by Werken Design; *Manta Dining Chair 349* by Matthew Hilton; *Muffin Pendant* by Dan Yeffet; Chromogenic prints, 1976, by Hugh Holland

**154 & 155** *Sierra Desk* by Christian Liaigre; *#7 Chair* by Jens Risom

**156** *Sea Urchin* pendant by Coup Studio

**158** *Harp Chair* by Jorgen Hovelskov; Custom sconce by Kevin Reily

**159** Custom hanging daybed by NICOLEHOLLIS, fabricated by Julian Giuntoli Custom Furniture

**160 & 161** Custom bed and headboard by NICOLEHOLLIS, fabricated by Julian Giuntoli Custom Furniture; *Concordia Chair* by George Nakashima Woodworkers; Custom pendant by Kevin Reily; *Weight V*, 2010, by Richard Serra

**162** Freestanding tub by Concreteworks

**163** *Craftsman Chair* by James Perse

## KAHUWAI BAY

**165** Custom table and benches by NICOLEHOLLIS, fabricated by John Houshmand, Kamuela Hardwoods, and Dovetail Gallery & Design; Custom *Vellum Suspension* pendant by Michael McEwen Lighting

**166 & 167** Custom barstools by NICOLEHOLLIS, fabricated by De Sousa Hughes

**168** *Le Bambole 07 Armchair* by Maria Bellini for B&B Italia; *Carmel Coffee Table* by Tuell & Reynolds; Custom sofa by NICOLEHOLLIS, fabricated by Bespoke Furniture

**169** Towel ladder by Jacobs May Design; *Elevation Sconce* by Holly Hunt

**170 & 171** Custom bed by NICOLEHOLLIS, fabricated by Hilde Brand Furniture; Custom side table by NICOLEHOLLIS, fabricated by Custom Furniture Design and John Lewis Glass; *Fontenay Sconce* by Jonathan Browning

**173** Custom table by NICOLEHOLLIS, fabricated by Concreteworks and Julian Giuntoli Custom Furniture; *Iroko Dining Bench* by Piet Boon

**174** Custom bench by NICOLEHOLLIS, fabricated by Bespoke Furniture

## TIBURON

**180** *Sud Bench* by Christian Liaigre

**181** *Boom Boom Burst* chandelier by Lindsey Adelman; *Untitled* 2012, by Liu Wei; *Biblioteca Uffizi Firenze* 2008, by Candida Höfer

**182** Custom bronze screen by Michele Oka Doner

**183** *Branching Bubbles* chandelier by Lindsay Adelman; *Craiving and Flaws*, 2011, by Li Songsong

**184 & 185** *Sofa Club 1930* by Jean-Michael Fran; Custom *Aland Wing Chair* by Jean de Merry; Custom coffee table by NICOLEHOLLIS, fabricated by Julian Giuntoli Furniture; *Walnut Bench* by William Emmerson; *Plank Series* ottoman by Plane Furniture; *Jeweler's Table* by Alison Berger; *Lustre A Faucettes 283* by Hervé Van der Straeten

**186** *Rondelle Credenza* by John Pomp; *Burke Side Table* by Pfeifer Studio; *Zori* floor lamp by Vincent Collin; *Composition (Cards)*, 2017, by Tara Donovan

**187** *Unique Richard Ear Mini Beast*, 2017, by The Haas Brothers

**188 & 189** *Square Guest Stool* by BDDW; Custom table by NICOLEHOLLIS, fabricated by Custom Furniture Design; *Gala Chandelier* by Rich Brilliant Willing

**190** Custom pendant by Esque Studio; *Ever Blossoming Life - Dark, 2014*, by TeamLab

**191** *Eames Soft Pad Chair* by Herman Miller; *Saarinen Round Dining Table* by Eero Saarinen; *Sarus Mobile No. 428* by David Weeks

**192 & 193** *Augustin Sofa* by Christian Liaigre; *Drum* table by AMMA Studio; *Contour Low Back Lounge Chair* by Vladimir Kagan; *Nepal Side Chair* by Paola Navone; *Zaragosa Coffee Table* by KGBL; *Kraft Floor Lamp* by Ecart International; *Wintery Forest*, 2014, by Yang Yongliang

**194** *Chrysanthemum Table* from Stephanie Odegard Collection; *Spun Pendant* by Chris Lehreche

**195** Custom side table by George Peterson; *Family Lounge* by Living Divani; *MONIKA Pendant* by Naomi Paul; *Lightning Fields 227*, 2009, by Hiroshi Sugimoto

**196** *Sorraia Bed* by Holly Hunt; *Latin Chaise* by Christian Liaigre; *IMO Bench* by Pinch; *Self-portrait, White Sands, New Mexico, 1976*, by Richard Misrach

**197** *Sylvia* sconce by NICOLEHOLLIS for Phoenix Day

**198 & 199** *Ranch Settee* by Marmol Radzinger Furniture; Custom coffee table by NICOLEHOLLIS, fabricated by OHIO; *Concrete Ping Pong Dining Table* by James De Wulf; *Fora Outdoor Pendant* by Bover

## LARKSPUR

**201** Custom bed by NICOLEHOLLIS, fabricated by Julian Giuntoli Custom Furniture
**203** *Ile Club Bench* by Piero Lissoni; Hand-knotted rug by Stark
**204 & 205** *Rusa Chaise Lounge* by KAA Design for Design Within Reach
**206** *Rope Counter Stool* by DMDM
**207** Custom banquette fabricated by Room Online; *Balfour Dining Table* by James Perse; *Sundance* folding chair by Paolo Golinelli; *High Sticking Chair* by Frank Gehry
**208** Custom sofa by NICOLEHOLLIS, fabricated by Julian Giuntoli Custom Furniture; Recycled rubber coffee table by Montauk Sofa; *Log Side Table* by Gervasoni
**209** *Sling Chair* by Kyle Garner for Sit and Read
**210** *Macrame Work Lamp* by Robert Lewis
**211** *Rusa Lounge Chair* by KAA Design for Design Within Reach
**212 & 213** *Mongolian Lamb Vanity Stool* by Montage Modern

## STINSON BEACH

**216 & 217** *Groundpiece* sofa by Flexform; Vintage *Pine Coffee Table* from Galerie Half; Handwoven Moroccan rug by Tony Kitz; Custom *Tack End Table* by Uhuru; *Mionde Side Table* by Holly Hunt
**218** *Wire Bar Stool* by Overgaard & Dyrman
**219** Vintage chair by Hans Wegner; *Pins,* 2015, by Tara Donovan
**220 & 221** Custom table and bench by NICOLEHOLLIS, fabricated by Julian Giuntoli Custom Furniture; *Float Pendant* by Brendan Ravenhill; *Only by Chance,* 2016, by Idris Khan
**222** Custom headboard by NICOLEHOLLIS, fabricated by Uhuru; *Ajiro* rug by Beauvais Carpets; *Stacki* pendant by Articolo; *Bermuda Wallpaper* by Phillip Jeffries
**223** *Offset Bench* by Christian Woo
**224** *Single Board Rocking Armchair* by George Nakashima Woodworkers; *Ceramic Cylinder Stool* by Reinaldo Sanguino; *Jardin d'hiver & Fête de la Musique,* 2018, by Sheila Hicks
**225** *Portrait as a Big Haired Prophet,* 2018, by Sarah Hughes
**226** *Wander Light* by Jonas Wagell; *Balloon Dog* bookend by Jeff Koons; *Stay Strong,* 2018, by Stanley Whitney
**227** Custom built-in bunk beds by NICOLEHOLLIS, fabricated by Matthew Chase Woodworks; *Mangas Largas Naturales Rug* by GAN Rugs
**228** *Kayu Teak Dining Table* and *Bench* by Design Within Reach

**229** *Tinder Hemisphere Fire Table* by Concreteworks; *Westport Adirondack Chair* by Loll Designs

**239** Vintage mobile, cira 1970, source unknown

Principal photography by Douglas Friedman. Images on pages 4, 6, 12, 79–89, 100, 147, 151, 197–213, 232, 239 by Laure Joliet.

238

First published in the United States of America in 2020 by
Rizzoli International Publications, Inc.
300 Park Avenue South
New York, NY 10010
www.rizzoliusa.com

Copyright © 2020 Nicole Hollis
Introduction by Pilar Viladas
Photography by Douglas Friedman and Laure Joliet
Publisher: Charles Miers
Editor: Sandra Gilbert Freidus
Design: Victor Robyn
Production Manager: Alyn Evans
Editorial Coordination: Avery Carmassi Davison
Managing Editor: Lynn Scrabis
Editorial Assistance: Elizabeth Smith
and Andrea Danese

Printed in Italy

2021 2022 2023 / 10 9 8 7 6 5 4 3

ISBN: 978-0-8478-6467-6
Library of Congress Control Number: 2020938660

Visit us online:
Facebook.com/RizzoliNewYork
instagram.com/rizzolibooks
twitter.com/Rizzoli_Books
pinterest.com/rizzolibooks
youtube.com/user/RizzoliNY
issuu.com/Rizzoli

# *Copper Country* **1903** *Evening News*

*Several citizens of Calumet have at one time and another during the past week complained to the reporter of the orange and banana skins that are being thrown around on the sidewalks of Red Jacket. More than one person has been thrown to the walk by means of these bits of peel and sooner or later a serious accident will occur. It is hoped that in the future all persons peeling bananas or oranges on the streets will throw the peelings into the road way.*

JANUARY 5: Louis Gipp, while out hunting yesterday, had his right hand nearly blown off at the wrist by the accidental discharge of his gun. He was taken to the Calumet and Hecla hospital for treatment. Dr. A.B. Simonson, chief of the staff, found it necessary to amputate the index finger near the wrist.

The reporter visited the Gipp home this afternoon. Louis did not know just how the gun went off. His story is that he, with his father, John Gipp, and brother, George Gipp, went out rabbit hunting. They drove to Lake View where they put their horse in a barn and then proceeded into the woods on snow shoes to hunt rabbits. The dogs had been hunting for a time, but were driving the rabbits too far, so his father told George to catch the dog as he came past. George gave Louis his gun to hold while he caught the dog. Louis was holding both guns during the scrimmage of catching the dog and tying a piece of marlin about the animal's neck. Somehow one of the guns went off, the charge passing through the hand from the inner side and just through the knuckle of the index finger, totally destroying the articulation.

John Gipp, who delights in hunting and who has carried a gun ever since he was old enough to take aim, vows he will never take one of his sons out hunting with him again.

A large owl which measured about 3 feet in height and about 5 feet from tip to tip found its way into town last Saturday and perched on several of the residences in Blue Jacket.

JANUARY 8: Too much whiskey got William McKenzie, who is a bartender for Bat Quello, in Laurium, in very serious trouble…The affair created a great sensation. It was an unprovoked assault upon the Rev. William Coombe as he was passing the Michigan House at about 12:15 o'clock today, just after the Kilties band parade.

JANUARY 9: John Dunn, of the Michigan House, was in Justice Curtis' office at 10 o'clock this morning and paid the fine of $50 and costs, $6, for William McKenzie, who assaulted the Rev. William B. Coombe while the latter was passing the Michigan House. John Dunn and some of his friends made the rounds of the saloons last night and by contributions from a number of saloonkeepers raised sufficient funds to pay the fine and costs to give him his liberty for the brief period of one minute.

Marshal Trudell when the fine was paid went to the village jail armed with a warrant for William McKenzie's arrest for the second attack he made on the Rev. William

B. Coombe while the latter was standing in the doorway of Prosecuting Attorney Larson's stenographer's office. This was the attack that resulted in a general mixup of furniture, lawyers and ministers before Marshal Trudell and Night Policeman Jacob Puhek succeeded in arresting McKenzie and getting him out of the building and to the village jail.

JANUARY 17: It has become the duty of the reporter to chronicle the death of his friend and employer, the editor and proprietor of the *Copper Country Evening News*, Frederick Mackenzie; a man so well known to the residents of Calumet that his name is familiar to every English speaking person, young or old.

Frederick Mackenzie was born in London, England, October 27, 1832, his father being the celebrated architectural draughtsman of the same name. He came to the United States in 1865. Arriving in Chicago, he met a brother of Charles Dickens, the novelist, who advised him to buy a farm. Lack of experience in agricultural methods, and his health being impaired by malaria, he was forced to turn to the Lake Superior copper country.

…He enjoyed literary work, and when the opportunity presented itself in 1882, he became the owner and editor of the *Calumet Weekly News*. In 1892 he started the daily—*The Copper Country Evening News*.

JANUARY 30: For more than an hour before the appointed time for the McKinley birthday anniversary exercises to begin, hundreds of men, women and children stood in the storm and cold on the sidewalk in front of the Calumet theatre waiting for the doors to open. As soon as Janitor Morgan was notified that there were people outside he promptly opened the door and the crowd in a quiet and orderly manner entered and took their seats.

Without request nearly all the boys, and there were hundreds of them, went upstairs into the gallery and while they were boisterous, as boys will be, before the exercises began, as soon as the curtain raised, they were quiet and well behaved. The night was a very disagreeable one and the snow was falling as fast as it ever falls. There was every indication of a blizzard and a long walk home through the storm and deep snow for most of them, yet the theatre was packed with a living mass of humanity, who came to pay their tribute to the memory of the noble statesman who fell by the assassin's hand.

It will go down to posterity in the copper country that its people are patriotic and eager to honor and respect real statesmen, noble men and women, and the memory of the martyred presidents.

FEBRUARY 4: Superintendent William E. Parnall, general manager of the Bigelow syndicate of mines, died at his home at the Tamarack mine location, at 3:45 this afternoon of that dread disease, malignant cancer of the stomach.

Superintendent William E. Parnall was born in England June 5, 1839. He came to the copper country in 1860, landing at Ontonagon, where he obtained work as a miner in the National mine. From the National mine he went to the Franklin mine at Hancock, where he held the position of mining captain for one year. He then went to Rhode Island, where he had accepted a position as superintendent of a coal mine, a position he held for three years. He then returned to Lake Superior and accepted a position as captain at the Phoenix mine, where he remained until the spring of 1880, when the directors of the National mine again sent for him and offered him the agency of their mine.

He remained there until he resigned to take the position of assistant superintendent of the Tamarack mine under the late Captain John Daniell. He took charge of the Tamarack in June, 1890. When Captain Daniell retired from active work he succeeded him as general manager and director of what was then known as the Clark-Bigelow syndicate of copper mines.

MARCH 10: The large cross upon the steeple of St. Anne's French Catholic church which was blown over during the thunder storm of last week and which was suspended from the apex of the steeple by a mere shred of metal dropped to the ground yesterday during the noon hour, falling within a few feet of a bevy of school children.

A miner in the Tamarack mine last week having a lighted lamp on his hat stood under a dry stull timber long enough to set the timber on fire and walked away, never noticing what a dangerous thing he had done. When the fire was discovered some time later by another party of miners it had assumed dangerous proportions and took considerable effort to extinguish the blaze. Strict orders were given immediately after that no miners will be allowed to carry their lamps on their hats or to have a lamp holder on their hats on which to fasten a lamp.

Last week a party of ten miners had an experience in Tamarack No. 2 shaft that they do not care to have occur again. They were descending in the cage to their work when the cage came to a sudden halt by reason of a large rock having fallen against the timber and forced it inward. Before the engineer in the engine house could become aware that there was no load on the cable a couple of hundred feet of slack cable was coiled on top of the cage. Naturally enough the miners were too unnerved to return to work and so went home.

MARCH 12: *Notice To Owners of Dogs*
All dogs must be muzzled. Any dogs found running at large within the incorporate limits of the village of Red Jacket on and after April 8 must be killed.

P.D. MacNaughton,
Health Officer.

MARCH 14: The condition of Fifth street at the present time is the subject of much comment. Several business men are kicking and claim that it is the town's business to see that the sidewalks are clear. As one prominent Red Jacketite remarked, "It puts one in mind of crossing the Alps."

Commercial travelers who were walking east on Elm street from the Arlington Hotel yesterday were curious to know whether the numerous cows that were seen on South Seventh street could be taken as a reliable sign of approaching spring or whether the half dozen barrels of garbage, a portion of whose contents intermingled with the cow prints, were indications that the corner grocery had made its regular spring cellar cleaning.

MARCH 31: How humiliating it must be, not only to the actors themselves, but to the management as well, to see an audience prepare to depart before the closing scenes are enacted. It is to be hoped that Calumet audiences will bear this in mind in the future.

APRIL 10: Never before has there been such a representative gathering of the medical fraternity of the Lake Superior copper country as there was at the opening of the Northern Michigan general hospital in Laurium on Wednesday evening, April 8. Nearly forty medical gentlemen, besides the nurses and the students in the nurse's training school, were assembled in the handsome new edifice at 8:30 o'clock, the time announced on the invitations for the opening to take place.

APRIL 11: The Eagle drug store are still keeping up their reputation for window dressing. They have one of the prettiest Easter designs in the town. Their windows are decorated purple and white and the effect is the producing of a beautiful picture. When lit up at night the electrical appliances are made to form the word "Easter." The spectacle is superb and a visit to the store will repay the trouble taken.

Every spring when there is the largest volume of water running over the Houghton-Douglass falls many hundred people, old and young, go to see them. Of course, at this time of the year the roads are in bad condition and the walk of five miles or more in making the round trip was not all fun to many who made the trip.

APRIL 13: The promoters of the Cornish boys' supper and concert have reason to feel proud of themselves...It should not be forgotten that they were all Cornish folks, and as the Cornish have established a reputation by their vocal abilities success was assured in this direction.

APRIL 14: While speaking to a miner this afternoon the reporter was told that owing to the refusal of the trammers to go underground all work is suspended. There is no likelihood at present of the strike being settled, although the men go to the shaft houses every morning in the hope that work will be resumed.

APRIL 22: The sensation on the street this morning was a shooting affair, which occurred in the Asselin block on Sixth street at an early hour this morning. No person was injured by the three or four shots that were fired, neither is the man who did the shooting arrested, for the very good reason that the saloonkeeper who keeps the place where the row started says he does not know the names of the persons who started the row in his saloon and whom when put out, he claims, did the shooting.

Peter Palkala runs the saloon and from a number of stories that were told the reporter today, he keeps a saloon where men, women and children are allowed to mingle with each other and drink to intoxication. One woman and the saloonkeeper, Palkala, have been arrested.

APRIL 30: A solution has been discovered to the trouble the Red Jacket village council are in about the disposition of unmuzzled dogs. Sam Mawrence is a perfectly reliable business man who is known to the council and who volunteers to do this work to the satisfaction of all concerned. Sam Mawrence is the only man that can make money out of dead dogs and Sam will not hesitate to have his men kill such dogs as have not been taken out of the pound for reason that the dog tax has not been paid or the muzzle law not complied with.

Sam Mawrence has an extensive establishment several miles west of Calumet at which he boils down all the carcasses of horses, cattle or swine that are accidentally killed or die by other causes for their fat or grease, which is shipped away to lubricating oil factories.

MAY 4: A good catch was made at Tamarack dam Saturday afternoon when Mr. John Gipp, of Hecla, returned home with about twelve pounds of the speckled beauties, numbering about forty-five fish.

MAY 6: The "Headquarters for Birds, Specimens and Lake Superior Views" will be changed on Wednesday from 328 Fifth street to 194 Sixth street, in the Hermann building just at the Red Jacket terminus of the street railway. The large storeroom in that building will afford better facilities for displaying minerals, views and photographic materials. It will also be fitted up as a waiting room for the accommodation of ladies and others who wish to take the cars.

The dog catcher had one of the toughest jobs of his life on hand this morning. It happened thuswise: He proceeded with one of his canine catchers to the outskirts of the new Mineral Range depot. Arriving there, in company with two other men, he drew a revolver and fired three bullets point blank at the poor brute and finding this did not end its existence proceeded to hasten matters by jumping on the animal's head and neck. Even

this did not have the desired effect, as the dog, which was all this time held with a long rope, was whirled in the air for strangulation purposes, and then thrown on one side. But the laugh came when that dog rose up suddenly and bolted as fast as its legs could carry it. History does not record whether the poor brute was recaptured or not. It is hoped that it was not for the sake of its skin.

MAY 7: Is there no other way to take care of garbage in the village than by the use of the unsightly barrels? On one corner on Sixth street where the street car stops two barrels are usually kept full and the odor from them is usually offensive and unhealthy. Strangers coming to town on the electric cars wonder what kind of a board of health the village has. Other villages have zinc-lined boxes with tight-fitting covers, neatly painted and do not present the unsightly appearance that an old barrel does.

Ed Nara, the poundmaster, was feeling so spiritual at noon today that he wanted a job as a reporter. He thinks he can tell a better story about the killing of dogs than the regular reporters can. If he attempts to mutilate another dog in the uncertain way he has been doing, certain parties threaten to lasso him and take him out to the Tamarack dam for the fishes.

MAY 14: Paul Brenich and Caspar Dravich, two able-bodied, hustling men, who said they were Croatians hailing from Pittsburg, must have thought they had struck a bonanza when they ran up against Calumet yesterday. So beautiful did everything look in their eyes, and so well were the inhabitants dressed, that they decided that they would stay right here and work no more. They got the idea into their heads that Calumet and its environs was like the land of Canaan, flowing with milk and honey, and that all they had to do was to go after it.

In the meantime evil influences had been at work and Marshal Trudell was notified of their presence. Now, if the marshal has aversion for anything at all, it is a tramp or vagrant, and the marshal went after them this morning to stop their begging propensities. He soon located them and catching them in the act of soliciting, contrary to the laws of the state, immediately apprehended them and brought them before Judge Fisher.

Marshal Trudell has since found out that they sent away $130 to Austria, the proceeds of their begging in Calumet during the past week.

MAY 16: People standing in front of the Sterk block last evening were startled by hearing the scream of a woman. A moment previously they heard a dull thud, which was caused by a child falling from the side window of the second story of the Sterk building to the sidewalk between the buildings. Those who saw the child fall did not expect to pick her up alive, but today noon, when the reporter saw her, her condition was such that a complete recovery from her injuries is expected.

MAY 20: Fifth street had a fire scare last night. It was due to the gasoline lighting apparatus in the rear end of the F.C. Glocke cigar manufactory and store getting out of order. Mr. Glocke had just pumped up the gasoline machine preparatory to lighting the store lamps when flames enveloped the machine. Fortunately the supply of gasoline was turned off. The fire department responded promptly and it was the work of only a few minutes to extinguish the flames.

MAY 21: Two of the scavengers of the Calumet and Hecla company made a ghastly discovery in the early hours of the morning. They were cleaning out the pits at the bottom of 2129 and 2131 Log street, Raymbaultown, when they felt something bulky at the bottom of the pit. On bringing it to the light they discovered that it was the body of a baby girl in the first stages of decomposition.

MAY 22: Another case of small pox has broken out at the home of Mr. Mukkala on Caledonia street…That there are not more diseases about is a mystery, as the prevalence of waste heaps and defective drainage in the township is alarming.

JUNE 3: Hecla was all agog with excitement this morning. The reason was not far to seek, as it was soon ascertained that Josephine Regis, an elderly Italian lady, bordering on three-score years, had deliberately shot herself with a revolver.

JUNE 8: The manager and employees, and especially the bookkeeper, of the Keckonen hardware company, on Fifth street were greatly put out this morning over the antics of their great store window attraction, the two young bears that were captured and brought to town last week.

Although completely enclosed in a cage made of wire fencing fastened on gas piping, the bears have shown that when left alone they were onto the combination that secured them, for this morning when the clerk opened the store he found that the bears had been in the office investigating the books, found the accounts all straight and books kept neat and clean but they did not leave them that way. No department or corner of the store was missed by them and all the very handsome signs that the bookkeeper was so careful in making and placing in the cage to attract the attention of the ladies—not to himself, but the refrigerators kept in the establishment—were totally demolished.

JUNE 9: Several ladies are complaining of the actions of young men who congregate on the sidewalks of Fifth street every evening, and especially Sunday evenings, after the regular churching hours.

"It is bad enough," they say, "when they sit about on the street corners and expectorate on the sidewalks, but when it comes to squirting filthy tobacco juice on our clothes, then the matter become unbearable."

A general meeting of the members of the St. Joseph Austrian church was held Sunday afternoon at the Red Jacket Town Hall. Mr. John Vertin, of Vertin Bros. and chairman of the building committee, occupied the chair. After some discussion the tender of Mr. Paul P. Roehm for $46,000 was accepted and work will start immediately. The structure is to be built of red sandstone and when completed will be an ornament to that portion of the city.

JUNE 17: Ed Nara, the dog catcher, has rushed himself into prominence again. It is not through locating dogs without muzzles on the streets this time, but Ed has been throwing so much booze down his throat to the detriment of his wife and family, which consists of five small children, that the wife has at last made complaint to Judge Jackola.

JUNE 18: One of the most interesting departments now of the Calumet public schools is the school for the deaf, which has just closed its first year.

Peterson, Calumet's popular pitcher, has met with a nasty accident to his hand while at work underground at the Hecla mine, which will necessitate his laying up for a couple of weeks at least. Peterson was using a hammer and in bringing back his hand for a hard blow struck a jagged piece of rock behind, cutting the back of the hand open to the bone. His injury was so severe that he had to have the wound stitched.

W.J. Morgan, the former janitor of the Red Jacket theatre and Town Hall, returned yesterday from the Illinois College of Photography at Effingham, Ill., from which he graduated with credit. He is now a professional photographer, but where he will locate for business he has not fully decided.

JUNE 22: Sunday, June 21st, was a red letter day for the Croatian people of Calumet, the occasion being the dedication of their handsome new church on Seventh street. All the Catholic societies in Calumet and Laurium turned out in full regalia and headed by several brass bands paraded the principal streets of Calumet and then attended the dedication services. Fully a thousand men were in line.

A party of boys and girls went to a charivari at Mike Spehar's home in Cedar lane last evening, where a wedding was held. These young people had opened the window leading into the basement, and while the others watched, one, more bold than the rest, climbed into the cellar and passed the bottles out. Two of the youngsters were girls and they were as bad as the boys.

JUNE 25: A stranger stepped off a street car at the corner of Oak street yesterday and enquired, "Where's Calumet?"

The man who volunteered to give him the required information asked the stranger: "Do you mean Laurium?"

Stranger, "No, I just come from there."

"Well, do you mean Red Jacket? If so, you are in it now."

Stranger, "No, I don't mean Red Jacket."

"Well, then you want to go to the Calumet and Hecla location, do you?"

Stranger, "No, I just want Calumet town. I thought I was in it, but this thing looks mighty strange. Conductor yells out Calumet, then I can't find anybody that knows where it is."

He was told to go over on Fifth street and perhaps he could then locate himself if he was ever in the town before.

Curtis, one of Calumet's star players who made a home run yesterday is calling at Izzie Blumenthal's this evening for the purpose of obtaining the hat put up for the first man to make a home run.

JUNE 26: The Michigan Press Association has "come and gone," as far as Calumet is concerned. When the party came to measure the distance over the ground covered by just one mine, the Calumet and Hecla, they realized that it was a mammoth property. A tramp from the south end of the Calumet and Hecla, or Osceola depot, to the Superior engine house, seeing the sights as they went along, and then west to their train at the Calumet D.,S.S. & A. depot was too much for the "tenderfeet" of the party.

JUNE 30: "Let's get up a fat men's game between the residents of Laurium and Red Jacket." The others agreed and they decided to start right in and organize. The object will be a charitable one and the proceeds will be devoted to one of the churches, which one to be decided later on.

The extraordinary sight of a raving lunatic on the streets of Red Jacket this morning raised Fifth street from its almost lethargic slumbers. About 11:30 o'clock Fred Torreano, of Woodland avenue, with his little son, aged about 4 years, was proceeding quietly down Fifth street when he seemed to become suddenly bereft of his senses. The first intimation bystanders had that everything was not right was the seeming haste with which the poor fellow urged his little boy along. Then he suddenly let go of the little fellow's arm, who was badly frightened by this time, and commenced to rave and shout and brandished his arms around like a windmill.

A crowd soon collected around the poor demented creature and one man who knew him intimately picked up the little boy, who was sobbing bitterly, in his arms. Officer Murphy then arrived on the scene and pluckily hustled the man along to the lockup, where he finally ensconced him without any injury to anyone.

The Red Jacket fire department running team has commenced practice for the tournament at Hancock next August.

JULY 11: Several citizens of Calumet have at one time and another during the past week complained to the reporter of the orange and banana skins that are being thrown around on the sidewalks of Red Jacket. More than one person has been thrown to the walk by means of these bits of peel and sooner or later a serious accident will occur.

It is hoped that in the future all persons peeling bananas or oranges on the streets will throw the peelings into the road way.

JULY 14: Red Jacket and the neighboring locations have been infested with peddlers during the past month and it behooves the authorities to look into the matter and see that these people have the necessary license to carry on their business, as it is an injustice to the business men who deal in such goods to compete with the peddlers, who have no rent, taxes, insurance, clerks' hire and a thousand and one other incidental expenses to meet.

JULY 23: Joe Larochelle, of Rockland street, aged 20, a roller repairer in No. 7 shaft, Hecla branch of the Calumet and Hecla mine, slipped and fell while engaged in his work this morning and went down the shaft 700 feet. He was taken to the company's hospital where he now lies in a critical condition.

JULY 25: Jumping from a train while going at the rate of twenty miles an hour was the experience of a young Red Jacket clerk on Wednesday. He was coming back from Freda with the Congregational church excursion and was standing at the rear end of one of the coaches. While running from Laurium a sudden gust of wind blew his hat off and without stopping to think the young man jumped from the train after his hat.

Fortunately for him there were no rocks about or the consequences might have been more serious. As it is, he is complaining of severe bruises and a sore feeling over his body.

AUGUST 12: The newspaper plant of the Suometar printing company on Pine street was entirely destroyed by fire at an early hour this morning, causing a loss of $6,700, with $3,000 insurance, carried in the Faucett Bros. & Guck and Finnish Mutual fire insurance companies.

That the flames were confined to the building destroyed and that the damage to the rear part of the tenement portion of the Walz block is due to the strenuous work and heroic action of the Red Jacket and Calumet fire departments…

The fire loss and damage by water and the disturbance to the tenants is a source of a great deal of annoyance to Miss Walz, who has shown a great deal of enterprise in acquiring the property and in erecting the handsome sandstone building upon it, also in securing tenants for all the storerooms, offices and flats in a short time after its completion.

When the *News* representative saw her this morning she naturally was in an extremely unsettled state of mind, as her one great fear was for the disaster that had just taken place, and she was extremely sensitive on the matter of the origin of the fire.

While Miss Walz did not say that she thought the fire was incendiary in a direct way, it was evident that she had strong suspicions of foul play. What she did say was: "Before I was in the newspaper business I was not aware that I had any enemies, but of late certain persons have been causing me all kinds of trouble."

Miss Walz lost all her personal effects and in her anxiety to get her valuable papers and a few things that were priceless to her went back in the hall and lost herself in the dense smoke and had it not been for the heroic act of Night Policeman Puhek, who saw her go into danger, she undoubtedly would have lost her life.

AUGUST 21: Ed Naara, the dog catcher, has been served a dastardly trick by some one. On opening his barn door yesterday morning he found one of his farm horses lying on the ground quite dead and frightfully hacked.

On looking into the matter he soon came to a conclusion as to who did the deed. The night before a Finn well known to Naara, stalked into his kitchen swinging a big axe, and making use of dire threats, at the same time saying "Where is Ned? I will do for him." Four men were then eating supper, and they persuaded him to go away.

AUGUST 22: Marshal Trudell was notified yesterday of the appearance of a man who has been acting very strangely in the vicinity of Section 16 park. On Thursday he was seen by some of the people living around there in a practically nude condition wandering aimlessly about. This morning the marshal found the clothes of the man, including his underwear and boots, carefully stowed away, and brought them to the village. He failed to discover any trace of the missing man, but a thorough search is being made and when found he will be taken care of.

AUGUST 25: Five Polish women, who were out in the woods picking berries this afternoon, when on a short cut to the Section Sixteen park in the heavy timber near Martin's old charcoal kiln, they were startled by seeing the corpse of a man dangling from a rope fastened to the limb of a tree. One woman was so badly frightened that she fainted.

As soon as the others recovered from their fright and brought the unconscious woman to her senses, they walked as fast as they could and informed Sexton Olson at the Lake View cemetery. They then came to town and notified the marshal. Mr. Olson promptly telephoned the *Evening News* of the woman's discovery.

The body is undoubtedly that of Clawson, the young man who has been missing for about two weeks.

AUGUST 31: It is probable that the next six months will see the greatest immigration of Finns yet recorded for such a period in the history of our country. Oppression at home, says *Iron Ore*, has become unbearable and their American friends are advising their coming. Representatives of the Finnish people are going to Russia to induce a movement of desertion from that country.

America has millions of acres yet untouched by the plow, and the Finns are wonderful farmers. They are great workers and make productive tracts of land previously considered almost worthless. The Upper Peninsula of Michigan has many of them and they are gradually increasing in numbers. They not only till the soil and cut the timber, but they are found in the mines and they are displacing other nationalities to a considerable extent.

They are a saving, thrifty people, and they pay their bills. They seek to have their own homes, and these they keep neatly. Temperance workers are assisting them, and we find a better class of Finns coming to us than those of a few years since.

SEPTEMBER 23: An interesting case, in which Miss Maggie Walz figured as the principal defendant, and Carl F. Heideman as the plaintiff, was heard in Judge Jackola's court this morning.

The facts of the case as brought out at the trial were that Mr. Heideman, who was manager of the Suometar publishing company, issuing a Finnish paper and doing book work, whose plant was recently destroyed by fire, discovered that the company was indebted to him in the sum of $99.90 salary due him for services rendered.

SEPTEMBER 28: This issue of the *Copper Country Evening News* contains an account of the last of a brilliant series of games that the Aristocrats have played during the season of 1903. Today's game closes the season with 62 games won and 13 lost.

The visit of the Milwaukee American Association team that has played with its present members all the season and which puts up as good an article of base ball as any league in the United States or the world affords has demonstrated in its contests with the Calumet team that our amateur base ball team can be justly termed as skillful ball players as the professionals that have been amongst us.

One drawback towards bringing out the very best play that both teams were capable of in the series of four games played was the cold weather and high wind, the cold making the players fingers stiff so that neither battery nor fielders could handle the ball with that certainty and promptness that marked warm weather games.

OCTOBER 1: For the second time in an interval of less than a year, the Auditorium Hotel at the corner of Elm and Sixth streets, and which was christened by the last landlord the "Copper Range Hotel," is closed because the landlord is missing without previously having given any intimation of his intention to vacate. Landlord A.W. Hanson has not been seen in Calumet since Tuesday morning. Neither his wife nor his bartender or any of the servants in the hotel were aware that he intended skipping, for all of the latter claim money due them for wages.

OCTOBER 5: A good many people about town are relating their experiences during the wind storm of Saturday night.

One story goes that a certain young man, who is employed in a well known grocery store in the city, desiring to be sure that one of his many lady friends reached home in safety, hired a livery rig and started out with his maiden friend for the long drive to her home.

All went well until the couple reached the outskirts of the village, when an extra strong gust of wind carried the young lady's hat away. The gallant young man, defying the wind, got out and began a search for the missing headgear. The night was too dark to see objects plainly, and the hero began a thorough search by traveling on his hands and knees in the vicinity where he thought the hat had landed.

The young lady, meanwhile, had become impatient waiting for the return of the searcher and had driven home. Her brother brought the rig back to town and just as he arrived at the place the hat had taken wings, met the gallant young man and picked him up and drove him home.

Anyone finding a lady's hat any where within a radius of five miles of the mine office corner, will greatly oblige Fred by returning it to the store.

OCTOBER 8: Just as the Hon. Fred M. Warner, candidate for governor of this state, and the party of prominent officials of the Calumet and Hecla and other mining and business corporations of the county were at the Red Jacket shaft last evening to see the working of that most famous hoisting and crushing plant, six miners were being brought to the surface, who were seriously injured while at work in the shaft at or near the bottom of it.

The scene that the six miners presented as they were being taken out of the cage and transferred to the ambulance was indeed one that must have strongly impressed upon the mind of the aspirant to the office of chief executive of this great state the stern realities and danger of the miner's vocation.

The six miners were suspended in the shaft above the 75th level. They were finishing the work of placing the new guides, when a stick of timber which had been knocked out from the rock bin at the 63rd level, a distance of over 1,200 feet above them, came crashing down into and through the iron bonnet of their cage, the debris and splinters of iron and steel striking the miners and injuring them.

OCTOBER 14: The annual report of County Mine Inspector Josiah Hall for the year ending September 30, 1903, was submitted to the board of supervisors, which convened at the court house, Houghton, Monday. During the year covered by this report, the number of men employed at the various mines in the county was 13,629. The fatalities underground numbered 31, on surface two, making a total of 33 fatal accidents.

The sensation among the Finnish people on Pine street is the case of Herman Dahl, who has been living here for several months with a woman whom he claimed was his legitimate wife.

Yesterday his first wife and daughter, a girl about 16 years of age, arrived from the old country and at once hunted up her faithless husband. She found him and after some talk between them he agreed to leave his second wife and live with his first wife. Although he had done her a great wrong, she was willing to forgive him if he would now take care of his family of six children. He consented to this and the two were on the way to the First National Bank to draw some money he had deposited there, when they met wife No. 2 coming out of the bank. Wife No. 2 had been to the bank and drew out what funds, about $165, that were in the bank.

Right here is where the trouble began. Herman wanted the money, but wife No. 2 claimed the money was as much hers as it was her husband's.

OCTOBER 19: About 9:30 Saturday night, just when Fifth street was packed with a dense throng of shoppers moving north and south, besides the usual crush of young people who use Fifth street as a boulevard to promenade on, a scrap in front of George Shahen's fruit store caused considerable excitement for about ten minutes. Shahen was waiting on a lady customer in front of his store, when a Syrian who had a grudge against him, walked up to him and with out any polite preliminaries landed a right hander on the jaw and followed it up with three or four more blows on different parts of Shahen's anatomy.

Shahen ran inside to get away from his assailant and as he did so a young Syrian named Fenetus ran to his assistance, but a few stinging blows forced a rapid retreat. The spectators claim that the pugilistic stranger finished a third inmate of the store but this Shahen denies.

Shahen says that Hassid, the man who assaulted him, works on the street railway construction at Lake Linden, that he has been threatening to do him up and would have kept his word a week earlier had he not been prevented by Mike Tom, who also works on the street railway.

Shahen has been accusing his assailant of non-support of his family, who are in Syria.

OCTOBER 22: Mrs. Peter Verbanich, of Tamarack, was this forenoon made a widow for the second time by reason of a mine accident killing her husband. He had been killed this morning by getting accidentally squeezed across the chest and body between two of the large forty-five ton rock cars. Mrs. Verbanich's first husband, Mike Benichi, was killed in No. 1 Tamarack shaft in September, 1895, on the day that the thirty victims of the Osceola mine fire were taken from the No. 4 shaft.

NOVEMBER 11: The Osceola strike is ended, and it is a case of "As you were" as far as the mining company is concerned, the trammers going to work this morning without a single concession being granted. It was never thought for a moment that the company would listen to the men's demands for the reinstatement of the three trammers who were discharged, and it was the general opinion of the public that the matter would end abruptly and like "a flash in the pan."

…It would seem from past experiences that strikes in the copper country, badly organized as they are, are of no avail whatever and that a little tact at times would do more to reach the desired end than all the arbitrary methods that have been tried up here and which have always ended in a fizzle.

NOVEMBER 13: *The Laws Defied*
*Calumet Dog Owners Refuse To Muzzle Their "Pets"*
The law has never been pressed in Calumet and never will be unless some of the apathy that exists is shaken off. If only half a dozen dogs were caught and the owners made examples of, there would soon be a change and a radical one at that.

NOVEMBER 23: To be without a coat this weather and to brave the elements is not the most pleasant experience, but that is the kind of an ordeal that one of the dummies in front of the Savings Bank building had to go through the other evening, as a man passing that way who thought the coat might do him more good than the dummy deliberately appropriated the same and walked away with it. But the ever-watchful eye of one of the lady clerks detected him and she promptly informed one of the male clerks, who gave chase and caught the thief a few doors away going north. Seeing how easy he got left off, he will probably treat dummies with more courtesy hereafter.

NOVEMBER 28: Hosking & Co.'s cash store on Fifth street was burned to the ground this morning. This is the first serious fire since last fall, when the St. Joseph Austrian church met with a like fate.

NOVEMBER 30: It appears that Bobbie, as he was familiarly called, was playing with some of his playmates in the near vicinity of his home and the boys hit upon the idea of making a snow house. The next thing that was seen of the boys they were scampering across lots toward the Clark home to announce that the snow house had caved in on Bobby, although there were six or seven boarders in the house where two of the boys lived.

It appears that the cave-in caught all three, but the two got out and gave the alarm, uncovering the head only of Bobbie before they left. The little fellow was gotten out as quickly as possible, but life was extinct.

DECEMBER 4: Marshal Joe Trudell was re-elected chief of the Red Jacket fire department last evening, by an unanimous vote…The re-election of Chief Trudell to the post of honor has caused universal satisfaction generally throughout the city. He is looked upon as a most genial officer, and in the matter of fighting fires, the most capable man that the village possesses.

DECEMBER 10: Florida was given another visit by the fire fiend last night about 11 o'clock resulting in the total destruction of the double house at the corner of Quincy and Red Jacket streets, formerly owned by Albert Rasmussen, but recently bought by Will Nara, the photographer. Mr. Nara also lost a $100 camera in the fire.

…Mr. Nara had expected to have the house ready for occupancy by Christmas and had put in a complete set of furnishings for a party who contemplated renting part of the house. Mr. Nara has the sympathy of the community in his loss, which gives his bright prospects a severe setback.

DECEMBER 12: Miss Maggie Walz, of Pine street, has returned from Montreal and Quebec, where she spent about a week in the interests of a number of emigrants who had just come over and who had been detained at Montreal on account of affliction of the eye which was thought to be contagious.

DECEMBER 18: Izzie Blumenthal, who has been in business in Calumet for a great many years, expects to discontinue catering to the Calumet public about February 1 and will move to Kenosha, Wis., where he expects to go into business…In business circles, ever since his debut here under the firm name of Ruttenberg & Blumenthal, he has held the respect and esteem of all who know him, and since branching out in his own interest, he has by honest dealing, worked up a good trade. But, as Mr. Blumenthal says, times are not what they used to be and he has decided to try other fields, and for his success his friends extend him their best wishes.

DECEMBER 19: Jim Connors, a well-known frequenter of the various livery barns in the city, was found lying dead on the floor of the hay loft of Charles Mugford's livery barn at 1 o'clock today. Connors has always been an imbiber of spirituous liquors and it is without doubt that death was caused through excessive alcoholism.

DECEMBER 21: A meeting of the Finnish union was held yesterday afternoon at the Maggie Walz block on Pine street, when John Lakso was elected president, and Miss Maggie Walz secretary. There was a fairly large attendance. The meeting was called for the purpose of going into details with respect to the building of a suitable hall for meetings, etc., to be used by the various Finnish societies of the community.

The home of Mr. and Mrs. Charles Piggoine, of Tenth street, Yellow Jacket, was saddened Saturday afternoon by the sudden taking off of their darling daughter, the little one having had the misfortune to fall into a pan of scalding hot water, being scalded so badly that she died some time after.

DECEMBER 23: The brief announcement in last evening's *Evening News* that the committee handling the proceeds of the fat men's base ball game that was played in Calumet last summer, were giving away 500 pounds of turkeys to the poor of the neighborhood, has caused much satisfaction throughout the township.

DECEMBER 24: Christmas eve broke quiet over Calumet as far as shoppers were concerned, and it was not till late in the afternoon that things commenced to liven up somewhat. This was accounted for, to a certain extent, by the blizzard that was raging. As the evening wore on, however, Fifth street commenced to brighten up, and a lot of money changed hands…

Among the Xmas window decorations none call for special mention more than those of the Quello market. The window is tastefully decorated with cuts of beef, interspersed with a plentiful amount of parsley, the green of the vegetable adding much to the color of the juicy beef. But it is in the line of pork that the market comes in for special comment. Half a dozen young porkers are laid across the top of the window and in place of their natural eyes are inserted small electric globes of different colors, which give the whole window a beauteous effect.

Liddicoat's independent Carol choir will be on the streets of Red Jacket this evening and the residents will be treated to some rare old English Christmas carols…The music appeals specially to the large number of Cornishmen who are congregated here, and when they hear the strains of the old familiar carols floating on their ears, their thoughts are carried home to the old home across the sea. This innovation of carol singing by a number of Cornishmen has been in vogue for a number of years, but judging from the expressions of the listeners who congregate around the singers every year, its popularity never seems to wane.

DECEMBER 26: Christmas day broke cold and stormy over Calumet, the streets being practically deserted. The thermometer registered as low as 10 degrees (below), and was never higher than eight degrees for the whole day.

DECEMBER 28: Two brothers, named John and Matt Lund, of Calumet, set out Christmas eve to celebrate in the good old-fashioned way, and after imbibing pretty freely, commenced to get noisy. Then they thought a Christmas carol or two in the Finnish language would liven things up a bit.

Everything went all right for a time, but the same carols became so monotonous to some of the listeners that a few of the bolder of those present in the saloon went up to the brothers and asked them to change their tune. Now John and Matt thought they were doing all right, and they were not going to change to please anyone. And they were not backward in saying so. In fact, they spoke their minds so freely that they became insulting, and when they were ordered to leave the saloon, they wanted to know who was going to put them out. Then the row started, and in a moment clouds of dust were flying off the floor, and some of those present were busily engaged in licking it up, as the result of Matt's sledge hammer blows.

They were eventually run out of the saloon and into the arms of Officer Dickley who happened to be passing. The officer experienced some trouble in getting his men to the village jail, and had to place the "come alongs" on the wrist of one of them. This action on his part was the means of infuriating the crowd of young fellows who soon congregated around, and threats were made audibly to release the man from custody. The wiser counsel of the elder men present prevailed, and the men were locked up.

DECEMBER 31: A great deal of annoyance is being caused by the small boys at the Mineral Range depot…who congregate there for the purpose of taking up parcels, newspapers, etc., and has reached such an acute stage that the services of the marshal were requisitioned yesterday, and he cleared the depot of the small boys who were there in swarms…It is said that the boys indulge in tobacco chewing in the depot, and that around the place where they congregate the place is like a perfect swamp. They are also addicted to the habit of wrestling, and passengers on more than one occasion have been carried off their feet, and their protests against such conduct met with jeers by the boys.

---

### Photos, pages 78-80

Page 78: Top: Tamarack park? *Superior View*
　　　　　Bottom: Looking north toward Pine Street. *Grathoff*
Page 79: Looking north on Fifth Street. *Superior View*
Page 80: Top: Picnic at Waterworks park, August 10, 1907. *MTU-Copper Country Historical Collections*
　　　　　Bottom: Bianchi's "beer garden." *Marquette County Historical Society*

# Copper Country **1904** *Evening News*

*Sitting calmly in his automobile and steering just the same as if he was being propelled through the efforts of the machine, Captain Eric Abramson was towed through the streets of Red Jacket by a horse. Something had gone wrong with the mechanism of the automobile, and it refused to act.*

JANUARY 2: Neither the Osceola nor the Kearsarge miners went underground yesterday and consequently no rock was brought to the surface. It is claimed that the action of the men in not turning up was a protest against the action of the company in refusing to declare the day a holiday as is done by the Calumet and Hecla mining company.

There has always been a bitter feeling over the matter of New Year's day among the miners, the Osceola and Kearsarge men feeling that they were hardly dealt with in the matter. Their action of yesterday is causing a lot of talk in the town, the general feeling being that the men did the only thing it was possible to do under the circumstances to express their disapproval and that their action may establish a precedent.

JANUARY 4: The No. 3 engine house of the North Tamarack mine, which is controlled by the Bigelow syndicate, was visited by a serious fire this morning at about 3 o'clock, which resulted in the entire inside being badly scorched and the peak of the roof being burned through in several places, leaving large holes.

The Bisbee excursion on January 19 is proving immensely popular in all the Lake Superior region and people of many branches of life intend to go out to sunshine land. A good many will remain in the southwest in the hope that the mild climate will prove beneficial to their health, while others are going in the hope of finding better business situations.

Several people are complaining of the danger attendant upon the heavy blocks of ice and snow that are hanging from business places and private dwellings in and about the city. Up to the present an abnormal quantity of snow has fallen, and the roofs are simply overburdened with it.

JANUARY 5: "Two birds of passage," hailing from Chicago, who have been paying the village of Red Jacket a visit during the past five weeks, left this afternoon for their homes. That is, they had to, at the instigation of Marshal Joe Trudell.

They have been boarding at the home of Wo Chung, the man who washee-washees near the Mineral Range depot. Officers of the village have had the women under their observation ever since they have been here. Their mode of procedure has been to stay with the Chinamen a week at a time, and then they would go visiting and take in the sights of the county. Their last trip was yesterday and when they got back they were confronted by Marshal Trudell, who told them that their actions were not allowed

in this county, and that if they did not go back to their homes that he should make complaint against them.

JANUARY 8: It is considered by no means improbable that the list of dividend paying Lake Superior copper mines this year will be the largest for a long time. As it stands now it includes five mines, i.e., the Calumet & Hecla, Quincy, Wolverine, Tamarack and Osceola, and it is likely that two more will join the ranks before the end of the year.

Contractor Ed Ulseth, Architect Maas and Councilmen James Wiggins, James McHardy and John Gasparovitch, the latter three gentlemen comprising the building committee of the village council, met at the theatre on Wednesday evening last with a view of seeing what improvements could be introduced in connection with the playhouse.

It is probable that the gallery boys will receive special attention. At the present time in coming out, they empty to the main stairs and mingle with the people from both the balcony and lower floor, but it is the wish of the building committee, if at all possible, to cut a stairway leading to the town hall. This will be done, if it is at all feasible, the only difficulty the authorities are figuring on is whether the stairway will strike the roof on being cut. If it can be done without doing that, then a stairway will be cut and the "gods" will have an entrance and exit all their own.

JANUARY 9: Leap Year, the banner year for the young ladies, will be ushered in in this city in no mean way, as a large number of the young damsels of the city have arranged to give a leap year party at the Calumet Light Guard armory on the evening of Wednesday, January 20, for which the Calumet & Hecla orchestra will furnish the music.

JANUARY 13: If there is one thing more than another that will give a person an idea of the amount of snow that has fallen so far this season and hauled off the streets by the village teams, it is the large amount which has been deposited on the vacant lot back of Pine street near the railroad, which forms a runway ten feet high and makes a half circle from the alley entrance clear over to the Tamarack Junior road.

JANUARY 14: Mrs. Sarah Wilkins, of Fifth street, has been granted a patent on a novel hat pin which she has invented, the same going into effect from the 8th of last month.

Dr. Ana Heideman, of this city, is the only Finnish woman doctor in the United States. She came to the Lake Superior copper country several years ago, and has been practicing medicine for many years.

Last summer, at the instigation of local medicine men, she was arrested for not being a registered physician. A few weeks later she successfully passed the examination of the state board of examiners.

Dr. Heideman was graduated from the University of Helsingfors, the highest educational institution in Finland, and considered one of the best in Europe. She speaks fluently several languages, and is popular among her people in upper Michigan.

There are a few other Finnish women in the copper country who practice somewhat akin to medicine. They are known by the old name of "rubbing women."

The treatment now so popular throughout the United States, and practiced by the best medical schools of the world, known as "massage," was a favorite remedy and means of recuperation among the women of Finland centuries ago, and is still employed by them, a few of whom gain a good livelihood by it in this section.

JANUARY 19: A perfect hurricane raged over Houghton county during last night. The full force of the wind was felt in Calumet and vicinity, although there is little or no damage worth recording to buildings. The velocity of the wind was terrible, and literally shook several residences to their foundations. Instances are recorded of residents feeling the very beds they laid on shaking under them, and articles of crockery were heard rattling in the cupboards.

JANUARY 21: A shocking sight was witnessed on Seventh street last evening. This was no other than the spectacle of boys, varying in age from 14 to 16 years, rambling through the street in a state of intoxication. It is not known for a certainty where the boys obtained their liquor, but it is said that a chivaree was held by them in the neighborhood and that to stop the boys beer was placed on the sidewalk for them.

*Gospel Services*: Secretary George Westerman, of the Y.M.C.A., commenced a series of services today at the Tamarack mine, which he proposes to hold weekly. The service was held during the noon-day hour, and was well attended.

JANUARY 27: Operations are completely suspended at the Tamarack Junior branch of the Osceola Consolidated mine. The single drill which was in commission there for over a year sinking a winze in the lode from the twelfth level of No. 2 shaft has been withdrawn and it is unlikely that the Tamarack Junior will ever again become a producer.

The Tamarack Junior shafts at one time would have proved valuable to the Calumet & Hecla, in fact, it is understood that negotiations for their purchase were under way. They would be of little value now, however, as the Calumet & Hecla is sinking a blind shaft from the fifty-seventh level of the Red Jacket shaft to reach the ground in the five forties lying north, south and west of the Junior.

FEBRUARY 8: With the thermometer registering in the neighborhood of 20 degrees below zero and a stiff northeaster blowing, a state of affairs that is not hankered after by the average fireman when called out for duty, the Red Jacket and Calumet fire departments were called out at about 5 o'clock yesterday morning by an alarm from box No. 41, located at the corner of Fifth and Pine streets. The fire was in the building occupied by a bakery owned by Messrs. Lampinen and Erickson and Mrs. Brown, but which had just recently changed hands, being formerly owned by John Standell. The building itself was owned by Joseph Pinten.

FEBRUARY 12: The new Light Guard Armory was opened last evening, and the opening was attended by the elite of Houghton county. The nature of the opening was a grand ball, and it was one of the most brilliant functions ever witnessed in this part of the state. Punctually at 9 o'clock the full Calumet and Hecla band struck up and to strains of an overture the marchers paraded up the magnificent dance hall, arm in arm. Watched from the gallery overhead, the scene was an inspiring one.

…The present building is the finest of its kind in the Upper Peninsula. It is fitted with every essential that is necessary to the successful conducting of a militia company, and in addition is so laid out in design that it is a veritable paradise for social functions.

FEBRUARY 15: The storm of yesterday was one of the fiercest experienced in the copper country for many a long day. With the thermometer away down and a gale blowing the snow in blinding eddies, pedestrians who ventured out had a terrible time in battling against it…Passengers on the Copper Range road had a pretty bad experience, being confined on the train from 1 o'clock yesterday afternoon until well after midnight.

FEBRUARY 27: The habit that several of the small storekeepers have gotten into on Fifth street of depositing rubbish on the street in front of their stores, has made the marshal hot under the collar, and he has said pretty straight things to those who have been particularly lax in their observance of the village ordinances.

FEBRUARY 29: One prominent resident said to the reporter this morning, that never in the history of the village was a poundmaster wanted so badly as at the present time. The village, says he, is overrun with cattle and dogs, and no one seems to care or ascertain who is responsible for this state of things.

MARCH 1: The *Evening News* has been approached on several occasions by theatre goers who are disgusted with the actions of a certain crowd of young fellows who block the sidewalk after the termination of each performance, and make it necessary for people wishing to take the street cars to reach their destination, either to push through the crowd to reach the cars or to make a wide detour. The *Evening News* does not believe that these young fellows do so with any intention of creating annoyance, but rather from thoughtlessness, and a desire to see who were present and perhaps, with the hope of seeing their best girl.

MARCH 2: Marshal Joe Trudell then brought forward the matter of better facilities of escape in case of fire being afforded persons who attend the different halls in the city. The marshal in particular mentioned the Italian hall, which, in his opinion, was little better than a rat trap in case of emergency. There was only one escape from this particular hall in case of fire, and even then the doors opened inwards.

MARCH 4: The death rate for Calumet during the past six weeks has been abnormally high. Especially is this noticeable among young children and persons of more mature years. There is a great prevalence of pneumonia and la grippe in the township and it is due to the former disease mainly that the death rate has been so high.

MARCH 5: The present winter which we are passing through is responsible for more snow than has fallen since the winter of 1875. These are the words of one of the oldest residents of the copper country. In those days, said he, the snow would bank some thirty feet high, and it was no uncommon occurrence to see it on a level with the second story windows of the residences. Again, it would be a matter of impossibility to see dwellings on the other side of the street, owing to the heavy banks of snow.

Matters have not gone quite so bad as that this winter, but there are scores of residences in the township where the snow has drifted over the kitchen window, and it has been necessary to clear it away before the housewife could see to carry out her duties.

MARCH 10: Business is at a standstill in Calumet and the streets are practically deserted. The snow is drifting heavily, in some places running up to ten feet high.

MARCH 21: Count Carl Mannerheim, the Finnish exile, arrived in Calumet today from Chicago. He was met by Attorney Larson who immediately brought the count into

touch with some of the prominent Finnish people of the community.

MARCH 30: An accident which might have incurred serious consequences and probably proven fatal, occurred in the vicinity of the Arlington hotel this morning about 10:30 o'clock. The accident was caused by a lot of snow sliding off of the refrigerator building on the south side of the hotel. Solomon Rautio, of Newtown, who delivers milk at the hotel, was coming through the narrow passage at the side with pails in hand, when all of a sudden and without the least warning all the snow and ice that the roof contained came down on top of him, causing him to be completely submerged.

As luck would have it one of the lady boarders occupying a room on one of the upper floors happened to be looking out of the window at the moment the accident occurred and when she saw what had happened immediately notified the employees about the hotel, who soon got shovels and extricated the man from his perilous position.

MARCH 31: Another case of snowballing, this time in Red Jacket, was heard in Judge Fisher's court last evening. The accused is named Tom Rinowski and the complainant Frank Schulte. Rinowski is aged 23 and the complainant alleged that he was struck about the head with snowballs by Rinowski.

Snowballing on the streets of both villages has been pretty prevalent this season, but now that arrests are being made and parties are aware that the officers are determined to put a stop to it, the nuisance will be stopped without doubt.

APRIL 6: The D., S.S. & A., commencing on Sunday next, will resume their sleeping car service between Chicago and the copper country...The service has been out of commission since December 10, and was thus placed out owing to the great difficulty experienced in bringing through the heavy trains consequent on the heavy falls of snow that was being experienced.

APRIL 18: At the meeting of the Suomi society held at their hall in the Dunstan block last evening a move was started for the purpose of installing a library in connection with the lodge. Some of the best books in the Finnish language, as well as a few in English, will be placed on the shelves for distribution.

A distinct shock was felt in Calumet about 3:30 this afternoon. The *Evening News* hastily called up the different mining locations, but could get no clue as to its origin...In Calumet the windows in buildings shook violently and several business people thought that the explosion had occurred directly on their premises, so acute were the oscillations.

APRIL 19: All kinds of theories are being expressed today on the shock that was felt in Calumet yesterday afternoon. The *News* has heard one of the best solutions of the noise, and one that is more than probable, this is that a heavy fall of ground occurred at the old workings that have been abandoned for some time at the back of the Hecla…

The shock caused little short of a panic in the Quello block. A local wag in this block suggested that the price of meat had fallen, hence the distinct rattling of the windows.

APRIL 21: From the actions of a certain individual who is in the city, it is more than probable that a "cocaine fiend" is located here. He was in the Jackola drug store on Monday afternoon. His mode of procedure is to ask for the directory, follow the clerk to the dispensing counter, and pretend to be looking over it, with a view to taking down some names and addresses. He did this Monday afternoon, and while the clerk was attending to a customer he appropriated a bottle of cocaine.

APRIL 22: A.E. Winship, who delivered a lecture here on January 20, under the auspices of the Calumet Woman's club, has the following to say of Calumet in the *Journal of Education*, of which he is the editor:

The very oddest town I know
Is Calumet with its pack of snow,
And the mines so deep where the coppers grow.

There is no Calumet. To be sure there are 50,000 people there, and 10,000 of them are daily underground. To be sure the mines have for a third of a century paid 40 per cent on the par value of the stock—not watered, but highly condensed—and yet if you look up Uncle Sam's census man you will see that he could find no "Calumet," and so left it out of the enumeration. Instead of Calumet he found Red Jacket, and half a dozen other incorporated villages, and these he reported and I have added them and found about 50,000 persons, big and little, and these they call Calumet, and they have organized them into a miscellaneous conglomeration called a school district, which belongs nowhere, but is everywhere.

APRIL 23: Copper mining is a sure industry and one of the boys of the Yellow Jacket school in writing to a school fellow down in one of the lower states, told his school fellow so. In addition, however, he incidentally mentioned that another industry of Calumet was the cleaning of snow off the streets by the street commissioner. This is rich and will be food for much thought by residents of the township.

APRIL 25: It appears that some of the boys who hang around the theatre had discovered a loop hole where they could gain an entrance to the gallery without being detected by climbing to the top of the canopy affair in front of the theatre and walking along the cornice work to a window where they got in.

One young fellow managed to go through the daring piece of work successfully, as they had arranged to have the lights put out while they were operating. This is what gave the snap away, as one of the theatre hands suspected that something was up and went to investigate.

He came upon the scene just as the second boy was climbing through and let the window down on his head, which gave him such a fright that he would have fallen back onto the sidewalk quite a distance below had it not been that he was being held there by the closed window. He received cuts around the mouth by the squeeze.

APRIL 27: A movement is on foot in Calumet to celebrate the Finnish national holiday on midsummer day, June 24…At Eveleth, Minn., a big celebration is being planned and the Finns in the mining camps there are to be granted a holiday…The day has been celebrated before in the copper country, but has never been recognized among the Finnish population universally as a holiday.

Now that the snow is rapidly going off the village, unsightly heaps are being exposed to view. The nuisance is mostly apparent on Sixth and Seventh streets. The *News* had its attention called to the nuisance by one of Red Jacket's councilmen, and he spoke in no mild terms of the filthy condition of the streets.

It has apparently been the habit of several of the residents to dump their refuse on the streets during the winter time, and to trust to the drifts to cover it up quickly.

MAY 2: The ore reserves of the Calumet & Hecla are variously estimated at 10 to 30 years. The former figure is much too low, as the mine has ground opened ahead of the stoping parties for nearly that length of time, while the higher figure is based upon desires and hopes, rather than on tangible measurements and estimates.

MAY 3: A party of ten Finnish people, with their families, left today for Fitchburg, Mass., where they have purchased farms and on which they will locate. Quite a number of Finnish families who have been former residents of this place, from all accounts seem to be prospering, which has been the means of enticing a great many more to come. These people are well adapted for the work of tilling the soil and stock raising, so there is not the least doubt that they will make things boom.

MAY 5: Some of the alleys and yards of the village are in a disgraceful state and visitors coming to the city have often remarked of the farm-yard like appearance of the municipality as a whole.

MAY 13: Now is the accepted time. Calumet residents who are interested in the maple syrup industry have been visiting the camps of Keweenaw and Baraga counties during the past three or four days, and report quite a number of campers.

The sap is running freely as the result of the winter breakup, and from present indications the harvest should be a fruitful one.

MAY 16: Wildly gesticulating and shouting at the top of his voice, was a young Austrian named Plautz on Fifth street at noon time today. From the man's wild look and his extraordinary actions, it was apparent that he was demented, and he soon gathered a crowd around him. Marshal Trudell was soon on the scene, and with help, he secured the unfortunate young fellow and then it was found necessary to manacle him. Later he was removed to the county jail at Houghton.

Martin Naiman, a miner employed at the Osceola mine, shot his son Saturday afternoon, because he would not give over money at the father's request.

MAY 17: A force of men began this morning carrying out the contemplated improvements to the old *Evening News* office mechanical department at the corner of Fifth and Pine streets. It is the intention to erect a superstructure with a very complete set of offices, comprising the editorial business, reportorial, and part of the mechanical departments on one floor, while the heavy machinery will be in the basement.

MAY 18: Joseph Asselin, proprietor of the Palace meat market on Sixth street, had one of his valuable plate glass windows broken last night. The miscreant who did the breaking is as much of a mystery as in the Kinsman harness store case, and up to the present time no clue has been obtained as to the culprit. Each window was valued at $70 or $80.

In addition to these acts of vandalism, several of the private residences of the village have had the windows broken during the past few days, and even the windows of the Red Jacket school have come in for the small boys' rocks.

MAY 19: The commencement exercises of the graduating class of the Calumet high school will be held on Friday evening, June 17, at the Calumet theatre. Dr. George Vincent, of the faculty of the Chicago university, will deliver the address to the students. The full Calumet & Hecla orchestra has been engaged for the occasion and during the evening it will render selections.

The class will probably consist of 25 members, which is much smaller than other years.

MAY 25: Samuel Hippola of the lake shore, a well known fisherman, who has been missing from his home during the past three weeks, is on his way to Finland. He left his home three weeks ago, presumably to go to Hancock for

the purpose of purchasing material necessary in his work, and took quite an amount of money with him.

Instead of purchasing the outfit he was after, he went to Edward Waara, the Hancock boat agent, and purchased a ticket for Finland. This was on the same day that he left home, according to Mr. Waara, and while his family was wondering what had become of the erring Samuel, he was sailing contentedly over the waters of the broad Atlantic on a visit to the scenes of his childhood. Just what his intentions are in the future not even his family knows.

MAY 26: Invitations were issued today by the committee having in charge the Michigan College of Mines annual ball, to be held in the new Light Guard armory, Calumet, on Monday, June 6.

The choir of the Hecla Finnish church will give a concert and bazaar at the Red Jacket Town hall next Saturday evening, May 28. The principal event of the evening will be the raffling of the pipe organ which is illustrated herewith. This instrument was made by John Karshu, a local organ builder, and is a monument to his genius.

MAY 31: Memorial day in Calumet was observed with fitting solemnity yesterday. Many of the business houses and prominent buildings flew "Old Glory" at half-mast, and all business houses and banks were closed all day. Lake View cemetery was the scene of a reverent throng yesterday afternoon, when it is estimated that fully 5,000 persons congregated there to witness the exercises by the military organizations of the city.

JUNE 4: Eugene V. Debs, Socialist candidate for president of the United States and one of the foremost labor leaders of the day, addressed an audience of about 300 persons at the Red Jacket Town hall last evening on "Socialism." He spoke for two hours and was applauded quite frequently.

He dwelt principally on the standing of capital compared with that of labor, and brought out many points favoring both, although his leaning was strongly toward the working classes. Mr. Debs speaks with great force and is very fluent.

Quite a number of ladies were in attendance at last evening's meeting.

JUNE 6: The *News* reporter had a pleasant conversation with Mr. Debs at the Central hotel. He expressed himself as impressed with the improvement which this part of the country had undergone since his last visit here, in 1897. He noted especially the large number of buildings which have been erected, and he takes this as a good sign that the people in this locality were prospering.

Taking everything in a general way, Mr. Debs was unable to see how things could be otherwise in such a blessed country as the Keweenaw peninsula. He considered this section to be very fortunate in having such a staple product as copper to supply the world, and he compared some of the unkind conditions of the west and southwest with this section. What pleased Mr. Debs was the fact that everything here operated in harmony, with no cause for any decided change in the workings.

JUNE 7: Edward Wiatr, who robbed the Polish church on Seventh street last week, was brought before County Agent Mason last night in Judge Fisher's court, and after pleading guilty was sentenced to the Industrial School at Lansing until he reaches the age of sixteen. Young Wiatr admitted, when caught by the priest in the act, that he had been systematically robbing the Catholic churches for some time past.

JUNE 14: Carl Canth, an exile from Russia, has arrived in Calumet from New York...This man was driven out of Kopia, his home, by the Russian authorities on account of the sentiment he expressed regarding Russia's treatment of the people in general...

Mr. Canth is a son of the distinguished Finnish writer, Mrs. Minnie Canth. Her books have gained fame in this country as well as Finland. "The Workman's Wife," written by this lady and produced on the stage in the form of a drama, has been suppressed by the Russian government on account of the sentiment and spirit contained therein. This play has already been produced in the county by local talent.

JUNE 15: The manual training exhibition, which was concluded yesterday afternoon at the Calumet High schools, furnished a treat to those who took the opportunity of visiting the schools. During the two days the exhibition was open, the schools were visited by thousands of persons, many of them parents of the pupils who had exhibits on view.

JUNE 29: Agitation has again been resumed regarding the installation of a public water fountain in the village of Red Jacket. The drivers of delivery wagons are the most interested in this movement, and have been hoping against hope that the council would take some action. Pedestrians, too, might derive a great deal of benefit from it. At the present time there is no public means whereby a person might quench his own thirst or water his horses. The teamsters find a great deal of difficulty in procuring water for their animals when any distance from the stables, and are anxious that a watering trough be placed at some convenient corner.

JULY 1: *Number 13 resumes*
Calumet & Hecla Opening Up Osceola Amygdaloid Again at Southern End of Property.
MEANS MUCH TO TOWN
It Is Understood That Between 80 and 100 Men Will Be Put to Work at Present—Idle Since 1901

JULY 5: As usual, a number of accidents are recorded in Calumet and environments due to the use of firecrackers. An old man, named Danielson, of School street, near Roehm's barn, was firing off a cannon yesterday morning, as was his usual wont on the Fourth of July, when the powder with which he had the old weapon charged flashed in his eyes. One of his eyes is so badly burned that it is feared that he will lose the sight of it.

JULY 6: Mrs. Henry Hendrickson of Laurium has decided to open a school in the Walz block on Pine street for instruction in the culinary art. Mrs. Hendrickson will also teach laundry work and also embroidery.

A restaurant will be run in connection with the school on the ground floor where meals will be served at all hours.

JULY 7: Several of the Scottish-American residents of Calumet have begun to revive one of the national games of Scotland and England—football. A team has been formed and practice is indulged in every evening on the grounds near the Hecla cemetery.

The game is played with a round ball instead of the egg-shaped ball that is generally seen in the American game. The ball is kicked and is not allowed to be touched with the hands. This style of play was in vogue in this city before Rugby was introduced. It is known as Association football.

JULY 23: People came from all over the county this morning to witness the big parade of the Walter L. Main circus, which is giving two performances in Calumet today. Fifth street was a seething mass of sightseers. Long before the music of the calliope was heard throngs were lining Pine street, eager to get their first look at the mammoth show.

JULY 27: This is the time of the year that Calumet is visited by the tramp element to a certain extent, but the present influx is much greater than ever known before, and the menacing attitude of the tramps that are in Calumet at the present time has never been equalled in the history of the township. It may be safely said, however, now that the officers are acquainted with the true state of affairs, that the tramp pests in Calumet will get their "walking papers" inside of 24 hours, and the "place that once knew them shall know them no more."

JULY 30: It is not generally known that Frank Polish, the man charged with stabbing Marshal Joseph Trudell on Eighth street, six weeks ago, attempted to jump his bonds and was arrested by his bondsmen while in the act of escaping...

It will be remembered that Polish stabbed Marshal Trudell on Eighth street on a Sunday night in June. Angus MacDonald was escorting a lady to her home, accompanied by his wife, when Polish jumped out against them. Polish was handled rather roughly, and it is presumed that he waited for MacDonald to reappear. They met outside the residence of the marshal on Eighth street, and on MacDonald shouting for help, the marshal rushed out of his house and joined in the fray, attempting to rescue MacDonald from the infuriated man. In the melee that ensued the marshal was stabbed in three places, and the culprit got away. He was arrested the next morning.

AUGUST 1: At the present time it is impossible to find a person in the town answering to the tramp description, and the clean out has been a thorough one. Marshal Trudell has made up his mind that every suspicious character entering Red Jacket shall be placed under surveillance either by himself or some person in authority, and that on the least suspicious move, such a party will be run out of town in double quick time.

AUGUST 9: The reunion of the Finnish temperance societies of the copper country at the Tamarack park was participated in by a large number of the Finnish residents hereabouts. The exceedingly fine weather helped to swell the crowd. The program at the park consisted of speechmaking, reciting and singing by glee clubs. Representatives were present from 15 different societies of Houghton and Keweenaw. Prizes were offered. Mrs. Palmer won first and Miss Walz second prize.

AUGUST 15: George Antioho, the Greek fruiterer, who conducts two fruit stores, one at the north end of Fifth street and the other near the Mineral Range depot, had the fronts of both his stores daubed over with tar between Saturday night and early Sunday morning. Antioho was seen by the *Evening News* and he gave it as his firm opinion that the act was the outcome of his refusal to close his store on the occasion of the Red Jacket fruiterers' picnic yesterday.

Hazel Lemay was arrested last night by Marshal Trudell, charged with assaulting two men on Pine street. It is alleged that while walking down Pine street last evening, she met a man named Lachti, whom she knocked down without any seeming provocation, laying him out for some time. She was carrying a heavy handled umbrella, which was capable of giving a wicked blow. The woman is said to have then sauntered down the street, and meeting another man, she gave him a blow, also.

The woman, who is frequently known as "Big Hazel," has been a source of much trouble to the village.

AUGUST 19: Wilho Leikas, who has just arrived from Helsingfors, Finland, has purchased the stock of books from Miss M. Walz and will hereafter conduct the business at the same stand. He will also handle literature from the pen of Erro Erko, the Finnish writer at present located in New York, and August Anderson of Ashtabula, Ind. The new store will also have in stock all the leading Finnish periodicals published in the United States and on the continent.

AUGUST 24: It is understood that on October 1 of this year the business of the Calumet postoffice will be transferred from the present building at the south end of Fifth street to the Ed Ryan block on Sixth street.

AUGUST 25: The opening of the Calumet schools takes place next Monday morning. Since the legislature has just legalized the payment of tuition to outside districts, the Calumet High school extends a cordial invitation to the students of the surrounding districts, who are prepared to do high school work, to avail themselves of the excellent opportunity offered of securing a thoroughly practical education at slight expense. The charge for tuition is $10 per quarter, payable in advance.

AUGUST 26: It is not generally known that the Calumet Public school has a charity list. Such is the case, however, as many a poor family in this district can testify to. Charity as applied by the schools has reference to the granting of text books free to poor families who are unable to purchase them.

AUGUST 31: Data, covering a period of four years, has been compiled by Dr. R.B. Harkness of the United States weather bureau, at Houghton. Following is the summary: The mean or normal temperature was 56 degrees.

The warmest month (of September) was in 1901, with an average of 58 degrees, and the coldest month was that of 1902, with an average of 56 degrees. The highest temperature was 88 degrees on September 1, 1900, and the lowest temperature was 34 degrees on September 19, 1901.

The earliest date on which first "killing" frost occurred in autumn, was September 29, 1903, but the average date on which first "killing" frost occurred in autumn, was October 7. The average date on which last "killing" frost occurred in spring, was May 4. The latest date on which last "killing" frost occurred in spring, was May 16, 1904.

No snowfall has occurred during the month of September for the past four years.

SEPTEMBER 3: Colonel Somers of Chicago, and representing the Bijou Theater company, is in Calumet, and on Friday made arrangements with the owners of the Agnitch building on Fifth street, to rent the same on a three years' lease. It is the intention of Colonel Somers to run a theater in Calumet with popular prices prevailing, and with changes of programs daily.

The Bijou Theater company is on the syndicate plan, and has branches all over the country, with headquarters at Chicago...Colonel Somers is figuring on installing one of Edison's moving picture apparatuses, and the machine will be supplied with all the latest pictures of the Russo-Japanese war. In addition to the moving picture entertainment, there will be the vaudeville features, the whole forming an hour of cheap and profitable amusement.

A Tamarack miner placed a rat in his partner's dinner pail one day this week, and has lost his job in consequence. According to the story told in the justice court, the parties involved were partners underground. Some time ago trouble arose between them, which culminated this week in one of the men placing a live rat in the dinner pail of the other. The dinner pail was empty of food, the man having eaten his dinner some time before.

He took it home, and this is where the trouble started. The man's wife took hold of the pail, as was her wont, to cleanse it, preparatory to filling it again on the next day. As she took the cover off, the imprisoned rodent leaped out and gave the woman such a fright as to upset her nerves badly.

SEPTEMBER 19: Fire broke out at 1:20 this morning in the Jacka block on Fifth street, and before it was under control the building was a complete wreck. The ground floors of the block were rented by J.J. Ellis, jeweler, and Charles Fichtel, druggist and newsdealer. In the upper floors of the building offices were occupied by the Calumet & Arizona Mining company, Drs. Labarge and Watson, and W.W. Ellis, insurance agent.

The cause of the fire is believed to be the work of incendiaries committed for the purpose of covering up their tracks after committing a burglary.

SEPTEMBER 22: Hod Stuart has arrived in Calumet, and at a meeting of the new rink promoters, formally announced his intention to affiliate with the Laurium people. This will be good news to Calumet lovers of hockey as they are now assured exhibitions of the real article in this splendid game. Mr. Stuart, in addition to being captain of the team, has also been appointed manager of the rink, to which position he is well adapted.

SEPTEMBER 23: Hod Stuart is counted on as one of the best hockey players who has ever graced the ice since the game was introduced in copperdom, which is saying not a little. His playing with the Portage Lake champion team last year was a good exhibition of his mettle, and will go far in gaining the confidence of Calumet people as to his ability.

SEPTEMBER 26: Acting under instructions from Sheriff Wills, Marshal Joseph Trudell visited every saloon in Calumet on Saturday afternoon, and demanded the removal of all slot machines and other devices used for gambling. There is not a wheel, either horizontal or vertical, turning in the county today. The stud table, the faro deal box, the crap shooting, all these are done away with and if any man wants to take a chance on getting a bit of the other fellow's money he'll have to jump him for it or flip pennies or run him 100 yards for a side bet.

SEPTEMBER 28: The homeseekers who left Calumet some time ago for Manitoba to inspect the lands offered for sale by the Scandinavian Land company, have arrived in the city and express themselves as being well pleased with their trip. The party, which was in charge of Miss Maggie Walz, the local agent, left by steamer from Hancock for Port Arthur and the remainder of the trip was made by rail. Two weeks was taken up. The land in question is located about 300 miles northwest of Winnipeg, and though it is in an almost entirely uninhabited region, it is said to be very fertile. At the present time the land may be had at very low prices.

SEPTEMBER 29: Following the usual fall custom, the bovines of the village of Red Jacket have again started their daily and nightly meanderings, and evidence of their wanderings in quest of food is apparent on most any street of the village. Ash barrels are being turned over promiscuously, and their contents dumped in the roadway, presenting a most unsightly appearance.

Since the opening of the Bijou Theater company's branch theater in the Agnitch block on Fifth street, crowds of young fellows infest the sidewalk and approaches to the theater and not only cause annoyance to the manager of the theater and patrons who may wish to enter, but also block up the sidewalk so that persons wishing to pass have either to push their way through the crowd, or else take the roadway until the sidewalk is clear again.

SEPTEMBER 30: The bowling season has started in Calumet. The A.A. Miller alleys are fast getting in shape, and within a week bowling will be in full swing. Mr. Miller is having the alleys freshly oiled, scraped, and shellacked. When completed the alleys will be some of the finest in the county.

The Hecla dry house of the Calumet & Hecla Mining company, used for changing purposes for the miners, timbermen and trammers employed underground by the company, was gutted by fire.

Over 600 men use this dry and all found it necessary to purchase new outfits before they could return to work. There was a general stampede to the business houses which handle this variety of goods and the stores had a rushing trade for a while.

OCTOBER 4: Sitting calmly in his automobile and steering just the same as if he was being propelled through the efforts of the machine, Captain Eric Abramson was towed through the streets of Red Jacket by a horse. Something had gone wrong with the mechanism of the automobile, and it refused to act. It was useless as it was, and in order to get the machine overhauled, Captain Abramson had to call into requisition the services of a horse and teamster to pull the machine through the streets.

The novel sight of a horse pulling an automobile was too much for the risibilities of the generality of the residents of Red Jacket, and the scene furnished audible amusement for many who saw the turn-out.

OCTOBER 5: The Scandinavian Land company, of which Miss Maggie Walz is the local agent, is making arrangements for another excursion to Winnipeg and Manitoba. It is expected that the same rates will prevail as on the former occasion. Nine persons have already consented to go.

OCTOBER 12: Rumor has it that those in charge of the independent political movement in Houghton county are contemplating the publication of a Finnish daily from the near future to the eve of election. The *Paivalehti*, the Finnish daily printed in Calumet, is advocating the election of the straight Republican ticket, and the object of the proposed new daily will be to counteract the influence of the *Paivalehti*.

About 25 Calumet young people repaired to the Lake View club house Tuesday evening and spent the time dancing. Refreshments were also furnished. The club house has proven quite a popular resort for outing parties during the winter months and has been the scene of many gay gatherings. It is also a rendezvous for hunters, who find it quite convenient to refresh themselves after a long tramp. The club house is supplied with every accommodation for parties who wish to spend an evening there.

OCTOBER 17: Dominic Penucci was injured about 9 o'clock Saturday morning in the Calumet branch of the Calumet & Hecla mine and he died in the afternoon at the Calumet & Hecla hospital, where he was removed immediately after the accident. According to the testimony of the witnesses, Penucci was in the ladder way and for some reason he became frightened and jumped into the shaft.

OCTOBER 19: Several young ladies who have occasion to traverse the county road in the vicinity of Wolverine complain of the actions of certain young lads in the use of slingshots. One lady states that a boy deliberately shot at her and struck her, although she escaped serious injury.

OCTOBER 21: The society event of the year, the Light Guard annual party, has been announced for Thanksgiving eve. It is on this occasion that Calumet society turns out en masse and the evening is made the most notable of all the society functions of the year...This will be the twenty-third annual event.

The art exhibit in the large hall at the Washington school was thrown open to the public and there was a large attendance despite the inclement weather. The exhibit itself is very fine. There are on exhibition 200 exact copies of the great masterpieces in painting, sculpture and architecture.

OCTOBER 31: The two systems of horography which are maintained in the copper country six months in a year are a source of much confusion and have been characterized by many people as "a relic of antiquity." This is literally true. The custom of setting the clocks half an hour fast for the fall and winter months was instituted in the copper country before the days of railroads and electric lights, and nobody was bothered in those times by having to catch trains.

NOVEMBER 7: Tomorrow is election day and the day on which the deer hunting season opens. There are a great many hunters who would rather shoot deer on election day than cast a ballot for good government, but there are some who will wait until they have performed their obligation to the state. The business places in Calumet will be closed and the housewife will see to it today that she has a supply of meats and groceries to last until Wednesday. As it is a legal holiday, there will be no court held. Everything will be quiet except at the voting places.

Election returns will be received Tuesday night by the *Copper Country Evening News* and thrown upon a canvas by stereopticon on the side of the Walls building on the Oak street extension, east of Fifth street.

NOVEMBER 17: The Bijou theater continues to draw large houses both at the afternoon and evening performances. This is accounted for by the first class and up-to-date attractions provided for the entertainment of the public. Special mention might be made of Orville Pitcher, the blackface comedian, stump speaker and monologist. Pitcher's stunt is a sort of paradox. He says a whole lot and at the same time he does not say anything. The stump is quite amusing and original.

NOVEMBER 20: Between the handsome covers of the second edition of "Tyler's Souvenir of the Copper Country" are presented the most important scenes in this section. Coupled with the pictures of days that have long since passed, it forms a comprehensive history of the progress of the years. The views show the miners at their work and group pictures of the men in the day and night shifts of various mines are given so that their friends can pick them out with ease. The issue is the finest thing of its kind which has ever been given circulation in this part of the country. The work is finely executed on the best quality of enameled paper. It is a booklet which is worthy of preservation.

Butter and eggs are scarce and high in the Calumet market. Butter is especially so. All that is shipped in is creamery stock, not a pound of dairy being visible. Prices for creamery range from 30 to 32 cents a pound. Eggs are selling at a fairly moderate price, but the quality cannot be guaranteed. From 25 to 26 cents is asked per dozen and all are cold storage stock. The Calumet market is supplied entirely from outside and for that reason not the best of stock is received here.

NOVEMBER 24: "I never saw a November so warm or with so little rain," said Judge William Fisher, who has been in Calumet 41 years..."usually the snow comes a month earlier than this and stays all winter."

"I remember a green Christmas in Calumet over 30 years ago. The sun came out strong on Christmas day and the water was running in rivulets from recent rains."

NOVEMBER 25: The tenth anniversary of the organization of the Finnish Ladies' society was observed on Thanksgiving day night by a social and entertainment in the basement of the Finnish National church. Miss Maggie Walz reviewed the work of the society for the past 10 years and stated the object of the organization, that of protecting women's rights. She recited some poetry which was very pleasing. After Miss Walz had concluded, a violin solo was charmingly rendered by David Tolonen.

NOVEMBER 28: Carl Somers of the Bijou theater was on Monday made the defendant in a case brought against him by Sheriff Joseph Wills the charge being that he unlawfully engaged in business on Sunday, then and there offering for sale tickets of admission to a show, the same not being, then and there, works of necessity and charity.

NOVEMBER 29: If you have wheels prepare to shed them now. With the advent of Thanksgiving came a little snow, a sort of foretaste of what was to be expected. On Saturday, a sleigh was seen occasionally, but there were many spots in the roads and wheels were in the majority. On Monday, sleighs were more in evidence, but in the hustle and bustle of every day activity, many people had no time to make the change. But Tuesday's snow was too deep for wheels to wriggle through with any degree of comfort and few ventured forth without runners. It snowed a great deal all day and during the night and Calumet and vicinity is now clothed in a thick blanket of the beautiful.

For the purpose of purchasing new suits and other necessities for the coming season, the Invincible hockey team will give an entertainment this evening to raise funds. It will take place at the Red Jacket Town hall and a good program has been arranged, to consist of moving pictures, illustrated songs, vaudeville and other amusements.

DECEMBER 2: The first sand-lime brick building erected in the upper peninsula of Michigan will be called the Calumet block. The structure will be completed by New Year's day and although erected in an unusually short space of time the building is as substantial as though it had taken years to construct it. It is located on Fifth street between Portland and Scott streets.

Hockey enthusiasts in northern Michigan believe that in a few years this Canadian game will come to be looked on with as great favor, this side of the border as baseball. The recent organization of the International Hockey league, which includes both the Michigan and Canadian Soos, Calumet, Houghton and Pittsburg, is the first professional hockey league in this country.

DECEMBER 12: Many people in Calumet have been in the habit of going into the woods and cutting trees with their own hands, lugging them back home on their shoulders. But the head of the house in these days is generally too busy with other things. If he has no boy of his own he may engage one for 50 cents to bring in a nice tree. This amount is as big as a fortune in the eyes of some lads, and they usually lose no time in supplying the demand.

Mike Curto of the Wolverine chased his wife with a revolver Saturday afternoon, and in order to escape from the man's murderous intentions, the woman had to take refuge in the cellar of a neighbor's house...It appears that the stipulation placed upon his release by the woman was that he should leave the country, and accordingly Curto left for Italy last evening...

DECEMBER 14: The first Greek child born in the copper country arrived in Calumet this week. His name is George Antioho, Jr., and the little fellow seems to be just as well off far from the shores of the land of the oracles as he would be where the sun is always shining and where the earth is not covered with snow.

DECEMBER 22: They met at the corner of Elm and Sixth streets last night at seven. Both were unmarried. It finally developed that John was a prospective buyer of Christmas gifts. "I'm a victim, too," admitted James. It was then that John and James agreed to do their shopping together. They went into the barroom for a bracer, as it had been a year since they had been inside any of the department stores and it took a large quantity of nerve to enter and look at toys and other things.

Then they started out with a firm determination of buy or die. And so it went on all the evening. At nine o'clock they stood in front of another liquor shop, and talked the situation over seriously.

"Well, let's go in and have a consoling drink," said one, and the other assented.

DECEMBER 27: Calumet is in the throes of a genuine Lake Superior blizzard. The storm began on Monday and by noon today was raging with all its fury. Old settlers say that the storm king will rule for three days, if tradition is carried out.

DECEMBER 28: For the first time in the history of any Finnish church society in the United States, a sacred concert was held in the auditorium of a church. The church which made this new departure was the Finnish National church on Eighth street…Christmas was observed at the Finnish church on Eighth street and the Finnish church at Raymbaultown, as is the custom in Finland, by an early morning service on Christmas day. Christmas trees were placed in the church, and these were extensively lit up with candles.

Suomi college students of Hancock were in Calumet Monday evening and gave a concert in the Red Jacket Town hall. The hall was well filled, and an enjoyable program of music was carried out.

A furious snow storm broke upon Calumet yesterday and raged all day and night. One man was killed in a railroad collision caused by the storm and another man narrowly escaped death on Fifth street in Red Jacket, the gale turning his rig over and causing the horse to roll upon him. Many people lost their way in the blinding storm, but so far as known no one is missing, all having reached a place of safety. Hazardous experiences are related by the score.

During the night drifts of snow eight and ten feet deep were piled up in places and the occupants of some houses were completely hemmed in. Sidewalks were alternately swept bare or buried under an avalanche of snow.

Calumet was entirely cut off from the outside world by transportation, or telegraph, no trains being run on any road and the wires being down beyond limited distances.

DECEMBER 31: *A Season of Gyrations*
*The Walks of Red Jacket Treacherous This Morning*
Slip, zip, slide, zip again, crash! boom! **!! ***!!! **!! Ouch!

And the man was down.

It was yesterday afternoon when the snow began to melt. By morning, the temperature was cooled down enough to harden the path a little. The real run commenced this morning. It came with a suddenness that put many, even cool-headed, persons up in the air, most of them feet first.

---

## Photos, pages 92-94

Page 92: Top: Retail store, Red Jacket. *Houghton County Historical Society*
 Bottom: Butcher shop, Red Jacket. *Voelker*
Page 93: Top: Women in men's hats. *Finnish-American Historical Archives, Finlandia University*
 Bottom: Beer garden, Red Jacket. *Voelker*
Page 94: Top: Calumet & Hecla band (at Tamarack park?) *Voelker*
 Bottom: String band, Red Jacket. *Superior View*

# *Copper County* **1905** *Evening News*

*From the standpoint of the wholesale shoe dealer, Calumet is a "jumbo" town. The women of this section have larger feet than are found ordinarily. The reason assigned is that there is an exceptionally large foreign population and many of the women from foreign lands have unusually large feet.*

JANUARY 6: There are too many dogs running about the streets of Red Jacket. That is an expression heard frequently. Canines of all breeds and sizes roam the streets. Yesterday a drove of them shot down Fifth street and pedestrians thought a runaway had struck them. Dashing along, the animals, some of them weighing between 100 and 200 pounds, brushed against people, almost knocking them down and giving them a fright.

"It is worse than the cow nuisance," remarked one citizen. "That is bad enough," he continued, "but there are so many dogs that you notice it more. There is scarcely a stranger comes into the town who does not remark about the number of dogs running about. And this, in addition to remarks regarding the cattle…"

JANUARY 7: The Calumet Woman's club at a regular meeting in the Gately-Wiggins hall yesterday afternoon, took up the discussion of work for next year. There was a wide divergence of opinion on account of the many topics of interest which present themselves to the members of the club, but it was finally agreed that ancient history would furnish an abundance of material for discussion and would prove interesting as well as invaluable to the individual members for the reason that discoveries have been made which throw new light on manners and customs of the people who lived in the dim and distant past.

JANUARY 21: Whether gambling is allowed in Houghton county or not, some very heavy bets are recorded on tonight's hockey game. A $2,000 bet is reported to have been made at one of the principal hotels in Calumet last evening…The value of the total amount of bets on tonight's game will probably not fall far short of $10,000. All betting is even.

JANUARY 24: The first day of the Chinese calendar falls on January 22 and it is the greatest holiday of the year among the natives of the land of the poppy and John Chinaman and his brothers in this country. There are quite a number of Chinamen in Calumet and the day was observed by them according to the usual custom. New Year's day is the only Sunday in the entire celestial year and the people stop work, don their best clothes and take the only bath they indulge in during the year….Red, the Chinaman's favorite color, is over everything. All of the presents are wrapped in red paper of some kind and eggs after being colored red are offered to the gods.

JANUARY 28: A week from tomorrow, on February 5, the greatest musical and dramatic entertainment ever given by the Finns of Houghton county will take place at the Calumet theater under the auspices of the Finnish Musical and Dramatic Society…Arrangements have also been made to have the Finnish company of soldiers take part in the entertainment, and, last but not least, Big Louis of Houghton will probably be in evidence.

FEBRUARY 9: This is the result, so far as known, of the explosion of five tons of dynamite yesterday morning at the eighth level of No. 3 shaft, North Kearsarge. The entire mine is now sealed up, in an effort to smother the flames which are licking up the timbers.

Only one dead body is on the surface. It is the corpse of Peter Kulpa, who was brought out of the mine early yesterday afternoon in a dying condition. All efforts to revive him were futile.

Five men, William Pollitt, Jr., Peter Savala, John Karvela, Henry Missila and Matt Kaskala, are still missing, and there is practically no doubt that they are in the burning mine, dead. These men were all working on the sixth or eighth levels…

A pathetic scene was witnessed on the arrival of William Pollitt, Sr., at the mine. The senior Pollitt insisted on going underground in search of his missing son, and he actually proceeded down as far as the eighth level, the scene of the explosion. The wonder is that he was able to crawl through the dense volumes of smoke as he did. After a fruitless search of two hours underground, he returned to the surface. His first words were, "I can do no more. I have done my duty."

FEBRUARY 10: No more does the gentle, sad-eyed cow roam the streets of Red Jacket…The state board of health has decreed that the milk from cows fed with garbage is not conducive to the health of the consumer. The cows that wandered through the streets of Red Jacket made it an important matter of business to root into garbage barrels. And Marshal Trudell was instructed to make another effort to secure a poundmaster. But he struck the right man when John Chynoweth was "sworn" to the faithful performance of the important duties of the office. It is a step toward progress. The community is really becoming metropolitan.

FEBRUARY 13: Mrs. Clara B. Birk, whose husband was killed in Calumet on August 19, has been adjudged insane at Iron Mountain and has been taken to Newberry and placed in the asylum for the insane.

FEBRUARY 16: A baby will be given away Sunday afternoon at the Salvation Army meeting in the barracks, corner of Seventh and Portland streets. The parents of the little one are Mr. and Mrs. Richard Nelson. Everyone is invited to attend the meeting and to see who gets the baby.

FEBRUARY 21: About 3 o'clock yesterday afternoon part of the roof of the Superior ice rink caved in. Fortunately no one was in the building at the time...No other suitable rink is available, and from the present outlook the game of curling in Calumet is dead for the balance of the season.

FEBRUARY 23: At Park rink last night there was a nice crowd of people enjoying the sport. Everyone seemed to be having a good time. Upon entering the building, two large rooms open up. One is for the boys and men and the other for ladies and children. Stoves heat the place, so that it is very comfortable. Beyond these rooms is the stretch ice upon which some of the skaters stretch themselves once in a while. There are posts in the middle for beginners to hang on to. The interior is well lighted with big kerosene lamps. The ice is kept in as good condition as possible. The skaters dash here and there, alone and in pairs, making the scene one of complete movement and grace.

FEBRUARY 25: A street car strike affecting all parts of the Houghton County Street Railway company's system was inaugurated just after midnight this morning...There has been no violence by any member of the union, so far as can be ascertained, and the union disclaims any responsibility for any molestations that have taken place. The trouble has arisen over the importation of outside labor by the street car company, following immediately upon an organization of a union here.

There is no change in the strike situation at the Osceola branch of the Osceola Consolidated today. A number of the miners said they would go to work this morning if they were protected. Marshal Trudell and a number of men when to the mine this morning to afford the miners protection. There were a large number of miners in the dry, but they concluded not to go down.

It was impossible to learn what the grievances of the strikers are. A man who is in close contact with the trammers said that he himself could not get a clear understanding of their wishes. They have no committee or representatives, as far as can be learned.

MARCH 4: The strike of the trammers at the Osceola branch of the Osceola Consolidated was settled just before 4 o'clock yesterday afternoon. The men decided to go to work after a conference had been held with Superintendent Parnall and Captain Richards. No concessions were made to the trammers except it was promised that the matter of time would be considered after the men began work.

MARCH 11: The aggregation of printers from the *Daily Mining Gazette* which came down to the Palestra last night, style them selves hockey players today because they happened to defeat the team from the *Copper Country Evening News*. The score was 3 to 1 in favor of the type stickers from the Portage Lake town but that doesn't describe the game. The *Evening News* had all the best of it from start to finish and it was only by accident that the puck was shoved into the local team's goal.

MARCH 22: The snow is covered with a crust of dirt and it is hard sledding with runners. A buggy was seen on the streets of Red Jacket yesterday and the driver was not obliged to halt his horses to allow them to get their breath as humane drivers of sleighs were seen to do. It is about as hard for runners to slide over dirt as it is for a locomotive to run without a track.

MARCH 23: Hockey is rapidly drawing to a close in the copper country. Except for occasional amateur games which are being played at intervals the game is hardly ever talked about. With the closing of the big league interest died out almost as suddenly as it was aroused at the opening of the season. The fiasco in Wednesday night's game at Houghton last week and the brutality shown in the preceding game the night before at the Palestra did much to harm the game. In certain quarters in Calumet the name of hockey suggests bitter words and contempt.

MARCH 24: A bronze bell weighing 3,800 pounds was received yesterday afternoon at the St. Joseph's Austrian church on Eighth street, Red Jacket.

MARCH 29: The sound of the shovel on the cement walk is heard on Fifth street, but there are some other streets where the walking is not quite so good. The gentle tropical breezes of the past few days, warmed by the rays of the sun, have penetrated into the snow and ice of this far northern region, honeycombing it so that the pedestrians sink down and fill their shoes with water. Men and boys have been at work on the sidewalks, especially in business sections, the past few days. Huge blocks of ice are loosened with axes and bars and shoveled to the street where the accumulation is carried off by the village sleighs.

APRIL 3: In a valley among the mountains in the eastern part of the province or regium of Piedmont, not far from the banks of the great River Po which winds its majestic course through Italy, the land of perpetual sunshine, is the little city of San Giorgio. It is from this place that about

150 of the residents of Calumet have emigrated. It seems strange that such a large number of persons from that distant city, containing only about 3,000 inhabitants, should all meet in this northern place and call it home.

There was a slight demonstration on the part of the striking trammers at the Franklin Junior mine this morning when about 50 miners resumed work at No. 2 shaft. The mine has been shut down for about two weeks, the suspension being precipitated by a part of the trammers who asked a 10 percent increase in wages. The management stated at the time that the earnings of the company were not such as to warrant such an increase, whereupon the men walked out.

Sheriff Beck and a number of deputies were on the scene this morning and are at the mine today to protect the miners. The strikers blocked the way to the mine, but used no violence of any kind. It is expected that a large number of miners will begin work tonight.

Like a bubble in the water arose the story about a cannie Scot who in the morning descended into the depths of one of the copper mines with a smile of contentment on his face and a big dinner pail in his hand. At noon a few of his friends made it a point to be with him while lunch, and other things, were enjoyed. The first article which met the eyes of the Scotchman was a pastie. He expected to dissect it with his incisors and that is where he was fooled. His teeth met resistance as King Cotton reigned within. With a disgusted look he glanced first at the pastie and then at the pail. Perhaps he thought he had made a mistake and taken someone else's pail.

It was a good thing for the mistress of the boarding house that she was not there when he finally decided that it was his pail. His companions laughed so heartily and cried "Huntigouk," which means April Fool in Scotch, in such a gleeful way that he himself could not restrain from laughing.

The Houghton County Street Railway company is experiencing some difficulty with its Wolverine branch of the line. Owing to the tracks being greased by unknown persons the latter part of last week it was some time before the car coming from Wolverine to Red Jacket could negotiate the trestle just below Albion.

Saturday morning the Wolverine trammers and company account laborers approached Captain William Pollard, head mining captain, and asked a 10 percent increase in their wages. Superintendent Fred Smith is visiting on the Pacific coast at the present time, and is not expected to reach Calumet for two weeks.

APRIL 6: The Kearsarge and Wolverine miners and trammers are still out. Everything is quiet and so far as known there are no negotiations going on toward a settlement of the difficulties. There are about 1,000 men out at Kearsarge and 400 at Wolverine.

A cave-in from surface took place during last night in the vicinity of shaft No. 4, Hecla. The shaft is about 800 feet deep and it was abandoned some years ago on account of its close proximity to adjoining shafts....The hole is close to the railroad tracks of the Hecla & Torch Lake road and today waste rock and old timbers are being dumped in to fill the gap, which is about 15 feet in diameter.

APRIL 8: It may not be generally known that several Finnish residents of Calumet with their families have left these parts during the past 12 months for various parts of the United States. It is stated in reliable quarters that last summer fully 40 families left here for Peterborough, New Hampshire, and other districts in the immediate neighborhood, where they took up the vocation of farming...The Finns are natural born farmers, and take to a farm "like a duck does to water."

The striking employees of the Kearsarge branch of the Osceola Consolidated will return to work Monday morning. This decision was reached at 6 o'clock last night after a committee from the strikers had waited on Superintendent Parnall and had reported back to the meeting of the men. The committee presented a request for a 10 per cent advance in wages and the abolishment of the contract system. Superintendent Parnall said that the contract system will not be done away with but if the men returned to work their demands for an increase in wages would be taken up and given thorough consideration. The committee reported back to the strikers and the men decided to return to work Monday morning.

Last Tuesday morning, all the underground workers at North and South Kearsarge asked for an increase of 10 per cent in wages. The men were told that the request would be placed before the proper officials. They did not go to their work but returned to their homes. The trammers at South Kearsarge went to work but quit later.

APRIL 12: The miners at both North and South Kearsarge appeared for work this morning. The striking trammers were there and the miners finally decided they would not go down...There is no change in the situation today at the mine of the Wolverine Mining company. Last night the strikers at the Franklin and Franklin Junior mines resumed work. The strike was declared three weeks ago. The men go back at the same wages as was paid by the company when the strike was declared.

APRIL 13: Although Calumet is well supplied with mine hospitals, many realize the need of a public institution for persons not having access to those controlled by the mining companies. Therefore a movement is on foot to establish in this community a public hospital…The object of the committee is not in any sense to establish a "free" hospital, but rather by united effort to establish a place where needy hospital care can be secured at a reasonable rate.

APRIL 14: A notice was posted at the Kearsarge mine today to the effect that all men who are on strike can consider themselves discharged from the employ of the Osceola Consolidated company.

Frank Murphy and Roy Swinton, the two high school boys who have been experimenting for some time with a wireless telegraph outfit, have now succeeded in sending messages for a distance of over 1,000 feet. On the north side of the tower of the Washington school building they have a receiver which is a large sheet of zinc. Messages were sent this week from this station to a similar receiver in the tower of the Calumet Methodist church.

APRIL 15: The draw of the Houghton county bridge was knocked from its position on the pier and became a total wreck…the result of the failure of the machinery to act properly as the steamer Northern Wave approached…and her prow struck the draw broadside.

APRIL 17: Owing to the big drawbridge connecting Houghton and Hancock becoming a complete wreck, all traffic between Calumet and the Portage Lake towns is tied up. The freight traffic is absolutely at a standstill and will remain so until this evening…Several of the stores are completely out of meat, having ordered only sufficient quantities to last them until Monday morning.

Charles A. Anderson was awarded the contract Saturday to build the new block for the Bosch Brewing company at the corner of Sixth and Oak streets. The Bosch Brewing company some time ago purchased the Fox and Everts saloon, known as the Michigan House. It was known soon after the purchase that the company was going to pull down the present building and erect a handsome business block in its place.

APRIL 18: The only apparent change in the strike situation in the copper country to date is the announcement that yesterday the whole of the miners and trammers in the Kearsarge branch of the Osceola Consolidated Mining company received their time. This means that every underground employee of the company at the North and South Kearsarge branches were discharged…

This week is the eighth week of the street railway strike and beyond the fact that several people are using the cars for locomotive purposes, the fact is still prevalent that the strike is on with all its annoying features.

APRIL 19: Wolverine Strike Ends—The strike of the trammers and other underground men who are not miners came to an end yesterday afternoon when the strikers voted to return to work this morning at the same wages which they were receiving before the strike began. In a vote which was taken at the meeting, all but half a dozen trammers wanted to return to work.

APRIL 20: Pyrotechnic, enthusiastic, spectacular was the address of Mother Jones at the Red Jacket town hall last night. The room was about two-thirds full, there being a large number of mine superintendents present.

While she held the undivided attention of all by her graphic descriptions of what she has seen in districts and during bloody strikes where child labor was employed, she did not arouse the sympathy that she would, had such conditions ever existed here. Her talk was highly interesting but it was not appealing and contained nothing that would make one wish to see the conditions changed that have prevailed in the Michigan copper country for half a century.

Mother Jones is a white haired old lady, and the vim in which she gives utterance to her ideas surprises here hearers. She knows how to tell a good story well and presents it in a way that thrills. She said she had been mixed up with strikes for many years—all kinds of strikes. She paid a tribute to the Western Federation of Miners and said that all men are cowards.

"How a woman can degrade herself by marrying a measly man who does not dare to join a union is beyond my comprehension," she exclaimed. "A mine superintendent once hired men at $70 a month to watch me. A man can't watch a woman. The superintendent ought to have known that and saved the expense. I got in among those miners and beat the cowardice out of them. Don't you women ever be afraid of men. They are the biggest cowards on earth."

APRIL 21: Calumet may be relieved by Monday of the partial famine now existing by reason of the disaster to the Houghton bridge. The scow which is being rapidly converted into a car ferry to transport cars across Portage Lake will be ready for service tomorrow if present plans are carried out. This scow will have a capacity of two cars.

The Mineral Range railroad's Houghton yards are full and cars are being dropped off at Chassell, Baraga, L'Anse and other points down the line where sidetracks are available. There is now a congestion of 150 cars of freight for Calumet. There is an average of 50 cars of freight handled here a day, including logging trains etc., in and out. The logging cars are being held in the woods as much as possible.

The pontoon bridge which was rigged up Monday temporarily relieved the situation, the bulk of Sunday and part of Monday's shipments being brought across. The

Monday meat train was successfully run across the pontoon bridge. The Thursday meat train was stalled on the other side of the lake, however, and the meat was loaded on boats and brought across, there to be reloaded for Calumet, where it was delivered yesterday on the scheduled day.

Providing the ferry starts operations tomorrow, the metropolis of the copper country will have been cut off from freight traffic for approximately one week.

From the standpoint of the wholesale shoe dealer, Calumet is a "jumbo" town. The women of this section have larger feet than are found ordinarily. The reason assigned is that there is an exceptionally large foreign population and many of the women from foreign lands have unusually large feet. Then, there is another reason given by some that people in the north indulge in more out of door exercise than those in the south, such as skating, etc.

Two sticks of dynamite were found yesterday morning near the Wolverine location on the tracks of the Houghton County Street Railway company, cunningly concealed in cedar boughs. The dynamite had been placed on the rails, wrapped up in small boughs, and tied fast…Yesterday afternoon while the striking street car employees were parading up Hecla street, Laurium, a gang of youths threw some stones at a passing through car. One of the stones entered the window of the car and struck a lady, who was riding, a severe blow across the head…

Last night a scene occurred in Red Jacket. A local car of the Houghton County Street Railway company was proceeding from the depot of the Mineral Range Railroad company in Red Jacket to Laurium. When opposite the Calumet postoffice on Sixth street the car was bombarded with a fusillade of stone. Windows in the car were smashed. A deputy named Schulte was on the car and he proceeded to the vestibule, displaying his revolver. The car had then proceeded some distance on its journey up the street and further trouble was avoided.

APRIL 24: In the depths of the forest of this "island" peninsula, where the trailing arbutus is wasting its sweet fragrance under its covering of moss and leaves, there is a blanket of snow from 1½ to two feet deep. With two or three weeks of such weather as was enjoyed last week, the snow will disappear and the hills and gullies will blossom forth with those delights of spring, wild flowers. Already, on some of the hillsides exposed to the kisses of the southern sun, the arbutus may be found by those who know where to look. There will undoubtedly begin tomorrow an exodus to the woods which will continue as long as the arbutus may be found, a period of about six weeks.

APRIL 25: Two cars of the Houghton County Street Railway company were fired upon just before midnight last night near Boston. Fortunately, no one was injured, but the passengers had narrow escapes. The shots shattered the windows and some of the lead was picked up on the floor of the cars.

APRIL 26: A petition was signed extensively in Calumet yesterday by the business men of Red Jacket and Laurium declaring themselves in favor of using the cars of the Houghton County Street Railway company, and also asking the residents of the county to do the same by availing themselves of the transportation offered by the Street Railway company…The strike has been dragging on with seemingly no means of settlement and no prospects of conclusion…The corporation has no idea of acceding to the strikers' wishes, and the same authority says the company, rather than give in to the men's demands, would take off its cars and discontinue the use of the service.

MAY 5: While a crew of 36 timbermen and laborers was being lowered at the Red Jacket shaft of the Calumet & Hecla at 8:30 o'clock this morning, the rope broke near the hoisting sheave. The double-deck cage was down 1,500 feet at the time. Five men were painfully, but none fatally injured, and the others were badly shaken up…Inside the skip there was a scene of confusion. At the first lunge of the cage the men were thrown from their feet, some striking the top of the deck. Then with the sudden stop when the safety catches set they were hurled violently to the floor.

MAY 6: There is every probability that roller skating will become popular in Calumet. A number of skaters in the township are exceedingly anxious to get on roller skates. It is known that a large number have been ordered from various hardware firms, and there is every indication that the installing of a hardwood floor at the Palestra is a sound business venture by the management.

MAY 10: As the years roll by, followers of the ring often wonder what has become of the array of pugilists who have made fighting history in by-gone days. The recent visit to Red Jacket of John L. Sullivan, ex-heavyweight champion, and the proposition of the Sons of St. George to secure Bob Fitzsimmons for July 22 on the occasion of the annual reunion of the Order of the Sons of St. George of the state, has brought back reminiscences and the question of their present occupation and location is frequently expressed.

MAY 11: An interesting editorial under the caption, "Mine Maker and Scholar," appeared the other day in the *Daily Mining Record* of Denver, Col. It refers pleasantly to Alexander Agassiz, president of the Calumet & Hecla Mining company, who has just arrived in Calumet.

"…Alexander Agassiz, president of the Calumet & Hecla Mining company, is a notable example…in both mining and science. As superintendent for the company in the late sixties he had a considerable share in making what has been for many years one of the great mines of the world. Although he did not remain long in charge of active operations, he has retained his connection with the company, and the fact that he has been able to make gifts aggregating nearly a million dollars to Harvard university shows that he had faith in the great enterprise when the shares were a small fraction of their present price.

"But while his activity in finance and industry has been exceptionally productive, Alexander Agassiz has done equally good work in pure science. His contributions to the literature of marine biology have been voluminous, and based on the results of personal observations. Numerous exploring expeditions on land and sea have been conducted under his direction.

"For example, he spent the winters from 1876 to 1881 in deep sea dredging, the steamer Drake being placed at his disposal by the United States coast survey. Honors and prizes have been conferred upon him by the scientific societies of both this country and Europe, and while his investigations have not been of a character to attract as much attention as the work of his father, Louis Agassiz, the latter, if he were alive, would have good reason to be proud of his son. Alexander Agassiz is living proof of the possibility of combining success in money getting with high attainment in purely intellectual pursuits."

MAY 17: Joy Pollard, the well known labor union organizer, who has been working in the copper country in the interests of organized labor for the past 12 months, is under arrest in Cripple Creek, Colorado, on a charge of carrying concealed weapons. Pollard was in the copper country as recently as three weeks ago, and is known personally to many residents of this section.

MAY 18: President Agassiz of the Calumet & Hecla mine, who is at present in the copper country on one of his periodical visits, will lecture this evening in the Calumet school hall under the auspices of the Calumet Woman's club. This is Mr. Agassiz's first lecture before a Calumet audience and this fact alone should prove a good drawing card.

MAY 19: Miss Maggie Walz, who is bringing a colony of Finnish people to Drummond island, is doing a work that should call forth the commendation of the people of Chippewa county, editorially comments the Soo *News*. It is a work that will materially help the county, as the new settlers will be of a hard-working class to whom failure is an unknown word.

A Red Wing, Minn., dispatch says that Iver Davidson, a giant, who had been with Barnum for many years, died there. He was seven feet, two inches in height and 46 years old. Louis Moilanen, better known as "Sack's Louie," who recently left Houghton to join Ringling's circus, is but 19 years old and already had the better of the Minnesota giant by about six inches, being no less than seven feet, eight inches tall and weighing 370 pounds. If Louie continues to grow until he attains his majority he will reach a height of eight feet.

Probably but very few people in Calumet were aware of the fact that two weeks ago there was visiting in Calumet one of the greatest of Finland's playwrights and authors of modern times. His name is M. Kurikka. He is known personally to a select few of his countrymen in this section, and while here he visited with some of them.

On Sunday evening one of Mr. Kurikka's plays, "The Last Struggle," will be given at the Calumet theater under the auspices of "Wolma," the Finnish Workmen's society.

The play deals with the reign of Alexander II, of Russia, and the story is woven round the date of the freeing of Russian slaves. The drama is a soul-stirring one, and in the hands of some of the local Finnish residents, will be given due interpretation. The cast is composed of some of the most prominent Finns in the community.

MAY 20: During the summer months hundreds of Calumet residents daily take trips to the waterworks and vicinity at the lake shore. The temptation to take trips on the lake has never been great because of the fact that only one row boat has been available. Many timid persons do not feel like trusting themselves on the bosom of Lake Superior in a shallow row boat, and Mr. Nyberg has struck the right key in introducing gasoline launches. The venture is certain to be a paying one.

JUNE 6: D. Horwitz, the Calumet Russian furrier, is probably the most envied taxidermist in the country. Mr. Horwitz, who is at Glenwood Springs, Colorado, has been allotted the task of mounting and preparing for President Roosevelt several game animals and birds which the chief executive shot while on his recent hunting trip.

Big Louie of Houghton, whose correct name is Louis Moilenen, has the German measles at Cincinnati. He left here a few weeks ago to join Ringling Bros.' circus. He was taken to room No. 3, the largest in the institution, but when the bed was inspected it was found to be many feet too short. The difficulty was overcome, however, by putting two beds together, piling additional mattresses on them and then placing a table on one end with the pillows for his head to rest on.

JUNE 13: Newspaper readers are familiar with the name of Borchgrevink, but comparatively few know that M.L. Borchgrevink, a cousin of the great Anartic explorer, is an inventor of note and a resident of Calumet. With Fred Olson, who is also gifted in that line, they have just invented and brought to perfection a machine for washing dishes or clothes.

JUNE 14: Now that the fruit season is here the usual practice of throwing banana and orange peelings on the sidewalks of the village is in evidence once more. Last summer a crusade against the offenders was started and the marshal will continue it this summer.

JUNE 19: On Sunday, June 25, the formal opening of Electric park will take place. The full Calumet & Hecla band has been engaged to give a concert from 2 to 5:30 o'clock…New scenery is expected for the theater, an elaborate and expensive curtain being included. A new electric sign will probably be in operation on the opening night.

JUNE 24: Miss Maggie Walz of Pine street is back from Drummond island where she has been since the first of the month in the interest of the new Finnish colony which she recently established there on the land granted by the government.

JULY 11: The announcement in the *Evening News* a few days ago that Hod Stuart had received an offer from Yale university to coach the hockey team there during the coming winter has caused much talk in hockey circles in the copper country.

JULY 14: Although Calumet people have been reading of library robberies perpetrated in the upper peninsula it is not generally known that during the night of Wednesday, July 5, some unknown party or parties entered the Calumet & Hecla public library and helped themselves to money and did some damage to the building.

JULY 17: Laborers, numbering about fifty in the employ of P. McDonnell & Co. of Duluth, who are engaged in paving the streets of Red Jacket, went out on strike this morning, asking to be paid every two weeks instead of monthly as at present.

The work on the streets will not be delayed owing to the action of the strikers. As soon as the men's demands were ascertained the company decided to engage other men, and the work will be proceeded with as usual with another gang of laborers.

JULY 19: Signor Blitz and Madame Fay, with their vaudeville troupe, gave another performance last evening at the Calumet theatre.

The grand finale of the whole performance, however, is the illusion act in which a lady is hypnotized by Professor, laid flat in an ordinary box trunk and then made to slowly rise from the trunk to about four feet in the air where she remains seemingly suspended in air. While in the air Professor Blitz passes a wooden hoop all around the body, which adds to the mystery of the affair.

JULY 25: Superintendent William E. Parnall of the Bigelow group of mines has resigned his position, and will go to Denver, Col., where he will become associated with capitalists in the coal mining business…Mr. Parnall has been in charge of the Bigelow mines about two years, since his father died. As supervisor of Osceola township Mr. Parnall has done splendid work for the township in which he resides.

The Bigelow group consists of the Tamarack; the Osceola Consolidated; Ahmeek; Seneca; Dollar Bay Land & Improvement company; Hancock Chemical works; Lake Superior Smelting company; Dollar Bay rolling mills, and the Isle Royale property.

JULY 27: Calumet was shaken to its very foundations last evening. All sorts of rumors were afloat as to the cause of the unusual shock, but nothing authentic can be advanced to account for it. It is believed, however, it was an earthquake shock because of the extended area in which it was felt, the severe vibration being experienced all through the copper country and as far away as Marquette.

The shock was distinctly felt by every man, woman and child in the township, and residents were much frightened. It was at first thought the Dollar Bay powder mills had blown up.

JULY 31: If noise will count for anything there will be plenty of it at the approaching Fat Men's baseball game on Wednesday of next week. The official rooter for the Red Jackets has issued orders that cow-bells will be the standard noise maker. Local hardware merchants have ordered an extra supply in anticipation of the demand that is sure to be made.

All owners of automobiles, dogs, ponies, horses and all other quadrupeds are requested to line up outside the Arlington hotel an hour previous to the time for the parade, so that the procession may be gotten together. Owners of cowbells are also requested to be on hand…

Ed Merz is known to be easily exasperated and if some of the Laurium rooters attempt to disturb him while batting Red Jacket rooters are requested to ring their bells with vigor to deaden the sound of derogatory remarks which may be made.

The "fat man" is due for a home run and he says he is going to get it. He has a bat made especially for the occasion, and it has stamped on it, "A hit every time up, and more if necessary."

This summer has marked a new era in civic improvements in Red Jacket. Not only will Fifth street be paved this year, but Pine as well. The new sidewalks that are being laid on Oak, Sixth and adjoining streets are also doing much to better the appearance of the village and before another year ends, it is probable the whole village will have undergone a complete change.

AUGUST 11: Again the mad dog is in evidence in Calumet. A brute ran amuck on Woodland avenue yesterday afternoon, and bit three boys. It was eventually shot while running loose and foaming at the mouth.

AUGUST 22: Mrs. Nelson of Florida, wife of Mr. Nelson, "the Cornish pasty man," was handled very roughly last Saturday evening by an unknown man. According to the story told by Mrs. Nelson to the neighbors she heard a knock at her door about 9 o'clock in the evening.

She opened the door and was accosted by a man who asked her if she had any pasties for sale. Replying in the negative she informed him he could have some sandwiches if he wished. This did not suit the fellow, and he immediately became abusive.

Mrs. Nelson saw that she had a ruffian to deal with and attempted to shut the door in his face. The fellow placed his foot in the door and prevented it from being closed. Mrs. Nelson courageously tried to push him away and then the man caught hold of her and pulled her outside. A scuffle ensued. Mrs. Nelson screamed lustily and the fellow thinking the place was getting too hot to hold him immediately released his hold of the woman and ran away.

SEPTEMBER 1: The most disastrous fire that ever visited the Calumet location occurred last evening. The high school and manual training buildings were totally destroyed, and the Miscowaubik club, together with its handsome furnishings, were practically ruined by fire, smoke and water…

The fire was first discovered by a party of young people who engaged in dancing in the Washington school hall…

From 10:15 o'clock, when the fire was first discovered, until two o'clock this morning the conflagration was witnessed by thousands of persons.

SEPTEMBER 4: The recent storm of wind and rain which visited Calumet was responsible for much damage…A large leak was discovered at the Red Jacket theater Saturday afternoon during the matinee. The water found its way into the theater by way of the large tower. It worked through to the parquet. Fortunately the seats were unoccupied at the time, and although it was found impossible to stop the leak at this particular period, steps were taken to prevent a recurrence for the evening's performance.

In this the efforts of the employees of the theater were successful, and everybody was able to witness the performance of "The Girl from Kay's" without the slightest annoyance.

The members of the company, however, were not so fortunate. The dressing rooms were flooded so badly that it was found impossible to use them and temporary quarters had to be found for the company. The ladies had the dining room of the municipal building placed at their disposal, and other satisfactory arrangements were made for the male members of the company.

SEPTEMBER 6: Calumet was visited yesterday by one of the most entertaining writers in the country. Ralph D. Paine, whose name is a household word to readers of the popular monthly magazines, is in copperdom. He called at the *Evening News* office yesterday.

Red Jacket, Laurium and the Calumet location appear to him as a unique combination. Characteristic of the man was the inquiry as to the definition of the names of the villages.

"Calumet," said Mr. Paine, "is certainly Indian. It denotes the pipe of peace. Red Jacket also stands for an Indian chief, but Laurium, wherever did that aristocratic name spring from?"

…"I have had an entirely different impression of the copper country. Down in New York, this place is looked upon as sort of wild west. I shall try to remove that impression when I get back. You have a good telephone service and there is a decided air of prosperity about the place. The street improvements are doing much to improve Red Jacket, and the Calumet & Hecla library is a novel of neatness, it is a beautiful little structure.

"It is not the gift of Carnegie either?" This was said with a laugh and a shrug of the shoulders that meant more than words could convey.

OCTOBER 7: Laurium is fast becoming the residential center of Calumet. A prominent businessman stated last evening he had twelve applications for a vacant house inside of twenty-four hours when it became known that the house was unoccupied.

"There were so many I did not know whom to rent," he said. "Instances like this are happening daily in Laurium. Red Jacket cannot take care of the people that are continually flocking to Calumet and Laurium gets most of them…

"There is an air of prosperity about the village that was never so pronounced as now. I could cite several instances where wealthy people of the community during the past two years have purchased lots there and have erected for themselves magnificent homes."

OCTOBER 11: The annual report of the late mine inspector, Captain Josiah Hall, presented to and read before the county supervisors yesterday, gives some interesting statistics. The total casualties for year ended Sept. 30 were 58. The number of men employed at the various mines in the county was 15,255.

The casualties are apportioned among the different mines as follows: Atlantic, 1; Baltic, 4; Calumet & Hecla, 11; Centennial, 2; Champion, 4; Franklin Junior, 3; Osceola, 11; Tamarack, 9; Trimountain, 3; Quincy, 10. By nationalities the apportionment shows: Austrians, 7; English, 15; Finns, 22; German, 1; Hungarian, 1; Irish, 3; Italian, 8; Swede, 1.

Another table shows the number of men employed and the casualties in the active mines of Houghton county from Oct. 1, 1887, to Sept. 30, 1905. During that period the fatalities numbered 587 the past year ending. In the fiscal year 1904 there were 45 fatalities. In 1895 there were 44; in 1902, 44. The least number was 19 in 1896.

The number of men employed in the county during 1905 shows an increase of 9,034 over the number in 1887 when the first report was made. The number employed during the intervening years is as follows: 6,310 in 1888; 6,480 in 1889; 7,310 in 1890; 7,702 in 1891; 7,640 in 1892; 7,591 in 1893; 7,343 in 1894; 7,249 in 1895; 8,170 in 1896; 8,726 in 1897; 10,476 in 1898; 13,051 in 1899; 13,971 in 1900; 13,498 in 1901; 14,130 in 1902; 13,629 in 1903; 14,321 in 1904.

Houghton county was visited with its first fall of snow last evening.

OCTOBER 12: In keeping with larger metropolitan cities Red Jacket is to have a pawnbrokers' shop if present arrangements are carried out...One wit remarked that there are persons to be found in Calumet who will pawn their household goods in order to obtain money to buy stock so intent are certain persons to obtain it now that the boom is on.

OCTOBER 13: The first regular session of the Calumet Woman's club was held this afternoon at the Gately-Wiggins hall.

OCTOBER 16: Attorney Oscar J. Larson, now on the way home from his European trip, the greater part of which has been spent in Italy, was accorded a signal honor while in Rome. It was nothing less than an interview with the pope.

Mr. Larson has been in Italy on behalf of the people of Houghton county, versus one Igesto Cabbatini, who is in the Houghton county jail charged with murder. The defence asked for time in order to proceed to Italy to investigate the rumor that hereditary insanity prevailed in the Sabbatini family.

OCTOBER 20: "Schlatter, the Divine Healer," is in Calumet. He has a national reputation, at least as an interesting character. He claims to cure the sick by the laying on of hands and their own faith. He is a unique personage and with his flowing hair and beard is a marked figure on the streets.

Marshal Joseph Trudell will introduce the curfew in Red Jacket. His attention has been called to the fact that a number of youths and girls of tender age are on the streets at night, and he will make an earnest attempt to stop the practice. Every boy and girl under the age of sixteen years will have to leave the streets at eight o'clock unless they can give a reasonable excuse for being out.

OCTOBER 23: The interscholastic football championship of the copper country has been decided and the Calumet highs are the victors. They played the Hancock Central highs on the local gridiron at Athletic park Saturday afternoon and won by the score of 22 to 0.

OCTOBER 25: And now comes the statement that in all probability the bell of St. Joseph's Austrian church will be tolled every evening at eight o'clock as the curfew in Red Jacket. The bell of the St. Joseph's Austrian church is a large one and its sonorous tones can be heard distinctly in every part of the village.

OCTOBER 28: A local druggist stated this morning that the season for soda water was practically closed but some of the druggists and others who have operated their fountains during the past season will serve the dainty beverage hot during the winter...When soda water was first put on tap in this city several years ago it did not contain any ice cream and sold for five cents. "Sundaes" and other fancy mixtures are of a comparatively recent origin.

NOVEMBER 2: The latest form of sport talked of for Calumet is that of skiing. The project of organizing a club has been favorably received by a number of enthusiasts and there are great hopes of the success of the movement. There are a large number of Scandinavians in the district familiar with the sport, who will do all in their power to foster and help along any ski organization that might be formed.

The iron lamp posts ordered by McClure & Hosking for the village, to be located at business corners, arrived in Calumet last evening, and are now in the yards of the Copper Range railroad. The announcement that the poles are here will be welcomed by residents. The poles are well adapted for lighting the streets. They are made on the "gooseneck" plan, and will extend out from the sidewalk several feet, thus illuminating a large portion of the street.

NOVEMBER 20: Governor Fred M. Warner is in the county...Yesterday was quietly spent by the governor at Houghton. This morning he started out on a tour of the copper country, inspecting mines and mills and other points of interest and generally familiarizing himself with the industries of copperdom. This afternoon the governor arrived in Calumet, where he will stay for the remainder of his visit.

Two little boys named Jacob Hiltunen and John Radika were playing on the Wolverine No. 4 dam yesterday afternoon, when the ice gave way, and before Hiltunen could be rescued he was drowned. The other child was more fortunate, being saved just in time to resuscitate him.

NOVEMBER 23: Madame Helena Modjeska appeared in the title role of "Mary Stuart" last evening to a large and appreciative audience in the Calumet theater. Throughout Madame Modjeska gave a magnificent portrayal of the principal role.

DECEMBER 4: Red Jacket is getting more and more metropolitan. For the first time in its history it will this week have three theaters playing on every night stand. The theaters are the new Campbell Bijou in the Butler block, where a good bill will be put on; the Somers-Petersen Bijou house, also advertising an entertaining program; and the Pollard Lilliputian opera company, booked for popular operas at the Calumet theater, such as "The Belle of New York," its opening production tonight.

With the signing of a coverpoint for the Calumet hockey team and his arrival here the team will be complete...When the team lines up Monday of next week against the Canadian Soos for its initial game of the season it should be one of the strongest in the organization.

DECEMBER 5: The Calumet & Hecla company, which was incorporated and commenced business thirty-four years ago, has just declared a quarterly dividend of $15 per share, making $50 per share paid by this company to its stockholders for the year 1905. This is equal to 200 per cent, as the par value of Calumet & Hecla shares is $25 each.

The total amount of dividends distributed by this remarkable copper mine since its incorporation, thirty-four years ago, is $92,350,000. The highest dividend paid during the past ten years was in 1899, when 400 per cent was paid.

It is interesting to note that the dividend rate of Calumet & Hecla has been steadily advanced since 1902, during which year only 100 per cent was paid. In 1903 the rate was increased to 140 per cent, in 1904 to 160 per cent and 1905 to 200 per cent. At this rate of increase next year will see a distribution of 240 per cent.

DECEMBER 6: Some time ago it was reported that the Calumet & Hecla library had been burglarized, and money stolen from the drawers of the institution. Now it develops that the store of Frank B. Lyon, near the Calumet hotel, had been burglarized, bicycle bells and other small articles stolen, and in addition the Calumet Congregational church has been entered.

DECEMBER 11: Now comes the complaint that the Houghton county street railway depot at the Albion location is being utilized for purposes other that for which it was intended. It is claimed a number of youths lounge in the waiting room with no intention of traveling, and that the place is filled with smoke from cigarettes and cigars in the mouths of these young fellows a large part of the time. In consequence many ladies, it is said, find it impossible to remain in the waiting room, and prefer standing outside in the cold to waiting in room which is made insufferably obnoxious by tobacco smoke.

DECEMBER 12: The Salvation Army is making arrangements to give free Christmas baskets of provisions and clothing to the worthy poor on Christmas day, and ask all charitably inclined citizens to help them in the effort.

The committeemen of the Fat Men's baseball club are also preparing to distribute turkeys, provisions, and other necessaries and are now making preparations to obtain the goods so that they will be on hand to distribute during the festive season.

DECEMBER 14: Last evening there was considerable snowballing on the streets. Boys were the offenders, and as the curfew hour had passed the question was asked whether it was still in force or whether it had died a natural death.

A few days ago several pigs were observed running along Fifth street, and so funny did the situation appeal to some traveling men they stated they would have some fun over the matter when they "got down the road." This is the first time it is believed pigs have been seen on the streets, but they were allowed to remain.

DECEMBER 15: Two skiing clubs have been formed in Calumet. One of them has its headquarters at Lake View, and the other is located at the Tamarack. The sport is gaining in popularity, and there is every probability many enthusiasts will indulge.

DECEMBER 16: "Another summer Drummond island will be possessed of a brick kiln, sawmill, and a flour mill," said Miss Maggie Walz of Pine street to an *Evening News* man last evening. "A committee has been appointed to further these projects and an attempt is being made to form a company.

"During the next two months I shall wind up my affairs in Calumet preparatory to going to Drummond island in the spring to take hold of the new post office which is to be established there, and of which I am to be the postmistress. I shall probably spend the greater part of the year on the island but will visit Calumet at periodical times, as considerable business interests will call me here."

A special meeting of the members of the alumni association of the Calumet high school was held last evening in the high school assembly room in the Washington school building…Almost every class which graduated from the school was represented in the art collection in the old school and it was argued the members of the association should do their share to replace it.

DECEMBER 19: According to the present program the new Michigan buffet, corner of Sixth and Oak streets, the property of the Bosch Brewing company, will be opened for business Saturday in time for the Christmas trade.

The fixtures now being installed are of quarter-sawed oak and very elaborate. The designs are magnificent, and the bar proper will be one of the finest in the upper peninsula. The fixtures are being put in position by the Northwestern Furniture company of Milwaukee.

Perhaps the most striking feature of the bar room will be the handsome hand-painted design, representing a scene in the Alps. It will occupy the whole length of the bar in an alcove directly above the bar fixtures. The interior decorations has been done by the Milwaukee Associated Artists, and the work furnishes a splendid illustration of the expert decorator's art. In the "den" leading from the bar, which is a little gem of a place, some of the prettiest designs ever seen in copperdom have been introduced, and when this room is completed it should prove most attractive.

DECEMBER 30: It is said that during the past few months the force of the Calumet & Hecla Mining company has been increased by at least 1,000 men. What this increase means to Calumet only those directly interested can estimate.

The fact that the management is working three shafts on the Osceola amygdaloid and two on the Kearsarge lode in addition to those on the conglomerate has called for the employment of many additional men.

This fact has made itself felt in business of all kinds. Houses at the present are almost unobtainable. The boom in real estate in Red Jacket and Laurium has recalled the palmy days of 1899, and is likely to eclipse it.

The advent of new capital into Keweenaw county will have its reflection in Calumet. The metropolis will be the distributing center, and the results should be apparent as developments in Keweenaw progress. The completion of the Keweenaw Central railroad with its terminal in Red Jacket, and subsequent connections with other local roads, will have a good effect. The development work in Keweenaw will mean the employment of more men. This will mean more business for Calumet.

---

## Photos, pages 105-108

Page 106: Top: Broom-making blind man G. Victor Johnson and William Goraczniak, 1906. O. Gardner. *National Park Service, Keweenaw National Historic Park, Jack Foster Collection.*
Bottom: Ozanich Bros. Tailor shop, 407½ Fifth Street, Red Jacket. Mike Ozanich, front. Joe Ozanich, rear. *Houghton County Historical Society*

Page 107. Top: Calumet High school library. *Agnich*
Bottom: Maggie Walz and friends at Schoolcraft? Cemetery, c. 1908. *RCM/Mantel*

Page 108: Top: Red Jacket work place. *Superior View*
Bottom: Calumet & Hecla library children's room, February 24, 1906. O. Gardner. *Keweenaw National Historic Park*

Calumet High School

# *Copper Country* **1906** *Evening News*

*A novel and unique method of testing whether foul air and gases still existed in the underground workings of the shafts of the Tamarack mine was tried this morning. Just as the skip was descending a dog was dropped into it and lowered to the underground levels. After being allowed to remain some time, the skip was hoisted to surface. The animal was dead, showing conclusively that gas still exists...*

JANUARY 1: The Copper Range railroad company has altered its railroad schedule considerably during the past few days. Several additional trains have been put on since navigation has closed, and this fact will be appreciated by patrons of copperdom.

One of the most convenient trains that has been placed in service is the 7 o'clock train out of Calumet every night for Houghton. This train goes to Laurium, and persons wishing to skate at the Palestra may take this train. The fare is five cents, the same as the street railway. It is for patrons of the road wishing to visit Houghton, however, that the train will be most convenient. On the return it will not leave Houghton until 11:15 p.m., thus giving Calumet residents a chance to witness all hockey games at Portage Lake in addition to any social functions that they may wish to attend at any time.

JANUARY 2: The year 1905 was memorable in Boston financial history in many ways...Calumet & Hecla, Boston's leading copper company, this year inaugurated a new policy of buying the securities of other companies and took unto itself the Manitou and Frontenac properties in Keweenaw county.

Left homeless and dependent upon herself by the death of her grandmother Miss Maggie Walz of Calumet left her native home in Finland...writes a correspondent. A mere girl of 16, she arrived a stranger among strangers, in this cosmopolitan settlement, with only $7 in her pocket.

...She secured a position as a domestic and the agency for some books and papers.

This was 25 years ago.

After a few years she had saved enough to take a trip to Europe. Upon her return she took a position as clerk in a store, which occupation she followed for 12 years, with the exception of two years at college.

A few years ago she erected a $40,000 business block in Red Jacket where she carries on her business. She is publisher of a Finnish Ladies' Journal and has many other interests. In a quiet way, she does a great deal for charity, taking care of many unfortunates in her own home at times.

Miss Walz was recently appointed by the government to colonize Drummond island, in the upper part of Lake Huron, and quite a community has sprung up through her efforts.

"The past year was a prosperous one for the people in the Michigan copper country," said John D. Cuddihy of Calumet, at the Spalding in Duluth. Mr. Cuddihy is president of the First National bank at Calumet and manager of the Calumet theater...

"All signs point to an unusual activity during 1906 in the upper peninsula of Michigan. The high price and heavy demand for copper has much to do with this condition."

"...The new road called the Keweenaw Central is opening up the country, to the north, and the prospects are that this section will contain from 10,000 to 15,000 more people within the next two years.

"At present the Calumet & Hecla Mining company is employing 1,000 men more than a year ago. It has now two veins known as the Osceola and Kearsarge, which alone promise at least fifty years of activity."

JANUARY 3: Red Jacket has secured a poundmaster. Marshal Joseph Trudell has supplied both...There has been a considerable falling off in the number of the bovines on the streets during the past few weeks due in a great measure to the marshal's vigilance, and it is believed that now the fact has become known a poundmaster and pound has been provided owners of cows will be more careful in the future and keep their bovines in proper places.

JANUARY 5: For the benefit of those unable to attend the hockey games at Houghton between the Portage Lakes and Pittsburgs which are being played this evening and Monday evening of next week several of the hotel and saloon proprietors of the township had had private telephones installed, and are receiving reports direct from the Amphidrome.

Among this number is Dunn Bros., of Fifth street, whose place of business was crowded last evening. Mr. Dunn states that he will receive returns of all hockey games in the future whenever copperdom teams are engaged.

"The Wizard of Oz" will be the attraction at the Calumet theater January 13. It promises to be one of the very best of the local season to date and undoubtedly will be well received. One of the most interesting characters in the production is the "scarecrow," who has to stand motionless for eighteen minutes at a stretch, while a scene is taking place in the foreground...His outstretched arms are supported by a cross piece nailed to the pole, and during the first performance of "The Wizard of Oz" both the scarecrow's arms went sound asleep, and when Dorothy came to take him from the pole he really needed her support until he could restore the circulation.

JANUARY 8: On Thursday evening, January 25, St. Andrews' society of Calumet will celebrate the anniversary of the birthday of Robert Burns, the most beloved of all Scotchmen. The celebration will be in the nature of a banquet and social evening. The vocalists will sing old familiar pieces and there will also be Scotch dances. General Manager James MacNaughton of the C.&H. probably will preside.

JANUARY 11: A roaring, crashing mass of flames was discovered in the twenty-second level of No. 2 shaft of the Tamarack mine today. The fire is still burning but what headway it has made since first discovered is not now known. Every possible effort is being made to get the blaze under control and both No. 1 and No. 2 shafts have been closed, the mouths of the shafts being sealed to prevent any draft which might fan the fire.

The fire was discovered at about noon by Mike Milanovich, a timberman, who was eating his dinner with two drill boys. They heard the roar of the flames at the end of the level and went to investigate. They found the overhead timbers a mass of flames.

Last evening the officers of Sampo Tent, a Finnish branch of the Knights of the Modern Maccabees, installed its officers for the ensuing term. The remarkable feature about the lodge is that it is without exception the largest Finnish fraternal society in the country.

JANUARY 12: Missing men, undoubtedly dead: Michael Simonovich. Samuel Bozovich. Frank Harvidish.

At noon today Captain Thomas Maslin and a party of mine officials who accompanied him underground at the Tamarack No. 5 penetrated as far as the crosscut in No. 2 shaft, where the gases were so overpowering that the men were driven back, being unable to proceed farther in their search for the three missing men.

A public hospital has just been opened in Calumet. It is located on the top floor of the Corgan block in the Wills House and is owned and controlled by several local physicians.

JANUARY 13: As far as it is possible to ascertain conditions underground at the Tamarack mine are the same. No searching party went into the mine today, it being the general belief that further efforts to locate the three entombed miners would be futile. The fire is still burning in No. 2 shaft.

At least three private parties will take a trip into Keweenaw county next Sunday. It is the intention to spend the whole day roaming about. The easy manner in which the fields of snow are traversed, and the rapidity with which ground can be covered favors the sport. That skeeing has come to stay in this district is the general verdict.

Some time within the next four weeks, at a date to be announced later, the Laurium and Red Jacket fat men will play hockey at the Palestra in the cause of charity. The game promises to be equally as attractive as the fat men's baseball match that is played annually.

JANUARY 16: Rooms 21, 24 and 26 in the Washington school building have been closed for fumigating purposes. This step was taken as a precautionary measure this morning. Scarlet fever still exists in the township, and there is a probability it may spread.

JANUARY 18: Inquiry at the Tamarack mine office by an *Evening News* man elicits the information that it will be at least a week before the shafts that have been sealed will be opened again. Considerable smoke was seen coming through the small openings at Tamarack No. 1 yesterday, even after the shafts had been closed, showing conclusively that the fire is still under way.

Charles F. Nelson of Laurium, the well known "pasty" man, has a grievance. He approached an *Evening News* man this morning with the announcement he is prohibited from sitting in any street car with his pasty basket if objections are made by the passengers…It is claimed the pasties have a plentiful sprinkling of onions and that in a heated car the odor at times is very annoying.

…Mr. Nelson is a very old gentleman, and an irate one if matters do not run smoothly for him. He is aware of the fact the company only objects to the odor of the pasties, "but, do you think," said he, "that I would leave my pasties out there with the smokers and have them spat upon." The cloths that covered the dozen or more pasties snugly laid inside his basket were then turned carefully aside and the pasties were exposed to view.

JANUARY 19: Many Calumet residents expect to attend the ski tournament at Ishpeming on February 22, Washington's birthday…It is reported President Roosevelt may be present and this is adding to the interest.

JANUARY 23: The Calumet & Hecla is perhaps the largest holder of timber lands in the upper peninsula, being credited with the possession of 900,000 acres of pine and mixed timbers. This company used over 30,000,000 feet of timber yearly in its mines in Calumet, most of which is bought in open market from dealers, although some of it is cut from the company's lands.

That the scarcity of timber is making itself felt, is shown by the increase in the amount of cement used in the mines of the copper country. The Calumet & Hecla company was among the first to use cement in place of timbers in its workings, and the use of this material has increased yearly.

JANUARY 25: It will be but a short time before the mining companies of Calumet and vicinity will return to standard time. "Mine time" is used only during the short days and when they have lengthened somewhat standard time will again be used.

Monday, February 5, marks the opening of the second semester of the school year in Calumet. At that time a new class of forty-five pupils will be graduated from the eighth grade into the high school. This class will bring the total enrollment of the high school up to 347, making it the largest in the upper peninsula.

JANUARY 31: Although three weeks have elapsed since the outbreak of the fire in the underground workings of the Tamarack mine, no successful attempt to reach the lower levels of the mine has yet been made. This morning a timberman expressed a wish to go underground at Tamarack No. 5 to look for the bodies of the three missing men, but his request was refused by one of the mining captains on the ground.

One of the most exciting events ever pulled off in Red Jacket took place last evening. It was sport of the most fascinating kind. Sport that caused the blood of those present to tingle with excitement.

Imagine upwards of fifty men gathered in the sample rooms of the Arlington Hotel, everyone of them intent on keeping his eyes on a box that weighed at least twenty-eight pounds. Underneath that box was a magnificent specimen of the badger species. He was credited with weighing at least thirty-six pounds. To kill him two of the best bull dogs in the township had been secured.

FEBRUARY 2: Marshal Trudell announced this morning that…All dogs found running the streets without muzzles will now be shot without the slightest hesitation. According to the marshal at least three hundred were killed in the township last summer, but this fact seemingly has made no difference, as there are still numerous brutes on the streets, a large number of them apparently ownerless.

FEBRUARY 5: A novel and unique method of testing whether foul air and gases still existed in the underground workings of the shafts of the Tamarack mine was tried this morning. Just as the skip was descending a dog was dropped into it and lowered to the underground levels. After being allowed to remain some time, the skip was hoisted to surface. The animal was dead, showing conclusively that gas still exists.

FEBRUARY 6: Early this morning there were no less than five dead dogs on the streets of Red Jacket. All bore evidence of having been poisoned. None of the dogs were tagged or muzzled. This means that the dog crusade has been started, but by whom no one seems to know.

FEBRUARY 9: Data compiled from the official reports of the mine inspector shows that during the past nineteen years 587 men have lost their lives in the copper mines of Houghton county.

FEBRUARY 10: Two dogs were lowered in No. 5 shaft of the Tamarack mine this morning. They were kept there for some little time and when brought to surface it was found had been overcome, showing there is still considerable gas underground. Everything possible is being tried to purge the mine of gases known to exist. Fans are being worked at No. 2 shaft and air from other sources is being pumped into the mine regularly.

FEBRUARY 12: This morning ten men were lowered into No. 5 shaft of the Tamarack mine. They went down as far as the twenty-ninth level but nauseous gases prevented their going further.

Amateur hockey has taken a firm hold of the community. Matches are frequently played. Yesterday's contest was played in the Red Jacket rink, and according to one of those who took part it was a very "vicious" affair. Slashing was in evidence throughout.

MARCH 1: It will be news to many that the Calumet Brewing company intends to declare its first dividend some time this year…The company was organized six years ago. It acquired an excellent site near Lake View and built a plant that is one of the most complete and up-to-date in the northern country. The company's main business offices are located on Pine street, Red Jacket.

MARCH 2: At 1:45 o'clock this morning fire was discovered in the rockhouse at No. 3 shaft of the Wolverine mine by the rock house boss. The fire department at the mine responded immediately to the alarm and did effective work, saving the shaft house and keeping the fire from working into the mine. It was seen at once that the rock house was doomed and no attempt was made to save it.

MARCH 3: Covered with snow from head to foot, with every bone broken, the body of Erick Stukel, a miner employed at the Kearsarge branch of the Osceola mine, was found attached to the plow of a Mineral Range locomotive by the engineer and fireman this morning.

MARCH 10: After many fruitless endeavors to penetrate the underground workings of the Tamarack mine a party headed by Captain Ed Waters was successful yesterday afternoon. It proceeded as far as the 28th level of No. 2 shaft comparatively easy, meeting with little gas. Pushing on the party climbed to the level above where after a short search the bodies of two of the unfortunate victims of the recent fire were discovered. The party came to surface after discovering the men, and later another party went down headed by Captain John Rowe. It located the last of the missing men. The bodies were so blackened by gas and smoke that it was impossible to recognize them. All three were within two hundred feet of each other. All appearances pointed to death by suffocation.

On the outcome of tonight's hockey game at the Palestra depends the disposition of the pennant...Hod Stuart and Lorne Campbell of the Pittsburgs will be in the Calumet line-up this evening, it is expected, and if so they will strengthen the locals considerably...If Hod is in anything like his old-time form, there should be something doing tonight, and there are many who venture to predict Calumet will win out.

Three exciting races were pulled off at the Palestra last evening. They were the novelty race in which Matt Gipp was to run five laps while Albert Davey skated seven, the ladies' race between Miss Lillian Archer and Miss Amelia Fred, and the backward race between K. Malleh, Schneller and Johnson.

MARCH 13: An authoritative statement was made today that Red Jacket probably will purchase a bell to toll the curfew hour. There is a belfry on the municipal building which is considered an ideal place for a bell. Sooner or later a village clock also probably will be installed in the belfry over the town hall. Four blank spaces were left by the architect for the purpose of placing a clock there. The faces of the clock could be seen from all quarters of the village.

MARCH 14: The upper peninsula hospital for the insane at Newberry, opened in 1896, is now taking care of 643 patients, with total record of about 1500. A large percentage of the present number of inmates are from the copper country. This is not surprising as Houghton county with 70,000 people is the largest in the peninsula.

MARCH 15: A protest meeting is called for Sunday afternoon at the Italian hall, Red Jacket, under the auspices of the Socialists of Houghton county for the purpose of passing resolutions protesting against the enforced imprisonment of C.H. Moyer, president of the Western Federation of Miners; William B. Haywood, secretary of the same association; and George H. Pettibone, at one time a member of the National committee of the miners' union. The men will be prosecuted for the assassination of Governor Steuenberger of Idaho.

The Michigan State Telephone company, the Houghton County Electric Light company, and the Western Union Telegraph company have already removed most of the poles owned by them on the streets of Red Jacket. By the end of the month all poles will have been removed, and the work of placing the overhead wires underground will have been started.

MARCH 30: "My fingers take the place of my eyes," said Blindman Victor Johnson to an *Evening News* man yesterday, and so they do. Mr. Johnson was engaged in trimming a broom when the reporter entered the little broom factory in Yellow Jacket, and the visitor marveled

that the blind man did not cut his hand. There are four or five little machines in this little factory and every one of them is manipulated with the greatest ease by Blindman Johnson and his assistant, another totally blind man named Gronzenok.

APRIL 2: The ravages of scarlet fever has played havoc in the home of Peter Ozanich, who resides at the rear of Sam Mawrence's store on Fifth street. The third and only child died this morning, after a comparatively short illness, the three dying within ten days, all, presumably, from scarlet fever.

APRIL 7: Miss Maggie Walz of Calumet, one of the best known Finnish lady residents in the country, will leave for Drummond Island, accompanied by at least fifty settlers...The island is an ideal place for patients suffering from hay fever, and Miss Walz states the more the island becomes known the greater its popularity will be.

APRIL 8: For the first time in twelve months it was possible yesterday to cross Portage Lake via the county bridge, traffic by that means having been suspended for a year in consequence of the destruction of the draw, the result of a collision by steamer.

APRIL 9: Last night shafts Nos.1 and 2, and No. 5 of the Tamarack branch of the Osceola Consolidated Mining company were closed and sealed for an indefinite period, owing to the fact that fire was discovered to have broken out afresh in No. 2 shaft, the scene of the original conflagration...This means that at least one thousand employees will be temporarily out of work.

APRIL 12: The Bosch Brewing company has awarded a contract to Myers & Thielman, well known contractors of Laurium, for the erection of a two-story frame structure on the Munch property on Pine street. The company now owns considerable property in Red Jacket, and has always followed out a line of erecting modern business places. The new Michigan house is an instance in point. This property at the corner of Oak and Sixth streets, is one of the handsomest blocks in the copper country. Its interior decorations are said to be equal to any other buffet in the state.

APRIL 14: A burglary was committed some time during last night at Vertin Bros.' store, corner of Oak and Sixth streets...It was the first burglary that has ever occurred at Vertin Bros.', and it is likely to be the last if precaution in the future will count for anything.

APRIL 17: The closing down of Nos. 1, 2 and 5 shafts of the Tamarack mine has thrown about one thousand men out of work, and although many of the skilled miners are finding employment elsewhere there are still several hundred left unprovided for. Many of the unemployed can be found on the street corners of Red Jacket, and at periods throughout the day may be seen wending their way to and from the Calumet & Hecla and other mining company's properties in quest of work.

To add to the situation the strike in the anthracite coal fields of Pennsylvania is having the effect of supplying the copper country with a large number of miners.

APRIL 23: Fire broke out in the Wickstrom, Neimi barn this afternoon shortly after two o'clock, and by the time the Red Jacket fire department was able to respond to the alarm, the building was a mass of flames…The building occupied by the Wickstrom, Neimi grocery department which adjoined the barn soon caught fire, and at this writing is a mass of flames. The building, which is a frame structure sheathed in iron, will undoubtedly be destroyed.

A west wind fanned the flames and the bakery next to the grocery store was the next to become food for the flames. A blacksmith shop adjoining the bakery to the west then caught and fire is also lodged on the roof of the Commercial house. A barn adjoining the residence of Mr. Korteneimi is also aflame, and will probably be entirely destroyed.

As the *Evening News* goes to press the fire seems to be under control and will be confined to the district now burning.

APRIL 24: Troubles never come singly. This is true in the case of the Mooti family of Calumet. Yesterday afternoon Joseph Mooti, aged about 50 years, a trammer at No. 3 shaft, Hecla, was killed by a fall of rock. The accident happened while the Vienna bakery, where Mooti's daughter was employed, was being destroyed by fire, forcing the girl out of a position.

APRIL 27: The Finnish Socialists will convene in the Red Jacket town hall where a lecture will be given by a well known Chicago lady Socialist. At the Italian hall a play will be presented by local Italian talent, illustrating the coal strike and other matters of public interest in the country. The Italian effort is in charge of Mr. Petrielli, a well known local Socialist.

### IT WILL BE LARGE
CALUMET'S 'FRISCO RESPONSE WILL REACH SEVERAL THOUSAND.
### CHINAMEN ALSO SUBSCRIBING
Fifth Street Committee First to Report—Amount Was $591.50, Which Included a Counterfeit Dollar

MAY 5: It will be remembered that a week or so ago a band of gypsies arrived in Calumet and located at Tamarack No. 5 location. Matters were made very warm for the band, reports being circulated that the gypsies had fleeced some of the local residents of hard-earned cash on a previous visit. "Once hit, twice shy," went this time, and the gypsies had to hike out without doing any "business."

Previous to going they called down vengeance on Calumet, and predicted the township would be visited by an earthquake. This report was circulated around town, and a number of local residents went to the Portage Lake towns in the hope that if Calumet was visited with an earthquake they would be safe. They returned home last evening with the laugh on them.

MAY 8: This morning there arrived in Calumet from Ford Bros., Minneapolis, the well-known church decorators, a consignment of windows for the St. Joseph's Austrian church. The value of the windows is given as at least $4,000…It is estimated the church will cost in the neighborhood of $100,000, and that when finished it will be one of the finest Roman Catholic edifices in the diocese, not excepting the Cathedral in Marquette.

MAY 9: Miss Maggie Walz, who is colonizing Drummond island with Finnish settlers, was in the Soo this week on business…"In the last party which came here there were about forty people all told and several more will arrive soon. Many of the new comers are from Ohio. Many of the colonists will go to Sanilac county this summer to work in the sugar factory. Next fall they will use the money they earn to buy lumber for houses and barns."

MAY 15: Friday of this week marks the thirty-sixth anniversary of Red Jacket's big fire. It occurred on May 18, 1870, and when the fire had finished its ravages there was little of Fifth street buildings. There was no Sixth, Seventh or Eighth streets in existence then.

"At least fifteen hundred laborers have left the copper country for other parts during the past four months," said G.L. Perreault, the employment agent, this morning, "and at present there is not a single laborer to be secured…"At least four hundred Austrians have left this country during the past few months, and as many Finns. The latter came in from the lumber camps in large numbers, stayed around the county for a day or two, and then went to Duluth and other large centers from where they were sent out west."

JUNE 2: Rapid progress is being made with the work on the Scott hotel.

JUNE 6: John Tachell sent a communication to the Red Jacket village council last evening requesting that the council award him damages for the loss of a horse which Mr. Tachell claimed was killed by falling into an excavation that had been made in connection with the street improvements…It was stated at the council meeting that it was impossible for the horse to get killed by falling into the trench which was only eighteen inches deep, and it is said that with reasonable care the horse could have been gotten out safely. The council finally decided to table the communication.

JUNE 7: Calumet is being visited by George H. Sutton, known as the handless billiardist because of the fact that he has lost both wrists and has made arrangements to give exhibitions at the Arlington hotel and Schroeder's saloon on Oak street, this week.

Governor Fred M. Warner and staff will reach Calumet tomorrow morning on the 6:30 train. He will be met at the depot by Representative William J. Galbraith and a number of other influential residents of this community. The governor's reception will be purely of an informal nature. It is understood he will dine at the Miscowaubik club.

JUNE 13: In describing the extent of the interest in the primary election held in Calumet township yesterday, it is only necessary to state that out of a total of 2,899 enrolled voters only 525 voters took advantage of their prerogative, less than one-fifth.

JUNE 16: The Socialists of Calumet will hold their annual picnic tomorrow afternoon at the Tamarack park.

JUNE 22: In 1898 there appeared at the copper mining village of Calumet a certain John Graham, an old Butte miner, with beautiful malachite and azurite specimens from Bisbee, Arizona, which he wished to sell. He had been a fellow miner in Butte with Captain James Hoatson of the Calumet & Hecla, and sought out his old friend. Hoatson was much interested in the beautiful copper rocks, and was told that "there was just as good as the Queen at Bisbee." So Hoatson went to Bisbee…Hoatson returned to Calumet to raise money for development. He approached his associates and superiors in the local management of the Calumet & Hecla, who at first decided on carrying the enterprise, but soon after remained outside. Scores of the former mine laborers in Calumet and vicinity are today amply supported by dividends from the Irish Mag shaft, and owe their competence to the fact that they believed in "Cap'n Jim" Hoatson.

JUNE 23: While the Copper Range train was coming to Calumet from Lake Linden last night it struck a cow and killed it. The engineer did not see the bovine. A peculiar circumstance in connection with the affair is the fact that the cow when struck by the engine was tossed into the air and landed on the coach next to the locomotive. Cows have been killed on local tracks before but never has any been tossed into the air in that manner.

JUNE 28: Joe Pasconen of Red Jacket, has a most voracious appetite for ice cream. This fact will be appreciated when it is stated that to win a bet last evening he ate ten large dishes of ice cream within a period of thirty minutes. He ate at the expense of the proprietor of the store. He is now acknowledged to be the champion ice cream eater of the copper country. He has any girl beaten a mile.

JUNE 30: "This is probably the quietest time of the year in the immigration business," said E.A. Lindgren of Duluth, immigration agent for the South Shore road for northern Michigan and points through Minnesota, to an *Evening News* man this morning.

"Many of the Finnish and Scandinavian immigrants come north," said Mr. Lindgren. "A large number of them go to points in Minnesota, while hundreds come to the copper country. Many Finnish and Scandinavian immigrants go home during the winter months. They reach this country early in the spring, work hard all summer farming, mining, and in other occupations, and being naturally of a thrifty disposition save considerable money.

"The greater part of that money is taken back to the old country, where Christmas is spent at the home fireside. I expect a big rush for European ports this fall. There are very few immigrants coming in just now, and I can say that the immigration season is now practically over as far as this country is concerned. The next movement will be the return to the old country."

JULY 5: A serious accident to a Finn occurred while he was witnessing a performance yesterday afternoon at the Bijou theater. During an act a boy seated in the gallery was leaning over the partition with a loaded cane in his hand. Without any warning the cane fell from the boy's hand and alighted on the head of a Finn who was seated on the main floor of the building. As the cane struck the head of the Finnish resident it exploded, badly frightening the man and the audience in general, and necessitating his removal to a nearby surgery where it was ascertained he had sustained a fracture of the skull.

JULY 7: While proceeding up Fifth street yesterday afternoon with a team of horses Simon Lasanen, the driver, was thrown from the rig, and badly injured, sustaining a broken collar bone, and several fractured ribs, the horses becoming frightened by an automobile passing at the time. Eyewitnesses state that the unfortunate man was thrown at least fifteen feet in the air, and that he landed on the ground with terrific force.

A strike of concrete workers, fillers and graders in the employ of James J. Byers & Co. in Red Jacket was declared this morning. An increase of pay and an eight-hour day are demanded.

JULY 10: "Many wealthy people go abroad annually, not knowing that within the state of Michigan they can visit a city in which resides people from all parts of the world. If anybody wants to see specimens of foreigners in their native garb from everywhere, go to Calumet. There are seven Catholic churches in Calumet of Italian, Bohemian, Austrian, Croatian, French, German and Polish.

"There are probably as many Finlanders in the upper peninsula today as there are in Finland, and nearly all of them dress in their native costumes, with shawls or other clothes for headgear."

JULY 12: The circumstances of the case, which was one of assault and battery, as told in the court yesterday was to the effect that Nevola in company with a party of Finns and their wives was proceeding to his home at Centennial Heights on the afternoon of the Fourth of July. While passing along the main road to the Red Jacket shaft the party passed a number of men who were playing a game of ball. The game was played with large wooden balls, and just as one of the men was throwing a ball Nevola got in the way of it and was struck on the legs. It was stated he took the blow good naturedly, and threw the ball back to the players. The players, however, were not so jubilant, and accused Nevola of interfering with the game. This he denied when one of the party advanced upon him with a ball in his hand, and in a moment had struck him on the head with it, knocking him insensible.

JULY 16: An *Evening News* representative had the pleasure yesterday of a ride on the "Freda Flyer," the Copper Range railroad's new train between Calumet and Freda park on Sundays

JULY 20: The R.S. Blome company experienced another small strike of graders and fillers yesterday afternoon. This time the men were not striking for higher wages and shorter hours, but strongly objected to having a foreman in charge of them discharged.

JULY 24: Of interest to Calumet people is the announcement that the Calumet & Hecla Mining company intends in the near future to change the Hecla and Torch Lake railroad from narrow gauge to standard.

JULY 26: "We could use 3,000 miners in the copper country if they could be obtained," said a prominent mining man this morning…On the streets of Red Jacket and in Keweenaw county where railway operations are on, the demand for labor is unprecedented, and it looks as if it will not be met. Harvesting operations also require a lot of men just now, and while many have gone into the hay and corn fields there is a demand for many more. The Finns as a class monopolize the farming industry in this and other counties in the copper country, and hundreds of them are engaged on farms at present.

AUGUST 2: Up to yesterday over 15,000 people had visited Electric park this summer, the largest number having gone there last month when the grand total reached 7,694…The grounds are provided with swings and settees for a tete-a-tete. Every evening moving pictures are shown from first-class films and free dancing with music by the Calumet & Hecla orchestra is furnished three evenings a week and Sunday afternoon the Calumet & Hecla band furnishes a concert.

There was considerable excitement in the depot for a few minutes just previous to the departure of the little circus. One of the colored employees engaged in a dispute with another of a lighter hue and eventually came to blows. It was a regular Fitzsimmons-Corbett mill for a couple of minutes with the coon getting the worst of it.

AUGUST 9: Kreetan is the name of the newest postoffice in Chippewa county. It is located on Drummond Island at the Finnish settlement and is already doing a flourishing business. Miss Maggie Walz is postmistress.

…"I could live in Paris on the money I am spending on the island," said Miss Walz, "but I don't want to leave this country. This is good enough for me."

AUGUST 13: One of the finest school buildings in the northwest is being erected at Calumet to replace the structure destroyed by fire last winter. The school is constructed according to plans prepared by Architects Charlton & Kuenzli, Marquette and Milwaukee, and will cost complete, $150,000.

AUGUST 16: The circumstances surrounding the rise of Maggie J. Walz of Calumet, well known to local people, are now attracting attention in other places. Anent this remarkable woman, a Lennox, Mich., correspondent of a Detroit paper says:

"Miss Maggie J. Walz of Calumet, who will entertain the Michigan Women's Press association on Drummond island, leaving Detroit next Friday, is one of the brightest business women in Michigan. When she arrived from Finland 25 years ago she was a poor girl. Today she is owner of a business block which she built in Calumet at a cost of $40,000; is publisher of the *Naisten-Lehti*, the oldest Finnish ladies' journal in America, and owns considerable real estate and mining stock.

"Miss Walz is a fine type of independent womanhood, about 40 years of age. She has a good physique and possesses a frank, friendly manner, inspiring confidence in her ability. She is actuated by a desire to benefit her countrymen. The United States government has recognized her faithfulness by appointing her colonization agent for Drummond island, Lake Huron. The population now exceeds 1,000 persons, mostly Finns, although anyone seeking a home there is made welcome.

"A significant illustration of the esteem in which Miss Walz is held was the selection of the name of the first town on Drummond island.

"'Kreetan! Kreetan!' shouted the hundreds of Finns who gathered to make the choice and "Kreetan," which is Finnish for Margaret, won the day and the town forthwith given that name."

AUGUST 18: A meeting of the Fat Men's baseball committee was held last evening at the Arlington hotel when further arrangements for the annual game in Calumet was made…A suggestion was made at last night's meeting, and will probably be acted upon, that an invitation be sent to Roosevelt to be present...It will be remembered that Teddy visited Calumet last year, and his welcome was of such a vociferous nature that a second invitation will probably be extended. If he decides to come he will arrive over the South Shore road on a "special."

What has been this summer the most popular dancing pavilion in the county was found this morning a mass of smouldering ruins. The large frame structure owned by the street railway company at Electric park was consumed by flames early this morning.

AUGUST 27: The Calumet-Telluride Gold Mining company recently held its annual stock holders' meeting in Telluride. A board of nine directors was elected for the ensuing year, eight of them being Calumet or other copper country men.

SEPTEMBER 8: It will be surprising news to many that in one of the saloons in Red Jacket there are as many as two back rooms, kept for "private" purposes, which women and girls often frequent.

Matters have now reached a crisis. Yesterday afternoon Marshal Trudell arrested two girls in a saloon on Sixth street, who were in the company of two young men and drinking wine and smoking cigarettes. Their presence was known to the proprietor of the place, and he had served them with liquor, according to the report of the marshal.

SEPTEMBER 11: The Calumet & Hecla Mining company has established a pension system for its old employees...When an employee has reached an age where the company considers him unfit for manual labor he is placed upon the pension list and given so much per cent on the wages that he had been earning.

The plan is considered a magnanimous one. It is believed that no other corporation in the state of Michigan is making such provision for its old employees. Considering the fact that the Calumet & Hecla Mining company has something like 5,000 employees on its pay rolls, it can readily be seen the plan is likely to entail a big expenditure.

OCTOBER 12: The settlements are stretching and the deer and wolf are being driven into smaller confines each year. Where he hasn't the latitude in which to elude his enemy the deer must fall a victim to the greed of the wolf and that greed is to all indications never satisfied.

Calumet and Hancock is to be visited by two prominent Socialists on Sunday and Monday evenings, October 21 and 22. They are J. Walker of Muskegon, Socialist candidate for governor, and William T. Biggs of Chicago, the well known Socialist orator.

Dr. Helenious Seppala, the well known Finnish temperance orator, gave an admirable address last evening in the Red Jacket town hall to a large Finnish audience.

OCTOBER 13: There is now not the least doubt that the Calumet & Hecla Mining company intends disposing of all of its lots in Red Jacket. Applications are in for every available bit of land the company owns in the village, and it is said that favorable action will be taken on the same.

It is understood that the lots on Eighth street are to go to residents willing to build homes there. The idea is to make that street the boulevard of the village.

OCTOBER 15: Manager Sloane of the Calumet Gas company stated this morning that he expected to be able to turn on gas for the first time in Calumet during the holidays. It is expected that the company will furnish its first gas in this community to fully six hundred users, that number having practically agreed to use the commodity.

Ground was broken this morning for the proposed new Y.M.C.A. building that is to be erected next summer in Red Jacket.

OCTOBER 17: Rabbi Nachman Heller of Philadelphia, a noted Jewish scholar and writer, has arrived in Calumet and will probably locate here permanently to work among the Hebrews of this community.

OCTOBER 18: Active temperance workers say the greatly increased consumption of beer in this county is a good sign of progress toward real temperance. It shows that beer, a healthful beverage, is fast taking the place of strong alcoholic drinks.

Harry H. Greece, state manager of the White steamer autos, Joe S. Smith, sporting editor of the *Detroit Journal*, and A.D. Hallock, a mechanic, are making a unique automobile trip, being bound from Detroit to Calumet in a White steamer. From Calumet they will go south to Chicago and from Chicago to Detroit. The distance to be covered is about 2,500 miles.

OCTOBER 22: As was his custom every night Andrew Themo, a well known Finn of Red Jacket, went to sleep in a back room of the Kivari saloon on Pine street last night, and this morning was found dead.

A meeting of the Jewish citizens of Calumet was held last evening in Dunstan's hall, when ways and means for the maintenance of the Jewish school and its initiator, Dr. Nachman Heller, were discussed.

Basing its protest upon an article published in a Socialist organ, the *Ontonagon Herald* decries the attempts being made to turn public sentiment in favor of the Finnish strikers under arrest for participation in the riot at the Michigan mine. The *Herald* claims the courts should determine the fate of the men, and if they be guilty they should suffer accordingly.

OCTOBER 23: While it is generally believed—and statistics attempt to prove the theory—by far the larger ratio of accidents in mines are due to falls of ground.

These casualties are inevitable, yet their frequency may be lessened by greater care on the part of the miner to sound the walls and roof and using sufficient timber.

Another cause to which is attributable an unusually large number of accidents is explosion.

Falling down a shaft, resulting invariably in death, is often due to negligence on the part of the miner.

It would probably be a good idea if mine managers posted a list of "don'ts" at convenient places above and underground, so that the miner would become accustomed to practice greater care to safeguard himself and neighbor while attending to his duties.

OCTOBER 25: This week Marshal Trudell found two women lying intoxicated near a saloon on Fifth street. The edict prohibiting the allowing of women in saloons went forth some time ago, and the officers are making efforts to see that it is respected. The two women, who were found intoxicated this week, were in a disgusting condition and had evidently secured the liquor from a saloon.

OCTOBER 26: "I want you to take me to the county jail, and keep me there for thirty days so that I may have a chance to sober up," Peter Matheson is reported as saying to a Red Jacket police officer yesterday afternoon.

OCTOBER 31: There are approximately 5,000 Italians in Houghton county, according to Consular Agent James Lisa of Red Jacket. Mr. Lisa estimates that Calumet alone has at least 3,000 of the 5,000 estimated.

NOVEMBER 1: There are in course of erection in Calumet some of the most palatial residences north of the straits. The majority of these, in fact, practically all, are located in Laurium.

NOVEMBER 3: Ernest Thulin was killed while at work in the condenser room at the North Tamarack mine yesterday afternoon. It is surmised that he must have become caught in the machinery in some way, and whirled to his death, the body being found several yards away from the condenser.

NOVEMBER 12: It is estimated that Calumet consumes about 3,000 turkeys on Thanksgiving, and as this is considered conservative, it may safely be stated that the number consumed in this township during the Yuletide period easily amounts to 6,000.

NOVEMBER 13: Mrs. W.S. Campbell, owner of the Bijou theater, has made arrangements to give the newsboys of Calumet a treat by admitting them free to the performance next Friday evening. As the colder weather approaches, the crowds at the Bijou increases and each evening the little playhouse is crowded. The people of Calumet have always greeted vaudeville well, but the coming winter promises to be a record breaker in point of attendance at the Bijou.

Three gypsies, names unpronounceable, were arrested yesterday afternoon and brought before Justice Jackola charged with telling fortunes contrary to the village ordinances, and were fined $5 and costs each and also ordered to get out of town.

NOVEMBER 15: Considerable local interest will be taken in curling this season, and it is expected that Calumet will have two good "rinks."

The regular quarterly dividend announcement on Calumet & Hecla stock is due within the next week. The fact that the price of the stock is now close to its high record figure—$895 per share, touched in 1899—and the added fact that the company has at the present time a surplus in cash and copper of something over $10,000,000, it is only natural that "the street" is talking about a further possible increase in the distribution then to be made.

NOVEMBER 23: When Calumet people gather at the Calumet theatre next Tuesday evening they will see and hear the one man who has done more for the poor of New York, more for moral cleanliness, more for improved conditions in the tenement house districts in the great city than any other man living...Jacob Riis.

NOVEMBER 27: Sunday afternoon several ladies met in the Maggie Walz block on Pine street and revived the Finnish Ladies' society, or "Nais Yhtisdys," as it is known in Finnish.

DECEMBER 1: With the Christmas holiday less than a month away, Calumet people are already beginning to puzzle their brains over a suitable present to make to the wife, the mother, the sister, the brother, the cousin, the aunt, and the friend...in fact, that it is generally postponed from day to day until the anniversary of the grand chorus when the morning stars sang together is but a few hours removed. And what a rush is there then, my countrymen! They all hie away to the big department store or the clothing house, the toy shop and the confectionery, and the jeweler's emporium, in search of an indefinite something.

DECEMBER 3: It is expected that the travel out of Calumet during the holidays will be heavy this year, as it always is. The teachers form a good proportion of the Calumet population which spends its holidays outside of the copper country. Of the teachers in the Calumet schools a large number live in other parts of the country and they make it a point to spend the holidays at their homes.

DECEMBER 10: All labor troubles are over at the Osceola branch of the Osceola Consolidated. This morning the miners and trammers met an official of the company, and agreed to accept the company's offer of an additional 5 per cent increase made last week.

DECEMBER 11: Another mining company has just been organized in Calumet. It is the Finnish American Mining company, with a capitalization of $750,000 at a par value of $1 per share. Shares will be placed on the market in the near future for public subscription.

DECEMBER 14:…changing the date of the children's special night in connection with the local Salvation Army corps observance of Christmas night to Christmas eve, Adjutant MacHarg stating that the change is unavoidable owing to unforeseen circumstances. Christmas night as a rule is spent by the majority of the Army members in their own homes.

Adjutant MacHarg has a list of over fifty poor families which will be aided on Christmas day, and the encouragement his plans have received during the past few days has been such that he believes everyone will be supplied.

DECEMBER 15: One of the most palatial residences in the copper country is in course of construction in Laurium for Captain Thomas Hoatson, general manager of the Keweenaw Copper company.

DECEMBER 17: The strike of the section hands in the employ of the Mineral Range Railroad company in the copper country came to an end this morning, the officials of the road conceding to the men's demands for $1.75 per day, instead of $1.50 as paid previous to the trouble.

DECEMBER 21: Jessie Lytie, colored, is seemingly up against it. A warrant has been sworn out for his arrest on the charge of making threats against the life of John Huggins, also a colored resident of Calumet.

DECEMBER 24: There is at present only one child at Good Will Farm. The Good Will Farm & Home Finding association will hereafter conduct the institution purely as a home finding enterprise. No boarders will be taken.

The farm will accept no illegitimate children. The association encountered much unfriendly criticism for taking such cases in former years, and hereafter the churches will be expected to provide for little ones of this class.

DECEMBER 28: Township Clerk William Johnson expects to record a total of at least 600 births in the township for the year just ending. He stated this morning that 597 births are recorded to date.

With the 600 mark reached a record will be established for Calumet. In the village of Red Jacket it is expected a total of 120 will be recorded, also a record figure.

Laurium is populated considerably more than Red Jacket and in consequence the number of births will be greater. While Village Clerk Charrier has not completed his returns as yet, still it is pretty safe to assert that the figure will reach 250.

Summed up the total is nearly a thousand births for the year in this district, outside the township of Osceola.

The death rate is small in comparison with the birth rate, there being probably not more than four hundred deaths in this district during the year, thus showing a gain in population of at least six hundred. The population of Calumet is variously estimated between 40,000 and 45,000 persons at the present time. It should not be far from the 50,000 mark by 1910, taking the present increase as a basis.

DECEMBER 31: "Houghton county, and Calumet in particular, was never more prosperous than it is just now," remarked a Calumet resident this morning to an *Evening News* man…

It is a remarkable thing, said this particular resident, that once foreign-born residents come to this country, secure work, with its attendant good pay, and begin to enjoy some of the luxuries of life that never could be obtained in European countries by workingmen, that the feeling for the country of their adoption is strong. "It makes good citizens," he said, "and that's what we in this country want. Good citizens in any community make for the uplifting and bettering of conditions and Calumet may certainly be classed in that category."

---

**Photos, pages 119-120**

Page 119: Newly-arrived Italian immigrant to work in Calumet mines. By Nara. *MTU-Copper Country Historical Collection*
Page 120: At Red Jacket shaft, 1907. *RCM/Mantel*

# Calumet **1907** *News*

*Red Jacket is overcrowded, so badly in fact the condition is considered a menace to health. There are a number of homes in Red Jacket located principally on Sixth and Seventh streets, where in two, three, and four rooms something like twenty persons are living. The majority of these inhabitants are boarders. They are crowded in like cattle, and the atmosphere at night when these people are asleep must be of a very putrid nature.*

JANUARY 2: Without blare of trumpets the Hotel Michigan, owned by the Bosch Brewing company, and situated at the corner of Sixth and Oak streets, was opened to the public this morning.

JANUARY 18: The Calumet postoffice is still receiving many postal cards containing the endless prayer chain on them. In spite of the fact that the plan was started without authority, and evidently by some crank, many persons receiving them, particularly many women, are frightened by the threat contained in them, and are sending them out, "for fear."

JANUARY 21: The most severe storm of the winter and one of the fiercest Calumet has ever experienced was that of yesterday, the community being almost cut off from the outside world, few trains succeeding in arriving and those all very late.

Roadways and fences were covered deep with snow which drifted high and many residents almost had to tunnel out of their homes. One cannot now "cut across lots" in going to and from work as the snow is of sufficient depth to obliterate almost every obstruction but a two-story house.

JANUARY 22: It is believed this is the first time in the history of the local courts that only one case has been reported after a pay day. There are usually three or four, and at times the number has reached as high as twelve, within two days.

JANUARY 28: In the Calumet Protestant churches last evening the ministers of this vicinity took Temperance as their subject, each scoring the liquor traffic, presenting means whereby it could be destroyed and on the whole expressing great confidence in that ultimately the Prohibitionists will triumph in their campaign.

FEBRUARY 5: Anton Butovat, an Austrian trammer, met death last evening in the Red Jacket shaft, through an act of thoughtlessness on his part, according to the evidence.

Calumet patrons of the long distance telephone service to Duluth were advised this morning by the telephone company that beginning Feb. 1, the rate for a three-minute talk between Calumet and Duluth will be $4 instead of $1 as heretofore.

FEBRUARY 7: There is a great scarcity of labor in Calumet. The villages of Red Jacket and Laurium are hard pressed for men. Men are wanted to cope with the snow problem, and cannot be found, that is, not in sufficient numbers.

…said a railroad man to the Duluth *Herald*…"I never before saw such deep snow on the level as they have around Calumet and Houghton. There isn't much wind there, and consequently there are no drifts. The snow remains where it falls, so when it is deep in one place you may rest assured that it is the same depth all over the district.

"It is no exaggeration to say that in the streets and on the sidewalks of Houghton and Calumet, except, of course, where they have been shoveled off, the stuff is from three to four feet deep, and packed hard at that by the people and teams that have passed over it. In walking along the main street of Calumet, I found my feet were half way up to the store windows, on a level with the heads of the clerks inside. The street car tracks appeared as a tunnel, so far were they below the level of the street."

FEBRUARY 13: "Calumet has hundreds of thousands of dollars in business blocks and flats at the present time and more will be built this spring. There are no finer flats or apartment houses even in many of our larger cities than can be found right here in Calumet," said a Calumet property owner this morning.

When one names the Bollman block, the Schroeder-Nelson block, the Vertin, Ruppe and one or two others…

Besides the above named buildings there are the Coppo, Herman, Ryan, Schumaker and the Assylin blocks that contain many flats on a metropolitan order.

FEBRUARY 19: "Big Louie" Moilanen is coming to Calumet this week, and many who have never seen the big fellow will have an opportunity to do so. He is at present on his father's farm near the Boston location, and will make his home there until early spring, when he will accept one or the other of the offers he has received to travel with some show next season.

He has now reached his real height, standing about eight feet in his stockings. Louis told the *News* informant yesterday that he does not expect to grow any more.

MARCH 8: It is hardly to be credited that there are in Red Jacket's hovels which are in reality brothels, the like of which can only be equalled in the slums of some of the larger cities. A shocking case of this description has just been discovered by Marshal Trudell, who, in speaking of the matter, did so with a shudder and aversion despite the fact that he frequently comes across scenes of filth and vice. He arrested a woman named Annie Hanninen in a house on Pine street, yesterday afternoon, and charged her with being a common prostitute. When arrested she was too drunk to realize her condition.

MARCH 15: James Bartle, who was killed yesterday afternoon while at work underground in No. 14 shaft of the C.&H. mine, had, it is reported, a premonition that he was about to die. He had passed two or three sleepless nights previous to the accident, and it is said had actually selected the pall bearers to attend his funeral.

MARCH 19: Sakris Niemala, the well-known Pine street cattle dealer, had a close call from death on Oak street yesterday afternoon. He was gored by a cow he was leading and had the animal a pair of longer horns the chances are he would have been killed.

MARCH 25: The average citizen of Calumet knows that the local postoffices in Calumet and Laurium handle a large amount of mail daily, but few are aware of just the quantity. Inquiry this morning brought out the information that about 4,000 pounds, or two tons of mail was handled in a single day recently.

MARCH 26: The day shift miners of No. 5 shaft of the Tamarack mine refused to go to work this morning, and if the trouble is not adjusted by this evening it is said the night shift miners also will remain on the surface. The miners are the only ones who have grievances to make.

The trouble, *The Evening News* is informed, has arisen over proposed changes in the contract system and in the working time on Saturday.

APRIL 4: Early this morning while a skip load of men was proceeding down No. 5 shaft of the Calumet branch of the C.&H. mine Dominic Tomasi was instantly killed and John Richetta, Chas. Sundberg and Dominic Marvino injured, through the skip crashing into a pile of timber laid across the shaft.

APRIL 11: There were only six truants in the schools of Calumet, District No. 1 last month. There are between 6,000 and 7,000 pupils attending school in that district, so the showing is gratifying to the school officials. One feature introduced by the school authorities that has a tendency to keep children in school is that of making pupils bring written excuses signed by their parents or guardians whenever absent.

Three accidents occurred in local mines during the past few hours, one of which terminated fatally. The victim of one other is reported in a precarious condition at the Calumet & Hecla hospital, while the third man is painfully hurt.

APRIL 13: The night clerk in one of Calumet's hotels was troubled over the fact that the man who had sauntered in late and seated himself in a comfortable chair, had fallen asleep. He sent the bell "hop" over to tell him he was asleep, but the lobby lodger apparently did not believe the message. The lad listened to his rambling mutterings.

"He says to let him off at Lake Linden avenue," said the boy, as he reported to the night clerk.

"What does he think this is—a street car?" fairly yelled the clerk. Then a bright idea came into his head. He went over and shook the man.

"Thash airight, lemme off at Lake Linden avenue— noo," said the man.

"Fare!" cried the clerk in his ear. The man sleepily put a hand in his trousers pockets and pulled forth a nickel, handing it over to the clerk. The clerk let him sleep a little while and then returned.

"Fare!" again shouted the clerk, and again the man pulled forth a nickel and tendered it to the clerk, meanwhile keeping his sleepy eyes on the floor. Again he fell asleep and again the clerk demanded his fare. The collections were made at regular intervals for the greater part of the night, the boy failing to arouse the sleeper.

Finally as the gray dawn crept into the deserted lobby the man stretched himself and woke up, fully and wide awake. He walked leisurely around the lobby and then put his hand in his trousers pocket, drawing it forth with an air of surprise. He glanced over his shoulder at the desk. Then he walked up to the desk and lowering his voice, he said beseechingly:

"Say, c'n you let me take a nickel to get home, friend; I'm busted?"

APRIL 16: Despite the gloomy outlook for the summer the Copper Range railroad is already preparing for a big summer's excursion travel to its popular resort, Freda Park.

APRIL 17: James Lisa, Italian consular agent for the upper peninsula and the northern portions of Wisconsin and Minnesota, has practically completed his census of Italian people residing in those districts.

The estimate, according to Mr. Lisa, is at least 20,000, of which Houghton county supplies a large percentage. Houghton easily leads in the number of Italians in any one county, it being calculated by Mr. Lisa that there are at the very lowest 6,000 residing in this county.

APRIL 23: Calumet smokers consume 2,000 cigars daily.

APRIL 24: Time was when the restrictions placed on saloons in the copper country were practically nothing, but times have changed and the lid is kept on pretty tight, with the result that the pay day drunks and broils of other days are things of the past, to say nothing of similar incidents at other times.

APRIL 27: The greater number of the immigrants coming in now are Austrians and Finns, with a sprinkling of other nationalities. They usually come over here to make their home, with the intention of becoming citizens as soon as they are entitled to papers. They are willing to take any kind of work at first, and as rule, they make good laborers.

Just before Christmas each year there are large numbers of foreigners leaving for their native land to spend the holidays and in the spring they return to take up their residence again in their adopted country.

MAY 2: The number of births overshadowed the number of deaths more than two to one, so that if March is taken as any criterion there is not much cause to worry over race suicide in this county.

...the disclosures in yesterday's *News* of the unsanitary condition of the back yards and alleys of Calumet which in many instances are littered with ashes, tin cans, old stoves, bed ticks, decaying vegetable matter, tin cans and rusty wire.

Did any one smell gas in Red Jacket this morning? If not, why not? The illuminant is circulating through the mains today, and some consumers are already using it in the village. The first business house in which gas was turned on this morning was the saloon managed by Archie Hall on the south end of Fifth street in the Orenstein block. The gas flowed through the pipes in good volume, and the light obtainable was very satisfactory.

MAY 3: As usual in Calumet the Finns predominate in the number of births in the township...According to the records the last named nationality has added the first Swiss to this community in the history of the township...There has only been one Greek child born in Calumet township as far as can be ascertained.

MAY 4: While proceeding to the surface in Tamarack No. 5 shaft at noon today, Norman Johnson, a drill boy, through some means, fell from the skip he was riding to the bottom, a distance of several hundred feet.

MAY 6: The Copper Country has some of the deepest metal mine shafts in the world, and some of the largest.

Some of the shafts of note are the following: Calumet & Hecla shaft No. 4 has a single compartment; is sunk on an incline to a depth of 8,100, the slope angle being 37 degrees and 30 minutes; vertical depth below the collar, 4,748 feet. A winze has been sunk below the bottom of the shaft 190 feet additional, making a total depth on the incline of 8,200 feet.

No. 2 Calumet shaft, also an incline, is 7,000 feet in depth. Beside these there are several other inclined shafts at this great mine, which has over 200 miles of workings. These shafts range from 2,400 to more than 6,000 feet deep. The really great shafts of this mine are the newer

vertical working shafts. Of these the Red Jacket is 4,920 feet deep.

The Tamarack mine, adjoining the Calumet & Hecla, has the deepest vertical shafts in the world, the deepest of these being No. 3, which is 5,139 feet deep—141 feet less than one mile.

Welcome, Odd Fellows of Michigan, on this the fifty-ninth annual session of the Grand Encampment and seventeenth department council, Patriarchs Militant.

Calumet holds out to you that hospitality for which the copper country is famous. No gathering of importance in this region has ever suffered for lack of that feeling which makes a stranger within these borders of copper feel at home at once.

The local committeemen have worked indefatigably for weeks to make this gathering what it should be, one of the most notable ever held in Michigan. They have only one regret, and that is the condition of the streets which in places are still covered in with ice and snow.

MAY 9: A fire was discovered in the kitchen of the Dikinan flat at the rear of the Maggie Walz block on Pine street at the noon hour.

MAY 11: In contrast with Houghton and its few churches Calumet is a veritable "City of Churches." The finest edifice of the kind in the copper country, St. Joseph's Austrian Catholic church, is located there and practically every nationality in this community has one or more houses of worship.

MAY 13: The state fish car, Fontinalis of the Soo, arrived in Calumet this morning, and in consequence the streams and tributaries in Keweenaw county and fishing haunts in and around Calumet will be the richer in a few hours by about 150,000 brook trout.

MAY 16: Calumet may have a co-operative brewery shortly. A number of prominent Austrian residents have discussed the matter and have about determined to organize a company, having for its sole object the brewing of beer and selling of the same, to Austrian and other residents of this community.

MAY 18: The new theater on the ground floor of the Corgan block, Fifth street, Red Jacket, will be opened this evening. The new play house will be known as "The Star"...

With the entrance of "The Star" theater in the field, Calumet can now boast of three such places of amusement, as well as a regular vaudeville house, the Bijou theater.

The Bijou management promises a first-class show next week. The drawing card will be Woodford's educated animals...Included with the show is Tinymite, the smallest horse in the world, claimed to weigh only 21 pounds.

JUNE 6: The total assessed valuation of the township of Calumet, which includes several mining companies, has been fixed by the board of review to amount to $57,328,937, nearly four and one-half millions in excess of last year's valuation.

Charles Captel, assistant mill runner at the Tamarack mills, was caught in the pulley wheel of the shafting early this morning, and before the machinery could be stopped was whirled to his death.

JUNE 10: In his book "The Greater America," recently published, Ralph D. Paine, the well known special writer for *Outing* magazine, dwells at some length on the cosmopolitan nature of the population of the upper peninsula of Michigan, his description applying principally to Calumet. He finds nothing alarming in the immigration problem. For instance, this is the way he describes conditions in Calumet:

"In fact, the polyglot community is so singularly law-abiding, that the horde of sociologists that is rampant in the land should organize a personally conducted tour to this favored community. There is no municipal police force in the district. In the town of Calumet two-thirds of the public revenue is derived from saloon license fees, yet drunkenness seldom becomes disorderly. Calumet has a municipal theater, built by the public funds, at a cost of $100,000, leased to a manager who pays the town 4 per cent on its investment. In the eight school houses the children are fused as in a melting pot to become good Americans of the second generation, speaking English as their common tongue, and saluting the Stars and Stripes above their buildings."

JUNE 11: Red Jacket is overcrowded, so badly in fact the condition is considered a menace to health. There are a number of homes in Red Jacket located principally on Sixth and Seventh streets, where in two, three, and four rooms something like twenty persons are living. The majority of these inhabitants are boarders. They are crowded in like cattle, and the atmosphere at night when these people are asleep must be of a very putrid nature.

JUNE 29: Despondent, it is believed, from weeks of suffering from operations and a general breakdown in health, Solomon Kujanpaa, a Finlander of Swedetown, shot himself through the heart last night, dying within a short time.

JULY 13: Matt Gipp of Calumet, probably one of the best known hunters and trappers in Houghton county, is a candidate for the appointment of state fish, fire and game warden for this district…

Gipp has been known time and again to stop violations of the fish and game laws on his own initiative, and has often received the thanks of bona fide sportsmen.

JULY 16: It is a long time since a Cornish wrestling tournament has been pulled off in Calumet and the announcement one is to be held next month undoubtedly will be welcome news to the many followers of the sport in this section.

JULY 23: Gollmar Bros.' circus exhibited here this afternoon to a large and appreciative audience.

Whether the Calumet Woman's club, through its civic improvement committee, aided by the competition on "How to Make Calumet More Beautiful" is responsible for the decided improvement in the appearance of Calumet property or not is not certain. However, a noticeable change for the better has been commented upon fully of late.

JULY 25: Sheriff Beck in conversation with an *Evening News* man this morning stated that during the past month the record number of prisoners under his charge was reached, there being 52 in the county jail.

JULY 29: Yesterday's sham battle at Swedetown between the Calumet and the Houghton and Hancock companies was brought to a tragic termination soon after the troops were in battle formation and the firing had begun when Private Elmer Luokola of Company G, Houghton, fell suddenly to the ground at the side of his comrade Lieutenant Chapple, and expired within ten minutes.

A shot fired by a person as yet unknown had passed through the flesh of his left arm, entered the left breast, severing, it is believed, the large artery leading from the heart and passing from the body on the right side.

Since the tragedy, talk has been revived in regard to the great danger that has been experienced by those who have had occasion to walk in that vicinity especially on Sunday when the hunters seem to be out in large numbers. It is stated that bullets very frequently are flying around in a manner endangering the lives of the chance passerby to a great degree.

JULY 31: There were three hoboes in Red Jacket yesterday, two of them cripples. They came here to beg and for a time were successful in their efforts. Then Marshal Trudell got wind of them and within one hour had them up and ordered out of town. Almost needless to say they took his advice.

AUGUST 3: Teofila Petrielli, the man of the hour on the Mesaba Iron range, head of the Western Federation of Miners in that region, was formerly a resident of Calumet where he resided for several months, editing the local "La Sentinelli," now defunct.

Petrielli came to Houghton county in January, 1906, and filled ten engagements in this county, addressing audiences in English and Italian in the Socialist cause. Of anti-church tendencies, it is alleged that his editorials did not gibe with the opinions of local subscribers, and there was soon trouble.

AUGUST 12: John Jelinich, a track man in the employ of the Tamarack Mining company, fell 600 feet to his death.

Red Jacket has an Anti-Red Flag club. A number of Red Jacket citizens, mostly between the ages of 20 and 25, met Sunday in one of the public halls of the village, and organized for the purpose.

AUGUST 21:...early this morning when Fred Ford of the First National Bank of Calumet was walking down Sixth St. about two blocks north of the Copper Range depot, a huge bear reared its terrifying aspect directly in front of him in the moonlight.

SEPTEMBER 7: It is interesting to note that Calumet during the summer drawing to a close has consumed more than 11,000 cords of ice.

Calumet was stacked up against an ice famine two years ago when ice was shipped in here from Minnesota points at considerable big expense to meet every day wants. The local company learned a lesson at that time, and for the past two seasons has stored enough ice and plenty to spare to meet all demands.

Every Finn who comes into the copper country, Calumet in particular, is kept track of. The organization has for its object the patriotic education of the Finns, especially with regard to anti-red flag ideas.

When a stranger of the Finnish nationality comes to Calumet or any other town in the copper country his whereabouts are at once communicated to the parent organization in Calumet, and steps are at once taken to get into communication with him, and see that he is treated with every respect and an effort made to secure work for him.

From then on until he leaves this part of the country he is made to feel that life is worth living.

SEPTEMBER 10: The eight representatives of the R.L. Polk & Co., directory firm of Detroit, who have been working in Calumet and vicinity for the last five weeks and who will complete their work tonight, estimate that Calumet now has a population in the neighborhood of 55,000. The estimated population at the last census was 40,000 and the increase is the unusually large one of 37 ½ per cent. This is caused probably in large measure by the demand for labor and the immigration of foreigners to take places wherever there are new developments.

Most places on the globe of any size have more people by the name of Smith, with its characteristic variations such as Schmidt, Smythe, etc., than those of any other name and in many cases the Smiths will outnumber several of the other leading names combined. In Calumet, however, the Smiths are entirely overshadowed by the Johnsons as there are several pages of the latter name and few comparatively with the distinguished cognomen of Smith.

SEPTEMBER 30: The copper country rinks are business propositions, pure and simple. Business men own the stock, business men are managers and, though love of the sport was the original inspiration, the conduct of skating and hockey is on a businesslike basis. The rinks open each winter about December 31 and close about April 1. Every night for the four months, there is a band at the rinks, Sunday excepted, and crowds of from anywhere from 200 to 1,500 skate to the music. The copper country is not skating mad, but they love the sport for the amusement and the exercise and they enjoy themselves to the fullest.

When the ice skating season closes, the returns on investments do not cease. For three months after the end of ice skating, roller skating takes its place.

OCTOBER 1: Sometime during the past few days Calumet's splendid new high school and manual training building has been mutilated, presumably by thoughtless juveniles, the sandstone of the southeast corner of the east wing having been chipped in several places with some blunt instrument...

The Calumet & Hecla Mining company, which erected the structure, is offering a reward for the conviction and punishment of the culprits.

Calumet and the whole copper country generally was interested today in the curtailment of the force of men employed at the various Bigelow properties. This was most noticeable this morning at the Osceola mine. A number of men are being laid off there, and No. 6 shaft has been closed.

The reason given by officers of the corporation this morning was that it had been decided by the directors and the management generally not to overcrowd copper production because of the big surplus of metal on hand in this country.

OCTOBER 9: Not so very long ago it was stated in these columns that Mineral Range railroad cars had been broken into and cases of beer, the property of the Pabst Brewing company, stolen. Now comes the actual detection of Steve Duballa, a boy of less than fifteen years of age, pilfering a freight car and taking a quantity of apples consigned to a local merchant.

OCTOBER 10: That the Rev. Frederick Baraga, first bishop of the roman Catholic dioceses of Marquette and Sault Ste. Marie, Mich., which comprises the entire upper peninsula of Michigan, and whose body lies buried in St. Peter's cathedral there, contributed to philological literature the first and only dictionary and grammar of the chippewa language is an interesting but little known fact, says the *New York Herald*.

OCTOBER 11: Calumet can now boast of a musical organization composed entirely of Finnish residents. Calumet can now boast of a musical organization composed entirely of Finnish residents. It can lay claim to being the second town in the United States with a Finnish band. The organization has been named the Huma Finnish Band.

The organization of the Huma band makes the second musical organization in Calumet during the past month, the first being the Calumet Finnish Glee club, under the direct leadership of Prof. S. Mustonen.

OCTOBER 14: Casualties for the year ending September 30, 1907, are apportioned as follows:

| | |
|---|---|
| Baltic............................. | 1 |
| Calumet branch, C.&H.... | 5 |
| Centennial .................... | 2 |
| Champion..................... | 6 |
| Franklin Junior.............. | 1 |
| Hecla branch, C.&H. ...... | 3 |
| Isle Royale.................... | 2 |
| North Tamarack............. | 3 |
| Osceola....................... | 3 |
| Quincy........................ | 7 |
| Red Jacket shaft, C.&H..... | 5 |
| South Kearsarge............. | 1 |
| Tamarack..................... | 3 |
| Tamarack No. 5.............. | 4 |
| Trimountain.................. | 2 |
| Winona....................... | 1 |
| | |
| Totals......................... | 49 |

*Nationalities Affected*

| | |
|---|---|
| Austrian............ | 12 |
| English............ | 9 |
| Finnish............ | 10 |
| German............ | 1 |
| Irish............... | 3 |
| Italian............. | 8 |
| Norwegian....... | 2 |
| Swede............ | 2 |
| Swedish.......... | 2 |

*Casualties by Years*

| Year | Men Employed | Casualties |
|---|---|---|
| 1887 | 6221 | 22 |
| 1888 | 6310 | 24 |
| 1889 | 6480 | 21 |
| 1890 | 7810 | 36 |
| 1891 | 7702 | 28 |
| 1892 | 7640 | 21 |
| 1893 | 7591 | 25 |
| 1894 | 7343 | 22 |
| 1895 | 7249 | 44 |
| 1896 | 8170 | 19 |
| 1897 | 8726 | 26 |
| 1898 | 10467 | 23 |
| 1899 | 12051 | 27 |
| 1900 | 13971 | 36 |
| 1901 | 13498 | 33 |
| 1902 | 14130 | 44 |
| 1903 | 13629 | 33 |
| 1904 | 14321 | 45 |
| 1905 | 15255 | 58 |
| 1906 | 16506 | 44 |
| 1907 | 17579 | 49 |

The Western Federation of Miners on the Mesaba range is down and out and the only apparent vestiges of the strike, the deputies, are being removed.

OCTOBER 15: Now the copper country fans who staked their all on the Detroit Tigers or at least enough to make their bank accounts look emaciated for a month to come, will know whom to blame for the slump in their finances second only to that caused by the copper situation.

OCTOBER 16: Two men were arrested this week, and both called upon to pay fines for spitting on the sidewalks. The offense complained of occurred on Fifth street. Marshal Trudell arresting the men...Young men expectorate at random, tobacco juice often being squirted over ladies' dresses and in addition to the trailing dresses sweeping up quite a quantity of the filthy stuff.

OCTOBER 17: The body of a newly-born female child was found about 10 o'clock this morning about 300 feet from No. 5 shaft, of the Tamarack mine.

OCTOBER 18: In the midst of getting out its daily issue *The Evening News* is also engaged in moving into its fine new quarters at the south end of Fifth street.

*The Evening News* will be known as *The Calumet News* once it is settled in its new quarters, a change which its patrons no doubt will appreciate, as it is to be a paper devoted strictly to the interests and welfare of Calumet.

OCTOBER 19: The first class mail includes 3,000 sealed letters and about 600 postal cards. The second class matter is composed entirely of newspapers. Third class mail is made up of printed matter, circulars, and photographs, and reached the very creditable total daily of 1,500.

In addition there has been a total of 200 letters daily sent to foreign countries. The foreign mail, it will be noticed, is a very considerable item, in fact, is believed to be the largest in the Upper Peninsula.

OCTOBER 22: The program for the dedication of the new high school is practically completed.

OCTOBER 23: *The Calumet News* makes its initial bow to the public today, and in taking the place of *The Copper Country Evening News* in enlarged form and improved style...

Since the first of the week the *News* has been located in its fine new building at 104 Fifth street, Red Jacket.

OCTOBER 28: We do not believe the average Calumet theater audience is "cold and clammy" as charged…The average Calumet theater-goer is just as quick to recognize worth on the stage and just as courteous in acknowledging it as any place which is favored with high class attractions, and where plays must have merit to gain recognition.

The Calumet & Hecla Mining company assists the township greatly in macadamizing. It looks after practically all its own roads and Calumet avenue and the Red Jacket town road are evidence of the work of the big corporation in this respect.

OCTOBER 29: Miss Walz says that a large number of people of Calumet were hit by the recent slump in coppers. That some of these have repeatedly advised her to invest in these stocks, but that she preferred putting her money into real estate, where the returns may be slower, but surer. As a result of this she now has the laugh on a number of her friends and advisers.

NOVEMBER 4: "Your time has come. Whether you are in New York or Calumet, it will make no difference, your time has come. The Hand of Seven."

The above anonymous communication was received this morning by Gen. Manager James MacNaughton of the Calumet & Hecla, and shown to the members of the committee who interviewed President Agassiz and Mr. MacNaughton today regarding a petition prepared by a committee of the miners, asking for a modification of the order taking off 12½ per cent in the miners' wages and calling attention to certain grievances that the miners employed on the property believe they are working under.

Professional hockey has in the past two or more years suffered a loss of public interest. The winter of 1902-03 witnessed the zenith of hockey in the copper country. The next winter the Portage Lakes had a team which was invincible and the attendance fell off because a game was not a contest. The following winter the Calumet team— Hod Stuart's first managerial essay—was of similar strength and swept the International league. For the past two seasons the Portage Lakes were again so strong that their contests with other league teams were without interest for the reason that the result was inevitable.

NOVEMBER 5: It has come to be recognized that Mr. Howe has the best moving pictures that are presented, and, added to this happy circumstance, he presents them in an artistic manner. The audience hears the purling of the stream, the turning of the water wheel, and when, as it occurred last evening, a mighty waterfall is shown like that of the Victoria Falls, the very rushing of the waters is heard. The sound effects do not end here. Conversations are duplicated which make every movement in the pictures understandable and intensely real.

An order was sent this week to Vienna, Austria, for a new organ to be used in the St. Joseph's Austrian church, when that sacred edifice has been completed. The instrument coming from Europe will cost about $6,000, and it is expected that it will be the finest in the upper peninsula.

NOVEMBER 7: Apportioned by counties, fatalities occurred in the various mining fields as follows:

|            | Deaths | No. Men | Rate  |
|------------|--------|---------|-------|
| Houghton   | 49     | 17,579  | 2.79  |
| Marquette  | 37     | 6,744   | 5.49  |
| Iron       | 25     | 2,470   | 10.12 |
| Gogebic    | 22     | 4,693   | 4.68  |
| Dickinson  | 7      | 3,392   | 2.06  |
| Ontonagon  | 5      | 1,250   | 4.00  |

NOVEMBER 21: A foolhardy attempt to consume a given quantity of liquor within a given time for a bet occurred in a Red Jacket saloon last evening. The man it is said set himself to the task of swallowing 15 glasses of white brandy within the space of 15 minutes. He swallowed 14 glasses of the stuff, but before he was enabled to drink No. 15 he fell to the floor and had to be carried to his room in the building and medical assistance sent for.

NOVEMBER 23: *New High School Here Dedicated*

Mr. Galbraith referred to the burning of the old school building two years ago, and the impression it created among those witnessing its consumption by fire, stating that it had a favorable place in the hearts of most Calumet people because of its old associations and pleasing memories.

NOVEMBER 26: It has been ascertained, as accurately as it is possible to learn by means of a thorough census, that there are 27,238 persons in Houghton county who pledge their allegiance to the Roman Catholic church. Of these by far the greater number are found in Calumet and the immediate vicinity. According to the census enumeration just completed by the Catholic priests Calumet has a Catholic population of 13,141.

There are no less than six Catholic churches in Calumet. The Sacred Heart church at Hecla has in its parish, according to the enumeration of Father Casimir, 1,700 people; St. Anthony's, which is largely attended by the Polish residents of Calumet has a membership of 1,259, and the St. Joseph church, Slovenian, has probably the largest number in its parish of any in the copper country. It has been found to lack only fifty of being 3,000.

St. Anne's church has 2,032 communicants and St. Mary's 2,800. The Croatian church, St. John's de Baptiste, has a membership of 2,400.

DECEMBER 4: The gang of gypsies which has been operating in Red Jacket has been ordered out of town, and it is believed the visitors left yesterday afternoon for St. Paul.

DECEMBER 5: The Calumet road is one on which no improvements have been made for several years. It is the great avenue for vehicle travel between the two most important districts of the county, is some fifteen miles long and is constantly used by a great volume of traffic. Since the advent of automobiles this road has been used more than ever, and it is probable that the most important improvement would be to widen it, as well as rebuilding the roadbed itself.

DECEMBER 14: Had the average resident of Calumet known that within a few feet of the foundation of the new Calumet High school on the west side, there was a piece of float copper weighing 1,254 pounds within three feet of the surface, the chances are that there might have been some "sinking" there on a moonless night to get the souvenir.

DECEMBER 31: Copper Country girls, many of them at least, signify their intention of taking advantage of Leap Year, which begins when the clock has finished striking the midnight hour tonight. In fact, some of the young men who have planned to sit up and see the "old year out and the new year in" with their sweethearts need not be surprised if their fair friend pops the question the very moment the hours gives license.

---

## Photos, pages 128-132

Page 128: Uncle Tom's Cabin. Looking northeast on Fifth Street, Red Jacket, 1910. *Voelker*

Page 129: Top: Odd Fellows? Copper Range hotel, left, Calumet Theatre, background, 1909. *Voelker*

Bottom: 6th Street and Oak Street, Red Jacket, looking east at Vertin's department store, July 4, 1909. *Houghton County Historical Society*

Pages 130-131: Miners picnic at Red Jacket, 1907. *Voelker*

Page 132: Top: Central Hotel, Fifth Street, Red Jacket. *MTU-Copper Country Historical Collections*

Bottom: Houghton County Traction Co., Scott and Sixth Street, Red Jacket, 1908. *Agnich*

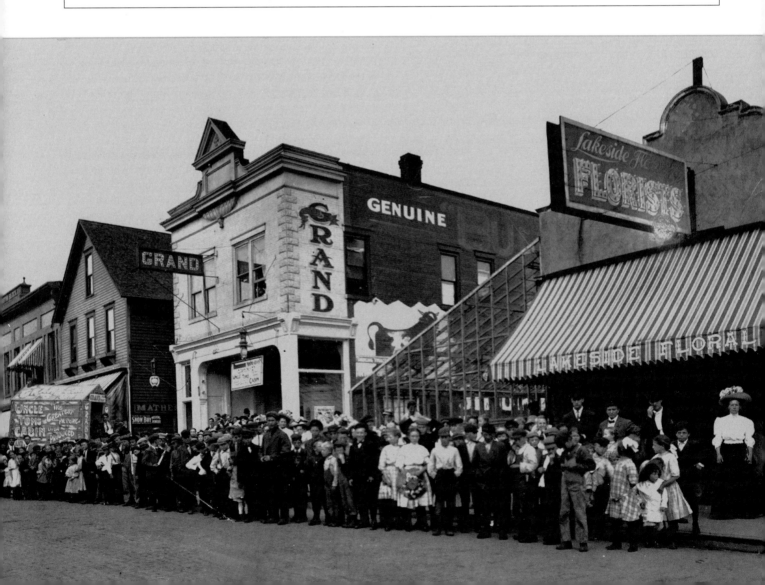

PICNIC SEPT 7TH 07.

LER

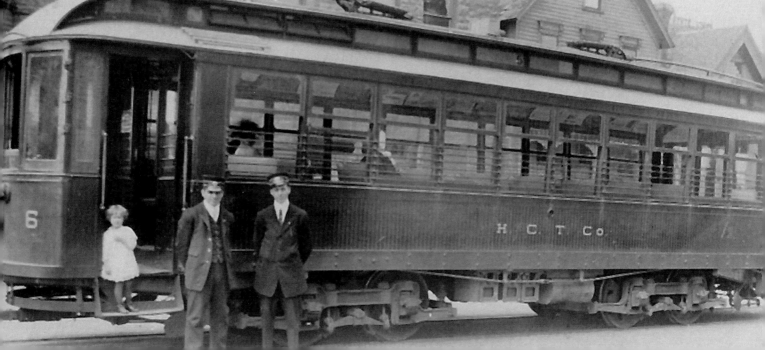

# *Calumet* **1908** *News*

*The old building is understood to have been a veritable death trap, but fortunately no one was on the second or third stories of the building when the fire broke out, and beyond the presence of two or three persons on the ground floor, who were gotten out of the building without danger, the danger to life from the burning down of the old Italian hall was obviated. With the erection of a modern structure, the architect will make provisions for exits and proper hanging of doors to swing outward that will make the building free from danger. The building will be made as fire-proof as possible.*

JANUARY 2: One of the most serious fires that have occurred in Red Jacket in several years took place early this morning, when the Italian hall on Seventh street, a pretentious frame structure, was burned to the ground. The loss is estimated to be $27,000 of which $14,000 is covered by insurance.

The Italian hall was owned by the Italian Benevolent society and was erected about 12 years ago. It was built entirely of wood. The ground floor of the building was rented by Tony Julio who carried on a liquor business on the south side of the building, and the Croatian Printing company, which occupied the north half of the ground floor for the purpose of publishing a weekly newspaper and doing job printing…

The hall was used yesterday afternoon and evening by the St. Joseph's Austrian and kindred other societies for the purpose of celebrating the 25th anniversary of the St. Joseph's Austrian society. Last evening a dance was held in the hall, and supper served. It is believed the fire had its origin in the kitchen, although just how will probably never be known.

JANUARY 3: So many burglaries have been perpetrated in Calumet during the past two or three months that a regular system of espionage apart from the regular night watchman service is about to be instituted.

Proprietors of some of the larger stores have made arrangements whereby one of their clerks will sleep in the store at night, taking turns on weekly shifts.

JANUARY 11: The *Moderator-Topics*, a Michigan educational publication, has the following in its current issue concerning Calumet's new high school:

"The new Calumet high school recently dedicated is probably the handsomest school building in Michigan. The state has nothing in the line of school buildings to compare with it unless it may be the new building for the Northern Normal at Marquette."

JANUARY 15: The $14,000…two-story stone and brick structure…will be erected on the same site, which is owned by the Italian Benevolent society. The old building is understood to have been a veritable death trap, but fortunately no one was on the second or third stories of the building when the fire broke out, and beyond the presence of two or three persons on the ground floor, who were gotten out of the building without danger, the danger

to life from the burning down of the old Italian hall was obviated.

With the erection of a modern structure, the architect will make provisions for exits and proper hanging of doors to swing outward that will make the building free from danger. The building will be made as fire-proof as possible.

FEBRUARY 7: "Has the copper country its own particular brand of snow?" queried a lower peninsula man this morning.

"I have been in districts where I believe as much snow fell and where the wind was blowing as hard as it was here day before yesterday, but it has never been my experience to see the beautiful pile up and drift the way it does up here. I think it must possess some quality that is absent in other brands…a train crew would drop dead of heart failure if they had to buck the embankments of snow that look easy to copper country trainmen."

FEBRUARY 28: It is the intention of the society to rent its hall for dance and other purposes. There is always a great demand for halls for social events in Red Jacket, and it is expected the Italian hall's second story will be in demand.

MARCH 18: A mass meeting of the Finnish people of Calumet is called for next Sunday evening, at 7:30 o'clock in the Calumet Light Guard Armory, for the purpose, it is said, of denouncing the actions of those of the Calumet Finns alleged to be of anarchistic tendencies…to go on record to show the English-speaking people of Houghton county, that they are entirely in discord with the sentiments and actions of all anarchistic people of their nationality.

MARCH 24: One of the advantages that the X-ray machine is to surgery was demonstrated a few days ago at the Tamarack hospital, when a nickel swallowed by a Tamarack child was discovered lodged in the esophagus.

MARCH 26: At about 4 o'clock yesterday afternoon, Marshal Trudell, who happened to be on a corner in this vicinity, was startled by seeing an old gray haired woman running toward him with hair flying and shawl trailing behind her.

"Come down here," she cried frantically in broken English. "I'm afraid my son is going to shoot me or somebody else."

Marshal Trudell hurried with her to the home but before he got there, perhaps before he received the appeal for help, the shot was fired which killed John Ahlgren. The officer states that he heard no report of the gun but when he stepped into the room to which the aged woman guided him, it was a gruesome sight that met his gaze. The little room was filled with powder smoke; a huddled, lifeless man lay prostrate, the blood and brains from his head still oozing out and into the boards of the floor…A dog, attracted by the odor of the warm blood, was eagerly sniffing the remains.

APRIL 18: Easter will be appropriately observed in all of the Protestant and Catholic churches in Calumet tomorrow. The new St. Joseph's Austrian church will be opened to worshippers for the first time and it is expected there will be crowded congregations throughout the day.

APRIL 24: Miss Maggie Walz left last night for Drummond's island, accompanied by a party of Finnish people from Calumet, Houghton, Hancock and South Range points. Others are expected to join on the way from the copper country to the Soo.

On arrival at the island they will take up land for agricultural purposes…It will be news to many to learn that Miss Walz has resigned her position as postmaster of the island. Her resignation was due to her inability to spend the winter there.

APRIL 27: The sleet and snow storm which set in during the night played havoc with the telegraph and telephone companies, to say nothing of the Houghton County Street Railway Co., and the steam roads, and as a result communication with outside points, out of the county, is almost completely at a standstill. The brokers have been up against it, although Paine, Webber & Co., had a wire to Milwaukee a part of the time and received some quotations. Both the Western Union and Postal wires are out of commission.

At a meeting of the Calumet & Hecla miners held Saturday afternoon in the John Dunstan hall on Fifth street, for the purpose of making arrangements for the next annual picnic, it was decided to engage the Tamarack park and to set the date after the committee confers with General Manager MacNaughton today.

A feature out of the ordinary occurred at the meeting, the editor of a Socialistic publication of Hancock, appearing before the miners and asking permission to make a short speech. A vote was taken and he was allowed five minutes. His talk was in effect an offer to secure William D. Haywood of the Western Federation of Miners, to come to Calumet on the date of the picnic and address the miners. The offer was turned down by the men en masse without discussion, it being deemed unwise to allow anything of that nature at the picnic.

APRIL 29: With an empty bottle, labelled chloroform, lying beside him, a man named Lehtikangas was found this morning, by Conductor Leveque of the Hecla & Torch Lake railroad lying beside the company's tracks near No. 21 shaft of the C.&H. Mining company, bleeding at the nose and in the last throes of death.

MAY 5: Several applications for liquor licenses will be made to the village dads this evening, completing the list for the village. A total of 61 licenses was granted at the special meeting last week, while there are several more on file, bringing the total number up to 74. This is about the average for the village.

MAY 6: It is quite probable that Calumet School District No. 1 contains a more cosmopolitan citizenship than any other school district of its population to be found elsewhere in the United States.

Calumet School District No. 1 includes the villages of Red Jacket, Laurium and what is familiarly known as the "location." The "location" is a property owned by the Calumet & Hecla Mining company and within its limits are found the massive machinery of that richest copper mining corporation and the homes of its numerous employees. The population of the district is about 40,000.

According to the report of the superintendent of the takers of the last school census, there are forty different nationalities recorded on the books of the census takers. These are as follows:

Alsatian, American, Arabian, Armenian, Australian, Austrian, Hollander, Hungarian, Indian, Irish, Italian, Jewish, Belgian, Bohemian, Brunswickan, Bulgarian, Canadian, Chinese, Croatian, Danish, English, Finnish, French, German, Greek, Holsteiner, Laplander, Negro, Norwegian, Polish, Prussian, Russian, Scotch, Sicilian, Slav, Spanish, Syrian, Swedish, Swiss, and Welsh.

The Red Jacket village council at its meeting last evening decided to honor past presidents of the village and the present president, by hanging pictures of these men on the walls of the council chamber. The presidents of the village since its incorporation and the present president are Peter Ruppe, William Hodgins, Francis Ward, Joseph Vertin, John D. Cuddihy, Henry J. Vivian, John R. Ryan, and Frank H. Schumaker.

MAY 8: General Manager James MacNaughton of the C.&H. has returned from Grand Rapids, where he went for the purpose of being present at the hearing of the C.&H. Osceola case. The proceedings were adjourned for two weeks.

The first cricket game of the season will be played tomorrow afternoon between the Kearsarge-Wolverine club and the newly-organized Calumet & Hecla club on the Kearsarge pitch.

MAY 9: Rev. Caroline Bartlett Crane of Kalamazoo, who is in Calumet for the purpose of addressing Calumet residents on topics pertaining to a more beautiful Calumet, will start her work tomorrow under the auspices of the Calumet Woman's club…

"You have a lot of nice things in Red Jacket," said Mrs. Crane, "and I am agreeably surprised. Your streets are in first class condition, and some of your buildings are very fine."

Mrs. Crane also had a good word for the municipal buildings and the Calumet theater. She expressed genuine surprise when informed that the latter was a municipal building.

MAY 11: An official photographer has been appointed by the Calumet Woman's club to visit all of the alleys and other places used for the dumping of refuse and the storage of sleighs and other things, and these photographs are to be used by Rev. Caroline Bartlett Crane in connection with her public lecture Wednesday evening in the Calumet theater.

However, alleys, back yards and other places are being cleaned up as fast as possible by property owners and others, Mrs. Crane's presence here proving the means of a quick clean-up this spring…

Eighth street, Red Jacket, in particular, presents a very pleasing appearance. This is looked upon as the principal residential street of the village, and those living there are doing everything in their power to make the street look its best.

…Owing to its cosmopolitan nature it is a difficult matter to educate some of the residents within its borders, as to what cleanliness means in back yards and alley ways. Some of these residents think it is their prerogative to dump all the ashes, empty bottles and other rubbish into the alleys.

The 25th anniversary of the Finnish Enlightenment society of Calumet will be held in the Finnish Temperance hall, on Eighth street, Saturday and Sunday, May 23 and 24.

The object of the society is to publish books and literature, in the Finnish language, of an elevating and educational nature and to send them to all branches of the society for distribution. Tons of this literature reaches Calumet from time to time. There are about 60 members affiliated with the society here, and attempts are about to be made to increase interest, and secure more members.

MAY 16: Two cases of smallpox were discovered in the Osceola school, and in consequence two of the rooms were closed yesterday for disinfection.

MAY 25: Among the delegates who attended the Michigan Woman's Press association, in Detroit last week, perhaps not one has done more for the benefit and uplift of her sex than Miss Maggie Walz of Calumet, editor of the "Nalstenlehti," the Finnish woman's paper, says the Detroit Times.

Miss Walz, known throughout the copper country and Drummond's Island as "Maggie Walz" was born in Sweden, across the river from Aavosaksa, the land of the midnight sun. She is of Finnish descent and speaks both English and Finnish fluently. When about 16 years of age she came to this country with friends, and being enthused with its greatness and freedom, decided to adopt it for her own. Ever since coming here she has been engaged in a splendid work among her people, and today is one of the best known women in the north country.

She owns a fine three-story stone block in Calumet, Mich., which combines stores, offices and flats. She is agent for real estate in the United States, Canada and Mexico, conducts a steamship ticket office and is a notary public.

Her special work, however, is Drummond Island, which is fast becoming colonized by Finns and Swedes and a few other provident nationalities who want a home and are anxious to become Americanized.

Rudolph Agassiz, son of President Agassiz of the Calumet & Hecla mine, left yesterday afternoon for Chicago, after a two weeks' visit here.

MAY 27: James Guglielmo and Peter Cicotte, killed, is the toll exacted by the falling of a piece of timber yesterday afternoon in No. 7 shaft, Hecla branch of the C.&H. mine.

…According to the testimony introduced into court Ahlgren drove to Red Jacket with a load of wood which he disposed of to Karinen and the two went to Karinen's home on Pine street, where they commenced drinking beer. A number of cans of the amber colored fluid were purchased and finally, both men being somewhat intoxicated, a quarrel arose as to who would go after the next consignment of the beverage. The quarrel waxed furious and finally Mrs. Karinen saw her husband, who by the way is less than 30 years of age, go into an adjoining room after a gun, with blood in his eyes.

She ran out of the house in search of a policeman and a few minutes later found Marshal Joseph Trudell. The officer returned to the house and found Ahlgren foully murdered.

JUNE 2: That he lost a bull frog out of an old tin can, and made an effort to catch it, falling into the old disused well at the Wolverine, is the story of how little Willie Prout, aged seven years, lost his life last week.

JUNE 4: Two fatal accidents occurred in Calumet during the past twenty four hours. The first happened about 4 o'clock yesterday afternoon, when Gust Monson, a foreman loader in the employ of the C.&H. mining company was struck over the head by a piece of timber, while unloading it from a railroad car, and was instantly killed. The other accident happened last night to Paul

Briar, a trammer who was crushed between a large rock, estimated to weigh at least 500 pounds, and the side of a skip at the 49th level No. 6 shaft, Calumet branch of the C.&H. mine. He lived several hours, lying at the C.&H. hospital.

JUNE 5: The following are the births by nationalities, compiled by Clerk Thomas, following former precedents. Finnish, 24; American, 12; Austrian, 10; Canadian, 8; English, 7; Norwegian, 7; Italian, 5; German, 2; Sweden, 2; Polish, Russian and Irish, 1 each.

JUNE 8: The first train of the big Wallace-Hagenbeck circus pulled into the local railroad yards about 5:30 o'clock in a shower of rain.

One of the biggest fraternal picnics that will be celebrated in Calumet this year will take place next Saturday when a joint celebration of six Croatian societies will be held. The picnic will be held at the Calumet & Hecla park, and it promises to be a monster affair.

The St. John Baptist, St. Rock, St. Jerome, Vina Dolac, St. Florien, and St. Nicholas societies, aggregating more than 1,000 members, will be in line in the parades.

A feature of the picnic will be a barbecue at the park, where 25 young lambs will be roasted and eaten. This is one of the Croatian's old country customs, and is usually introduced at their local picnics.

JUNE 12: A picture, "Just Like a Woman," coming tomorrow to the Grand, will be distinguished by having among the people that take part in the little moving picture comedy none other than D.E. Rice, manager of the Grand in Calumet.

JUNE 15: Robert LaFollette, candidate for the presidential nomination and famous as the senator who made the longest filibustering speech in the history of the senate, is to be in Calumet soon under the auspices of the Calumet Woman's club.

Red Jacket has secured a balloon ascensionist for the Fourth of July...The ascension at night will be a spectacular one, the balloonist shooting off fireworks while 1,000 feet or more in the air.

JUNE 16: A mis-step early this morning caused the death of George Brockovac, a young Austrian of 20 years, employed by the Tamarack Mining Co., at No. 2 shaft, plunging him from the twenty-ninth level where he was working to the bottom of the shaft into 24 feet of water.

JUNE 18: The national convention of the Finnish Apostolic church is being held in Calumet this week.

JUNE 22: "I feel something like Rip Van Winkle," said Roger Vail, a newspaper man of Minneapolis, as he walked down the crowded streets of Fifth street, Red Jacket, Saturday evening, after an absence of forty years

from Calumet. Mr. Vail could not be made to realize that this was the same village that he used to know back in the '60's.

...When Mr. Vail first entered Red Jacket there were only two stores here, five or six saloons and a butcher shop. There were a lot of "bush" between the village and the C.&H. location, and only about 25 or 30 houses on the big mining company's property. He returned Saturday night after a forty year absence to one of the liveliest little burgs in the state of Michigan, at least that is the impression the village of Red Jacket gave him.

JUNE 29: The old St. Joseph's Austrian church which was a frame structure, was destroyed the morning of December 8, 1902, owing, it is believed to the overheating of the boiler in the basement of the church.

The consummation of the laying of the foundation of the new St. Joseph's Austrian church in the spring of 1903 occurred yesterday when the splendid, costly edifice was formally dedicated...

As an instance of the length of the parade, it might be noted that the head of the marching societies, the St. Joseph's Catholic club, was filing into the church, while the rear end was passing the Italian church on Portland street, the parade having traversed all of Portland, Fifth, Pine and Eighth streets to the church. It will thus be seen that almost an entire circle was occupied by the paraders, of more than a mile in length.

JULY 1: At the last annual meeting of the Finnish Ladies' society it was unanimously decided to revive the publication of *Naisten Lehti*, or the Finnish Ladies' Journal. Miss Maggie Walz, the founder of the organ, assisted by Mrs. Warghelin, and another local lady yet to be named, will edit the paper.

JULY 3: If the Indians from the Chippewa tribe at Baraga do not parade the streets of Red Jacket tomorrow as they are scheduled it will be because two of the members of the tribe were killed by a passenger train out of Baraga shortly after midnight last night.

JULY 13: Officer Joe MacNamara, who arrested Tom Williams, late Saturday night in his residence on Pine street, on the charge of killing his wife, by shooting her through the right temple and neck told the *News* this morning a graphic story of the arrest...

Officer MacNamara said he passed two men on the stairs both flourishing revolvers, the glint of the barrels being plainly visible. Both men were sons of the murdered woman, and one of them was endeavoring to discharge his revolver, as Officer MacNamara could hear the click of the barrel as the trigger was pulled and the barrel revolved.

After locking up the prisoner, Officer MacNamara proceeded back to the scene of the crime, and in the parlor up-stairs found Mrs. Williams dead, weltering in her own blood.

William Thomas Dunstan, a young Cornishman, aged 21 years, met death by drowning in the Tamarack dam about noon yesterday. The body was not recovered until almost 24 hours later when Alfred Johnson and Chris Hoffman brought it to surface with the aid of grappling hooks.

JULY 14: Calumet must be infested with a gang of thieves who have lost all reason and thrown caution to the winds, or else they are taking awful chances, for last evening they entered the yard of Marshal Joseph Trudell and got away with his own and his daughter's bicycles.

JULY 17: A company has been organized in Calumet for the purpose of running a rapid motor car service between Red Jacket and Laurium. Two 20-passenger gasoline motor cars have been ordered and more will be added as occasion demands.

JULY 20:...Kostenchee was aware of the place his fellow boarders kept their pay books, and it is alleged that on Saturday morning after the others had gone to work, he went to the boarders' rooms, gathered up all their pay books, took them to the pay office of the C.&H. mining company, signed for them and later presented them at the First National and State banks of Calumet, where he received cash for them. He then must have returned to his boarding house, packed up his belongings, and going to the Mineral Range depot of the South Shore road, bought a ticket for Chicago.

A rehearsal of the C.&H. miners' band took place last week in the John Dunstan hall. A total of 43 musicians were present, and under the direction of J.C. Glasson, had an excellent practice. The band will likely hold another rehearsal next week when several more instrumentalists will be added, bringing the total up to the 50 mark.

JULY 21: "I could use 200 or 300 laborers right now, here in the copper country, if I could only get them," said G.L. Perreault, the well known local employment agent to an *Evening News* representative, in response to an inquiry as to labor conditions and the supply and demand.

"The several mining companies in and around Calumet are looking for laborers to work on surface, but the demand so far exceeds the supply in such numbers that I cannot fill the orders."

JULY 24: George Grigson, in the employ of the Houghton County Street Railway company, received a shock of 5,000 volts through his body this morning, and is alive to tell the tale. The unfortunate young man was working on the top of a street car at the corner of Sixth and Oak streets about 11 o'clock, when the accident happened.

The young fellow's hands are both blue-black in color, although they are singed only a little. As soon as he received the shock he was seen to stagger from the top of the car, and dropping to his side rolled off, striking the pavement with a hard thud.

JULY 25: The day of the plain soda, a pleasing concoction of water saturated with carbonic acid gas and flavored with a colored syrup, has passed. Now the dispenser who does not understand the mysteries of the "mint freeze," "frappes," of numberless sorts, all kinds of "sundeys," high-class beverages containing eggs and which in the mixing are poured from containers held in either hand of the expert at a distance of three and four feet, and many other soda fountain specialties, has a hard time to get a job.

JULY 28: A fire broke out about 3 o'clock yesterday afternoon at the Tamarack Junior mine and before it was gotten under control had completely destroyed No. 2 shaft house, the boiler house and the carpenter and blacksmith shops adjoining No. 1 shaft.

Tamarack Jr., was worked out and closed down about six years ago, and since that period the Osceola Mining company has removed all of the valuable machinery and tools from the property so that the loss in that respect is comparatively slight.

AUGUST 1: The parade of the C.&H. miners this morning through the streets of Red Jacket and Laurium, and the C.&H. location, was one of the striking parade features of the summer. A total of about 2,000 miners were in line, and accompanied by the C.&H., the Tamarack, Red Jacket, Laurium, the Finnish Humu, and the Miners' bands made a very imposing sight.

This afternoon two addresses were made to the men by General Manager MacNaughton and Attorney Will R. Oates. Following the speeches the sports of the day will take place. There will be boxing and wrestling bouts, hammer and drill contests, tug of war between the several miners' teams, concerts by the band, dancing during the afternoon and evening and a number of races for the children. Flags are flying on all of the shaft houses of the C.&H. company today in honor of the picnic.

AUGUST 3: Saturday's picnic of the C.&H. miners was a splendid success. One of the features of the day were the addresses by General Manager James MacNaughton and Attorney Will R. Oates.

Mr. MacNaughton was earnest and forceful and what he said rang true.

"Copper mining in this district," said Mr. MacNaughton, "started sixty-three years ago and the production of copper grew one hundred and sixty fold in the first ten years. Now the copper mines of Michigan are producing more copper in three weeks than they produced in the first ten years of the history of copper mining.

"During the past thirteen years more copper has been produced than was turned out in the first fifty years of the industry. You can see from this what is in store for the district in which you live and work; you can see what a bright and prosperous future there must be, regardless of every condition in the world without."

AUGUST 5: Work was started this morning on the demolition of the old Light Guard Armory off the south end of Fifth street. The building is owned by the Calumet & Hecla Mining company and has been standing for the past twenty-five years. Since the new armory was built a few years ago the old structure has been used as a warehouse. For many years it was the home of the Calumet Light Guards, now Company A, Corps of Engineers.

The C.&H. Mining company through its electrical engineering staff will start a gang of men at work next Monday morning stringing the wires from the C.&H. company's power station in Calumet to the Lake Superior water works, where an electric power plant for the pumping of water to Calumet and Torch Lake points is being installed.

AUGUST 12: Valentine Makki, one of the four unfortunate men who was injured in the accident yesterday morning during the work of demolishing the old Light Guard Armory, died about 8:30 o'clock last night without regaining consciousness.

AUGUST 13: James L. Nankervis of Calumet, commissioner of mineral statistics in Michigan, has compiled his annual report of the mines and minerals in the state...

This industry is on the increase in the state, there being a total of 1,931,011 tons mined last year as against 1,424,427 tons in 1906.

Mr. Nankervis shows in his report that the several mines in Houghton county employed a total of 17,509 men during 1907 as compared with 16,506 during 1906.

Copper country followers of hockey, the great Canadian winter sport, which for five years proved so popular in this district when it was played by professional teams, but which two years ago was dropped for the time being, are commencing to speculate as to the prospects of the professional game being revived the coming winter. Last year an effort was made to have amateur hockey take the place of the professional sport, and while it succeeded to some extent it is agreed that it did not compare with that played by paid teams and that, therefore, the latter article must again be forthcoming before the fans are satisfied.

Captain Hoatson brought back with him from Nipigon the largest brook trout ever seen in Calumet it is believed. The fish weighed, when dressed, a trifle over four pounds, and was placed on exhibition in the Glass Block store. It was seen by a large number of people. W.E. Steckbauer was commissioned to take a picture of the finny specimen. Last evening a party of Capt. Hoatson's friends dined off the fish at the Michigan café.

AUGUST 20: Trembling and distracted, his nerves shattered to such an extent that it was necessary to give

him morphine during the progress of his hearing in the court of Justice Fisher yesterday afternoon, Alfred Wilkinson disclaimed to the court and the officers that he had any intention of robbing the Kunnari barber shop on Fifth street last Thursday night. He declared that he was so crazed by the use of drugs that he was absolutely unaware of what he was doing.

Capt. Thomas Wills, who has just returned from nine weeks' visit to England in company with Mrs. Wills, speaks very interestingly of the trip, most of which was spent in England.

Capt. Wills left this country on the palatial steamer Lusitania and returned on her sister ship the Mauretania.

AUGUST 21: The gentle cow is allowed perhaps to roam more at its own will and pleasure in Calumet and Laurium than is permitted in the majority of cities but the limit was reached when one of the animals ambled down Sixth street, stopped a moment in deep thought in front of the harness and repair shop of Welder's and then deliberately walked in the front door, ignoring the several customers that were inside, and stalked to the rear of the building through the narrow aisle until she reached an auto that was stored in the back room temporarily for repairs.

AUGUST 22: It was two weeks ago that Miss Walz received a letter, written in her native tongue and in all respects similar to the famous "black hand" letters of the Italian Mafia. In the communication a demand for $400 was made, and Miss Walz was informed that should she fail to comply with this demand, her liberty, and probably her life, would be greatly endangered.

AUGUST 24: An amusing remark was passed by Miss Walz when she was rallied on the fact that she insisted on clinging to a life of single happiness. The conversation was in respect to silver weddings when some one remarked that Miss Walz would have to accept a partner for life pretty soon in order to live long enough to celebrate her silver wedding anniversary.

"Why, I have been bridesmaid at 129 weddings," returned Miss Walz, "and have been in attendance at I don't know how many more, so I think that is about enough for me."

There is a clue in the Maggie Walz "black-hand" letter case, which may lead to the identification of the sender of the letter, the contents of which were told in *The Calumet News* of Saturday. Maggie Walz, in a statement to *The News* this morning, said that one of her friends who is working on the case claims to have possession of some letters, the handwriting of which corresponds very closely to that of the letter threatening her freedom and life in the event she did not place $400 in a certain bottle as directed.

AUGUST 25: In his gratitude to Officer Trudell for taking him off the street and steering him for home when he was in an intoxicated condition, Frank Pudas turned about and abused the marshal roundly and attacked the officer with blows.

SEPTEMBER 1: The village of Red Jacket has an ordinance, which says, "Don't spit on the sidewalks"...between 2,500 and 3,000 persons die annually in Michigan from tuberculosis, one of the diseases caused by spitting on the sidewalks and in public places.

SEPTEMBER 2: Stanley Carter, a Calumet boy, mounted on a bicycle, took a notion this morning to race one of the auto cars of the Calumet-Laurium Motor company. Through his foolhardy conduct he collided with the car on Calumet avenue, and was thrown heavily, sustaining severe injuries to his head and one of his legs.

SEPTEMBER 8: One of the most serious forest fires that ever broke out in the copper country is raging today at the Ahmeek location. Hundreds of men are fighting the flames in an effort to save their homes and the property of the Ahmeek Mining company.

SEPTEMBER 15: Just why a piece of timber was being hoisted into position yesterday afternoon at the 52nd level, No. 6 shaft Calumet branch of the C.&H. mine, with the aid of tongs, instead of in the usual way by means of chains, was not explained at the inquest this morning having to do with the death of Joseph Nijra, a timber boss, who died about 11 o'clock last night at the C.&H. hospital after lingering about seven hours with a broken back.

Working below him just two levels at the time the accident occurred was the decedent's father, also acting in the capacity of timber boss. He helped take the unfortunate man to the C.&H. hospital, where his injuries were attended to.

SEPTEMBER 16: August Baggiore met death last night in No. 6 shaft of the Osceola mine by being run over by a skip and another fatal accident occurred at 9:30 o'clock this morning, Peter Gandino, a trammer being killed in the 49th level, No. 5 shaft, Calumet branch of the C.&H. mine, by a fall of rock.

SEPTEMBER 19: The activity locally of a copper country socialistic agitator, Frank Aatonen, has aroused the Finnish people residing in Sault Ste. Marie and they are seeking in every way to offset the effects of Aatonen's work, says the *Soo News*.

Aatonen is the organizer of a Finnish socialistic organization and is said to be one of the most radical socialists in the country. He is said to have taken part in socialist demonstrations in Hancock in which the red flag was freely displayed. His utterances locally have been directed not alone at the present organization of society but against the churches and Christianity in general. On last Friday he effected a local organization with a few members. This organization is looked upon by the bulk of the Finnish population in this vicinity as inimical to good order, to religion and the sanctity of the home life. Resolutions denouncing Aatonen and his beliefs have been adopted by the Finns.

SEPTEMBER 24: Today or tomorrow there will arrive in Calumet 20 carloads of ice for the Calumet Ice company, shipped by the Superior Ice company of Duluth. This represents 500 tons of ice, and despite reports to the contrary shows that unless this ice was shipped here there would be an ice famine.

Burglars held high carnival again in Calumet last night, ransacking three of the business places of the town, getting away with a considerable amount of valuable booty in one of them, the Savings Bank store on Fifth street. Evidently the thieves did not possess a very exalted idea of the efficiency of the policing of Calumet as most of their depredations appeared to have been carried on daringly in plain view of the street.

SEPTEMBER 25: Vogelstein & Co., say on the copper situation: "The copper market has recently remained rather steady but dull because domestic consumers are in a waiting attitude and have not been willing to buy beyond October owing to the uncertainty of the election..."

"If Bryan is elected copper will sell at 11 cents. If Taft is elected it will sell at 15 cents."

SEPTEMBER 29: The odor of the moth ball is abroad in the land. It is being shaken from milady's furs which are daily being taken from the dark corner of the closet where for the past five months they have hung carefully draped in a bunch of newspapers to keep the dust off and the odor in.

OCTOBER 8: Proof that the Calumet Miners' picnic, which is held annually in Calumet is a good thing for deserving needy persons was evidenced last week, when the several committees appointed to distribute aid among the widows and orphans of former employees of the company, distributed almost $1,000 in cash, wood and coal among 350 needy people.

OCTOBER 9: As the result of a number of boys using sling shots a number of the windows in the Finnish Apostolic Evangelical Lutheran church on Pine street have been broken. There has been too free a use of sling shots in Calumet township, complaints coming in from every hand of property damage caused by boys.

OCTOBER 10: That the fish of Lake Superior are being depleted at an alarming rate is the assertion of commercial fishermen. Where formerly tons of whitefish were taken at a lift, the fishermen now consider themselves lucky to get a few hundred pounds, and to a lesser extent the same conditions apply to the catch of lake trout.

Today marks the formal opening of the new Italian hall, a structure that is a credit to the Italian Benevolent society of this city. The new hall is located on Seventh street, Red Jacket, on the site of the old wooden structure that was destroyed by fire last winter. The ground floor is being used for saloon and store purposes, while the second floor will be devoted to lodge and hall purposes.

This morning the several Italian societies of Houghton county paraded the principal streets of Red Jacket and Laurium, previous to taking part in the formal dedication of the building.

OCTOBER 12: The formal dedication of the new Italian hall, referred to in Saturday's *News*, was a brilliant affair.

John B. Rastello, speaking in English, told of the history of the Italian Benevolent society, and the difficulties and misfortunes it had had to overcome, owing to the burning down of the old hall. He said that the society was founded in 1875 for the purpose of assisting the members and their countrymen in every way possible.

Mr. Rastello stated that in 1884 death claimed a number of the members, and that in 1889 when its hall was nearly completed, the building was blown down by a terrible storm and was a total loss. Mr. Rastello then referred to the fire on January 1 of this year, which destroyed the second building.

The Prohibitionist party held a rousing rally Saturday evening in the Red Jacket townhall, when Rev. Charles J. Johnson was notified of his nomination by the party for the state senate and William C. Kinsman of his nomination for representative in the state legislature.

OCTOBER 15: Capt. William Trethway, underground superintendent of the Osceola-Kearsarge lode workings of the C.&H. Mining company, met death instantly about 10 o'clock this morning in No. 21 shaft by being struck by a descending skip. It is supposed that Capt. Trethway was looking into the shaft when the skip passed. His head was badly cut.

OCTOBER 16: A forest fire on Section 16, C.&H. property, became so serious yesterday morning that at the noon hour the C.&H. Mining company sent to the scene every available surface hand to fight the progress of the flames.

OCTOBER 19: Nursery lore is recalled by the large variety of Hallowe'en novelties seen in the stores, and we are reminded that the season during which for a short time elves, fairies and ghosts are supposed to again inhabit the earth, is with us.

Many imported and domestic novelties are seen and nearly all are to be filled with bon-bons. There are quaint pumpkin novelties of all descriptions, including pumpkin dolls, large and small, jack-o-lanterns, heads with grotesque faces, witches, goblins and black cats, fruits of

all kinds, peaches, pears and apples; the plum pudding which is one of the newest novelties, as is also the moon face. There are dudes and policemen, cabbage men, brownies and the horrible skull and cross bones.

OCTOBER 24: Joseph Muhelich Puts Head Into Shaft While Waiting on the Fifteenth Level of No. 3 and is Struck by a Descending Skip—Succumbs to Injuries Soon After.

OCTOBER 26: One of the most flagrant breaches of the peace that has occurred in Calumet in a long time took place last evening, when a local resident while entering the Salvation Army hall on Portland street was struck over the head with a beer bottle by a man named Isaac Hill.

OCTOBER 28: Not everyone is familiar with the fact that Calumet has a broom factory, operated by blindmen. The little factory is in Yellow Jacket, in a building about midway between Portland and Oak streets. There are only two men employed, G. Victor Johnson and William Goraczniak. Both were former C.&H. miners, and became blind through powder blasts.

The C.&H. Mining company long had before it the problem of what to do to aid the men whose sight had been destroyed while in the employ of the company. The matter was taken up in Boston at first, and Alex. Agassiz becoming interested, a teacher for the blind, Charles Van Etten, was sent here from the east in July, 1903. A broom making plant was installed at the company's expense…

C.&H. and the Copper Range Consolidated company take all the warehouse brooms the men can turn out, while a large number of house brooms are handled by local merchants.

Frank Blaskovich, a trammer, was seen about ten minutes past 4 this morning standing by the side of the skip road north at the 38th level of No. 5 shaft of the Osceola mine, and about 15 minutes later was picked up dead in the skip way three levels below, or close to the 41st level.

NOVEMBER 3: Thanksgiving is coming and so are the turkeys…

One of the largest meat dealers in Calumet said this morning that he expected to sell about 3 tons and this he considered a very conservative estimate. There are about 14 meat dealers in Calumet and placing a very conservative estimate on the amount of consumption of turkey this Thanksgiving it can safely he said that 35 tons will be used locally.

NOVEMBER 10: The French-Canadians of Houghton county are organizing what is known as French Naturalization clubs. It is estimated that there are at the very least 2,000 eligible Frenchmen in the copper country who are not citizens and an endeavor is to be made to get every one of these eligibles enrolled under the flag, and to prepare those who will become eligible later on also to become voters.

NOVEMBER 14: The Calumet & Hecla band will resume its popular promenades next week by giving a party at the Light Guard Armory Friday night.

NOVEMBER 18: Thirteen hundred people crossed the threshold of the new Y.M.C.A. building last evening to inspect the magnificent structure.

Caught in a blinding snow storm, and bucking three foot drifts in places while covering the distance from Delaware to Calumet in an automobile was the experience of Mike Kemp and two other companions last Sunday night. Previous to leaving Delaware Mr. Kemp and his party were photographed by W.E. Steckbauer.

NOVEMBER 21: It is estimated that there are 10,000 Italians in Houghton county, and hundreds of these cannot talk the English language, while many of them are not citizens of the country. The night school that is to be started here will help these Italians to become citizens of this country and endeavor to teach them English.

NOVEMBER 23: At a meeting of the C.&H. Rod & Gun club Saturday evening, members pledged themselves to act as patrolmen until the end of the deer hunting season to assist Deputy Game Warden Gipp in his quest for violators of the law.

DECEMBER 1: Beginning at about 5 o'clock yesterday afternoon the wind started to blow a hurricane, and it gradually became colder. As the night advanced the wind increased in velocity, accompanied by snow, making it most uncomfortable to be out of doors. The mercury dropped rapidly and it was evident that the first real taste of winter had arrived.

DECEMBER 4: This morning marked the inauguration of regular street car service between Calumet and Mohawk, over the new extension of the Houghton County Traction company from Wolverine to Mohawk.

DECEMBER 8: Calumet has its geniuses. They are men in various walks of life. Numerous patents have emanated from this northern clime to lessen labor and add to effective devices. The most recent copper country man to enter the list of inventor is Oscar Ingman, a blacksmith carrying on business on Pine street. Mr. Ingman has invented what he calls a spoke gauge. It is a device, simple in contrivance that should be of great value to carriage making shops, blacksmiths' shops and in fact every place where spokes for wheels are used.

DECEMBER 15: A greatly improved wire service was inaugurated in Paine, Webber & Co.'s local office yesterday. A direct duplex wire with Boston will hereafter be used and it makes necessary the employment of another operator.

An amusing sight, though rather costly for the firm of Barsotti Bros., of Fifth street, occurred last evening. A member of the firm had just received from the Copper Range depot with several boxes of oranges. He had carried all but two of the boxes into the store, when the horse attached to the sleigh became restless and bolted. On reaching the Copper Range hotel on Sixth street, a spill occurred. There was a large crowd of Calumet's younger element standing around and while helping Mr. Barsotti gather up the oranges, which had rolled all over the street, appropriated some of the fruit. The horse when it started from the store had two boxes of oranges on the sleigh; when it was driven back there was one box only. Mr. Barsotti is thankful, however, that he managed to get one box back.

DECEMBER 17: The five Finnish ladies' societies in Houghton county have decided to take over the publication of the *Naisten Lehti*, meaning the *Ladies' Journal* in English, this decision having been reached at a recent meeting in Hancock. The *Ladies' Journal* is unique in that it is the only publication in the Finnish language in this country for women, and one of the only two in the world, the other being printed in Finland. The journal is issued quarterly and has been published for the past ten years in Calumet by Miss Maggie Walz of this city. Its headquarters will now be moved to Hancock, where it will be printed by the Finnish Book Concern of that city, and in the future will be gotten out monthly instead of quarterly.

DECEMBER 18: Miss Winnifred Salisbury, secretary of the Charities Bureau of Calumet, stated to *The News* this morning that she has found plenty of poverty existing here. Asked whether she could account for it, she stated that it was brought about through various causes in which sickness, drink, and bad management in some homes largely figured.

---

**Photos, pages 142-144**

Page 142: Top: Parade marching toward Laurium along Red Jacket Road. *Houghton County Historical Society*
       Bottom: "Going to Houghton." *Agnich*
Page 143: Top: Vertin's department store. *MTU: Copper Country Historical Collections*
       Bottom: Blum building fire on Pine Street, 1909. *Houghton County Historical Society*
Page 144: St. Joseph's Austrian Catholic church (now St. Paul's). Isler. *Keweenaw National Historical Park*

# Calumet **1909** News

*When meeting a team, the motorist will come to a complete stop, and cover his machine with a tarpaulin painted to correspond with the scenery. In case the team still exhibits signs of nervousness, the motorist will take his car apart as rapidly as possible and conceal the parts in the grass.*

JANUARY 2: The thirteen-months-old child of Mr. and Mrs. Victor Taurin, of Pine street, met with a shocking death yesterday afternoon, while playing with a tiny perfume bottle. As far as can be learned the child placed the bottle in its mouth and before it was noticed the bottle had slipped into the wind pipe, completely shutting off the child's breath.

JANUARY 6: As the result of an explosion while charging a "dry" hole at the 15th level of No. 3 shaft of the North Tamarack branch of the Tamarack Mining company, Herman Makki received such injuries that he died late yesterday afternoon in the Tamarack hospital, and Nickola Olesti, is in the hospital in a serious condition shocking injuries to his face and head and one arm blown off above the wrist.

JANUARY 7: *The Dead*
  Everill Curtis, aged 2.
  Marion Curtis, aged 3.
  Mrs. Douglas Bolton, aged 30.
      *The Injured*
  Miss Eva Bolton, Niece of Mrs. Bolton, aged 16,
    fractured skull and injuries about face and head.
    Will die.
  Angus Bolton, Brother-in-law of Mrs. Bolton.
    Broken leg, and internal injuries. Not expected
    to live.
  Mrs. Fred O'Dell, badly burned about face.
  Mrs. Fred Curtis, Sprained ankle.

The above is the list of dead and injured in a destructive fire that this morning ruined the Henry Blum building, on Pine street, Red Jacket…Realizing that their only chance was to jump from the burning building they leaped to the ground below with the result that Mrs. Bolton was killed outright, her neck being broken, and her brother-in-law and niece, especially the latter, received frightful injuries, her skull being fractured.

Had there been a fire escape attached to the building, it is probable that not a life would have been lost. It is noted that not one of the buildings in that district was provided with a fire escape.

Mrs. Fred Curtis, was seen by a *News* reporter this afternoon. She said she crawled out on to the porch of the building at the rear to attract attention and that Mr. Shimonich told her to jump and he would catch her. She did as directed, and as soon as she reached the ground, said "My children are in there." She was told that they would be all right, and was then led to a place of safety.

The bodies of the children were found in the ruins of the building this afternoon, both badly charred.

JANUARY 12: Miss Maggie Walz of Pine street has received word that Johnson's general store on Drummond Island was destroyed by fire on January 2.

The postoffice, of which Miss Walz is postmaster, was located in the same building. All of her effects and the postoffice equipment were saved, while the Johnson property was an entire loss, with exception of the feed which was stocked in a warehouse away from the main store.

The loss is a considerable inconvenience to Drummond Island people who have to go many miles now to get provisions.

JANUARY 13: Dr. Peter Roberts of the International committee of the Young Men's Christian association has been in Calumet for the past two days. Last night he met a number of prominent citizens and about fifty Finnish residents for the purpose of organizing a class among the foreign-born residents for the study of the English language, the institutions of the country, the duties and privileges of naturalization, and giving them glimpses into American history.

JANUARY 15: The Calumet Finnish Ladies' society held an interesting meeting yesterday afternoon in the Maggie J. Walz block on Pine street. Petitions were circulated at the meeting by Miss Walz, asking for signatures to be presented to Congress on the Women's Suffrage question. Miss Walz has been appointed Houghton county chairman of the State Suffrage association, and will endeavor to secure several thousand names of women in this county to be placed on the petitions now being circulated.

JANUARY 18: Chief Trudell informed *The News* this morning that the pay day just passed, was one of the quietest in the history of the village. Not a single arrest was made in Red Jacket, and the chief says he saw fewer "drunks" on a pay day night than he has seen in many a day.

JANUARY 21: Fewer boys are now to be seen on the streets smoking cigarettes. The merchants of this district handling tobacco have learned a lesson from recent prosecutions and Truant Officer Wills informed *The News* this morning that he gives the dealers credit for the way in which they are now handling the cigarette trade.

JANUARY 26: At The Bijou Theater—The star act at the Calumet Bijou this week is "His Nibs and Her Niblets." An exchange says of the act, "At the Majestic last night Knight and Benson gave the audience some of the heartiest laughs they have had this season. As soon as one reads the name of the act 'His Nibs and Her Niblets' you begin to smile, and by the time the act is over, your jaws ache."

Alfred Michaelson, a Red Jacket businessman accused of embezzlement, made a futile attempt this morning to break away from Deputy Sheriff William H. Vivian, while leaving a street car on Sixth street for Justice Jackola's court.

Officer Vivian despite the heavy fur coat he was wearing soon caught up with the man and a desperate scuffle ensued. The officer and Michaelson fought desperately. Owing to his coat being buttoned up the officer was unable to use his "billy" but eventually he landed on top of his prisoner and held him down until a citizen came along who was deputized to help take Michaelson to the Red Jacket village lock up.

JANUARY 27: A mass meeting of Finnish residents has been called for Friday evening this week at 8 o'clock, to be held in the Finnish hall on Eighth street, Red Jacket, for the purpose of making elaborate preparations to celebrate the anniversary of the birth of Abraham Lincoln.

Louis Sandretto of Sandretto & Peterson, saloon keepers on Portland street, was fined $20 and costs yesterday afternoon in Justice Fisher's court for employing barmaids.

JANUARY 28: A freak of nature in the shape of a two-headed calf was born this morning, the cow being the property of James Brennan, the well known Pine street cattle dealer. Mr. Brennen states he will have the calf mounted. It may be seen at his place of business on Pine street.

JANUARY 29: A Calumet man has prepared a unique set of rules and regulations for motorists. While they may be ideal in some communities it is not probable that the common councils of Red Jacket and Laurium will accept them. They read something like this:

When meeting a team, the motorist will come to a complete stop, and cover his machine with a tarpaulin painted to correspond with the scenery. In case the team still exhibits signs of nervousness, the motorist will take his car apart as rapidly as possible and conceal the parts in the grass. On approaching a crossing the driver must stop, blow his horn, bang a gong, fire a revolver, hallou and send up six bombs at intervals of five minutes.

Cars must be "seasonably" painted, so as to agree with the pastoral ensemble and not be startling. They must be green in the spring, golden in summer, red in autumn and white in winter. The speed limit on Main street will be secret, but a fine of $25.00 will be imposed on anyone exceeding it.

In case of a runaway, the nearest motorist will be fined $10 for the first mile and $5.00 for each succeeding mile that the team runs.

On approaching crossings at night the driver will burn a red fuse and wait five minutes for the road to clear; he will then proceed at a rate not exceeding 2 miles per hour; shooting a Roman candle every 100 feet.

Pedestrians crossing streets after nightfall must carry two white lights in front and a red light in the rear. Pedestrians must not carry in their pockets any sharp articles liable to cut automobile tires in event of a collision. Every pedestrian must demonstrate before an examining board his dexterity in dodging and extricating him from machinery. In case a motorist is made nervous by an approaching pedestrian, the latter shall hide behind a tree until the automobile has passed. Pedestrians must register at the beginning of each year, and pay a license fee of $5.00 for the privilege of living. There shall be no rebate if they do not live through the entire year.

JANUARY 30: More than one horse was observed standing outside of business places in Red Jacket and Laurium last night in the bitter cold weather. The attention of officers is being called to this violation of the state laws and owners of animals who are in the habit of leaving animals out in the cold unattended will be prosecuted. A wall of sympathy is going up from local residents on this question and renewed activity along lines of organizing a humane society is being advocated.

FEBRUARY 2: Isaac Johnson, aged 55, was found dead this morning about 200 feet off the main road near Lake Linden hill in the Florida district. Death was due to exposure. When found the body was frozen stiff and discolored, showing that death must have taken place at least a day or two ago. It is believed that during the heavy storm that was raging last Friday night he wandered off the beaten track while proceeding to his home. He must have staggered into a snow drift, and being overcome laid down and succumbed.

FEBRUARY 3: Members of the Ashtabula band of Ashtabula, O., are coming to Calumet. This band has made its name famous throughout the country by being one of the few Finnish bands in the United States. It visited Calumet two years ago, and made a decided impression.

The reason that the Ashtabula band is disbanding is because of the scarcity of work in the Ohio city. Much of the manual labor that was employed on the docks at Ashtabula is being replaced with machinery, and this is throwing a large number of men out of employment.

FEBRUARY 4: Rev. Father Frederic L. Odenbach, S.J., of St. Ignatius college, Cleveland, one of the only two priest astronomers in the United States, wants to come to

Calumet to conduct experiments in the deepest shaft of the Calumet & Hecla mine, and the seismic society of which he is a member has asked permission to permit him to install his wonderful microseismograph in the C.&H. to measure earth tremors.

FEBRUARY 4: Following the usual custom the births by nationalities have been compiled in the township of Calumet, the Finns again leading with a total of 24, or almost one-third of the total. The compiled list follows:

```
Finns .....................24
Americans ................11
Austrians..................11
English....................6
Swedes.....................5
Canadians..................4
Norway and Germany.....3 each
Italian......................2
Scotland, Ireland, Hungarian and
Polish                    1 each
```

FEBRUARY 5: Yesterday's attendance at the Calumet high school set a new high mark. The enrollment was 602, the highest since the school was built.

FEBRUARY 6: Agitation has been started among a number of leading automobilists of the county towards taking some steps to have an auto road between the copper country and Marquette. Now that automobiles are becoming quite numerous throughout the county the owners are commencing to feel a want for longer speedways. Here in copperdom the roads, with few exceptions, are ideal for automobiling, but the possibility of a trip to Marquette or other iron country points is remote, because of the absence of suitable roads through Baraga county.

FEBRUARY 9: Rumor has it that the Marathon craze has seized a number of copper country athletes and that already a number of those who are possessed of some running ability are betaking themselves to the byways and covering long distances after the Longboat fashion.

FEBRUARY 18: In the latter case Peterson, it is alleged, drove his horse at a fast clip through the streets of Red Jacket last evening, and in doing so collided with a horse driven by an employee of the Sullivan livery stable with the result that the latter horse met with such injuries that it had to be destroyed.

The court pointed out that there was too much fast and furious driving going on, and that the authorities were determined to put a stop to it.

FEBRUARY 24: Contractor Edward Ulseth has been awarded the contract to erect the large ice house in the yards of the Copper Range railroad in Red Jacket for the Crystal Ice company, recently formed.

FEBRUARY 26: With snow nowhere less than three and probably nowhere more than nine feet deep on the principal streets of the city yet, it probably is a little early to be considering the matter of building that is to go on here during the coming season.

FEBRUARY 27: Three fatal accidents have occurred in Calumet during the past few hours, two at the Red Jacket shaft of the C.&H. mine and the other in No. 4 shaft of the Calumet branch of the C.&H.

The most serious was that at the Red Jacket branch in which John A. Murphy, aged 50, and Charles Versiga, aged 35, both married men, lost their lives at 4 o'clock this morning through a powder explosion, and Stanley Stewart so badly blasted about the face and head that it is feared that he will lose the sight of both eyes.

The Calumet high school basket ball team played and lost to the L'Anse aggregation at L'Anse last night by the score of 50 to 26. The game was devoid of fine features and marked by rough play, both teams being inclined at time to play the man rather than the ball. The contest took place in the L'Anse town hall, which was exceptionally small and so arranged that the play was continually stopped because of the ball going into the audience.

One of the most dangerous and exciting runaways, accompanied by several miraculous escapes, ever witnessed in Calumet took place last evening about 6 o'clock when a delivery horse owned by E.R. Godfrey & Sons dashed through Red Jacket. The frightened animal started to run on Pine street, turned south on Fifth and on reaching Elm street took to the sidewalk. Continuing its mad pace the horse turned west on Oak and after proceeding some distance there was finally stopped. During its wild flight many persons narrowly escaped being struck and several were hit but unfortunately escaped injury.

MARCH 3: Doubtless few citizens as they are passing about the city and occasionally observing a team with a snow-plow or a gang of men loading snow onto a large box-sleigh, have anything like an accurate idea of the magnitude of the problem of keeping the snow off the streets of the city during the winter months, not even considering the great tasks of the traction company in keeping the tracks clear…

If nothing were done to remove the snow from the streets up in this country the towns would resemble remote spots in the Klondike wilderness before the winter were well started. Neighbors would have to abandon the back-yard fence and betake themselves to the chamber windows in order to indulge in the daily gossip and it would be like going down into a basement to enter the average place of business. Teams driving along on the snow-bed level would have to guard against tumbling over into the tops of the street cars in the middle of the streets.

The removing of the snow is a task beside which the plowing is child-play. After every storm Commissioner Ethier is kept busy with from four to six teams and a gang of from a dozen to 15 men for several days just at removing that surplus snow from the streets of Red Jacket, so that the citizens may not lose their village for several months during the winter.

MARCH 3: Perhaps few citizens realize the fact that Red Jacket maintains a peculiar record in the matter of fires. In practically all cities winter is considered the season of fires as it is then that the heating proposition comes in and overheated furnaces and stoves and defective chimneys get in their work, but it is not so with Red Jacket, according to the information handed out at the fire station. It is in summer that the firemen are kept busy here and winter is their easiest time.

"None of your d----- business" was the way a disreputable looking tramp answered Justice of the Peace David Armit yesterday morning when questioned as to his name and occupation on being brought into court on a charge of being drunk and disorderly. The court made it its business later to sentence the fellow to ninety days in the Houghton county jail without the option of a fine.

MARCH 6: Paul Bublic, single, aged 24, a resident of Seventh street, Red Jacket, met death at 2 o'clock this morning by a fall of rock at the 64th level, south of No. 4 workings of the Red Jacket shaft of the C.&H. mine.
According to the evidence the decedent was working as a trammer at the time the accident occurred. In company with others he was engaged in filling a car with rock, when a huge mass of rock fell away from the overhanging, crushing out his life instantly.

MARCH 12:...the remaining members of the old board and the newly-elected aldermen went into special session, and signalized their first meeting by deciding to have installed in the tower of the Red Jacket townhall building a 4-dial clock, and further to have permanent electrical lights installed on the townhall and fire department buildings.
The decision to install a town clock and permanent colored lights for display purposes was largely the result of the several conventions to be held here this summer.

MARCH 13: A mass meeting of the Italians of Houghton county is to be held in the Italian hall on Seventh street tomorrow afternoon at 2 o'clock for the purpose of hearing a report on the campaign for funds for the sufferers from the Calabria earthquake in Italy.

MARCH 15: Sam Hong, Hong Poy, Hong Sing, and Hong Din are a quartet of Chinamen, whose names suggest the approach of an automobile, but who are accused of being mixed up in a gambling deal of some magnitude. Hong Din is the complaining witness in the case, and he

appeared in Justice Fisher's court Saturday night and swore out a warrant for the arrest of the three first-named.
The "slant-eyed" natives of China appeared in court in due order to answer to the charge, and astounded the court with the remark, "Velley big lyee," when asked to plead. This did not satisfy Din, who alleges he had been "dinged" out of $750 by his fellow countrymen.

MARCH 19: Lake Superior water is again pure, an analysis having just been received from Ann Arbor which pronounces the water perfectly pure and safe to drink. This will be pleasing news to Calumet residents, nearly all of whom have their homes connected with the Lake Superior water system of the Calumet & Hecla Mining company.

MARCH 22: It has been suggested that Calumet set aside the month of June as "Home coming month." It is argued that such a step would be the means of attracting to Calumet many former residents who would take advantage of the cheap rates that will be offered on all railroads for the three big conventions that are to be held here during that month.

APRIL 15: The Calumet lodge has decided to use postal souvenir cards containing views of Calumet and the copper country in general and these are to be mailed to outside Elks and friends to boost the coming state convention of the order to be held here in June.

APRIL 21: The soliciting committee reported a total of nearly $6,000 subscribed toward the convention fund. The decoration committee was granted $1,800 for electrical wiring on the streets. Many strings of lights with designs, such as stars, circles, etc., will be hung, and there will also be electric arches at all of the gateways leading to the city.

APRIL 27: With the advent of finer weather the automobile business in Calumet will start with a rush. The Michigan Auto company of this city has already received seven Chalmers-Detroit cars, and three more are expected the latter part of the week.

John Plautz, editor of the *Glasnik*, published weekly in Red Jacket, has gone to southern Michigan on a short visit.

APRIL 29: The following is a complete list of the saloon keepers in Red Jacket, whose bonds were approved at last night's meeting: J.H. Schenk, L.G. Sewnig, F. Schroeder, M. Schmaizel, Paul Shaltz, J. Sunich, Joe Stefanez, J. Srebrnak, A. Tambellini, John Tambellini, C. Tomasi, J. Tomaez, J. Vercelli, John Wertin, William Wills, William Yauch, W.B. Aitken, B. Borgo, O. Bayard, B. Blum, N. Bianchi, T. Bucar, P. Belopavlovich, W. Chaput, Joe Curto, E.J. Dunn, J. Decker, J.G. Ervasti, M. Gasparovich, John Gasparovich, John Grym, A. Gurnoe, M. Grahek, A. Hall, A. Hilden, William Jones, F. Knivel,

S. Kasun, S. Klinowicka, John Karavala, John Koski, M. Klobucher, William Kehl, T. Kajala, Fred Kremer, M. Lucas, N. Lurie, P. Martinac, F. Messner, S. Michaelson, M.G. Messner, G. Martini, James Ormsby, J.B. Perencio, G. Paulson, P. Poikala, F. Poisel, C. Pasquinelli, S. Petlewski, M. Puhek, John Plautz, P. Revello, J. Rock, Thomas Shea, Schlitz Brewing company, John Shunich, L. Sandretto, Stukel, Marcus Sterk, and Peter Sauer.

Architect F.W. Hessenmueller, on behalf of the Calumet Business Men's committee, appeared before the Red Jacket village council to again take up the matter of temporary decorating of the public buildings owned by the village.

In making his plea for a reconsideration of the electrical displays on the opera house, townhall and fire station, Architect Hessenmueller paid the village a distinct compliment. He said it was one of the finest little villages in the country, having all of its streets paved, cement walks laid, and has the distinction of being one of two cities in the country owning its own theater.

APRIL 30: Jacob Saari, manager of the Finnish-American Mining company in Finland, cables the home office to the following effect: "Shaft has been sunk 60 feet below the third level. Struck a rich body of ore in shaft."

The stock in this company is held largely in Calumet, and the news from the property that general mining conditions are improving right along is welcomed. The company has been mining this property for about two years now, and has been developing considerable ore reserves.

Henry Martilla, of Pine street, is alleged to have chewed the nose, or a portion of it, off one Hjalmar Jankkila.

Twelve entries have been received for the dog race which will take place on Elm street Saturday afternoon, leaving the Carlton Hardware store for the Mineral Range railroad tracks. No whips will be allowed the youthful drivers.

MAY 4: Miss Walz is one of the busiest women in Michigan, and her time is already well taken up for the summer. She will first attend and take an active part in the organization of a Finnish ladies' society at Cleveland. Later she will attend a women's suffrage meeting in Detroit, where she will be one of the principal speakers. She is state superintendent of the petition favoring women's suffrage and has secured more than 5,000 names thereto. She will also attend the meeting of the Women's Press association at Port Huron and later deliver an address before the Christian Temperance Union of Michigan. Late in June she will represent the Calumet church at a convention of the Finnish Lutheran churches to be held at New York Mills, Minn.

MAY 5: At yesterday afternoon's meeting of the Calumet business men's convention and Fourth of July committee, Attorney August Moilanen reported that Attorney Saari of Duluth, a member of the Minnesota legislature and an orator of marked ability, has been secured as speaker of the day for the big Finnish celebration to be held here on June 24. Many Finns are expected here from the Minnesota iron ranges, Duluth, and the Michigan iron districts.

MAY 8: Automobile owners must keep within the speed limit of eight miles an hour in Red Jacket.

MAY 14: Red Jacket shaft, of the C.&H. Mining company, exacted a toll of three lives yesterday afternoon, when three timbermen, Louis Musso, John Dajeman and Louis Rosio, lost their lives…at the 65th level north of No. 4 shaft…engaged in what is known in mining as "heaving a pole" for timbering when a huge mass of rock weighing many tons, fell on them.

MAY 21: A well attended meeting of the bakers of Houghton and Keweenaw counties was held in the Nelson offices on Fifth street last evening for the purpose of organizing a U.P. branch of the National Bakers' association.

The meeting unanimously decided to organize, and Ed Keifu, of the Vienna bakers, Red Jacket, was elected the first president.

The Houghton County Traction Co. will open Electric park, its outing resort midway between here and Calumet, on Sunday, June 6…The formal opening will be attended by a concert by the full Calumet & Hecla band, which has been engaged to render a concert every Sunday during the season and for the free dances on Tuesday, Thursday and Saturday evenings.

MAY 22: Fire, which broke out in the boilerhouse at No. 4 shaft of the Wolverine mine shortly before 10 o'clock this forenoon practically gutted the boilerhouse without doing any great damage to the machinery and caused some damage to the roof of the compressor house near by. A shut-down until sometime Monday at the shaft will result while the necessary repairs are being made.

MAY 24: P.J. Norton, of Chicago, the oldest traveling man making this territory, is in Calumet today on his annual visit to the copper country. For thirty-eight years Mr. Norton has been calling on the Calumet trade, and he has seen this city evolve from a "bush" village with one street and a few stores to its present metropolitan appearance.

MAY 25: The *Paivalehti*, the well known Finnish daily newspaper, published in Calumet, has decided to suspend publication. This step was taken this morning on receipt of a wire from Attorney O.J. Larson of Duluth, president of the company.

The decision is the result of an agitation among the mechanical staff of the paper, in which union rates of wages and hours were demanded.

JUNE 1: Gambling is to be tabooed in Red Jacket this summer. Marshal Trudell will see that no gambling of any form whatever is permitted either on the streets or in any place of business during the convention month, or at any other time during the summer.

State Game and Fish Warden Chas. Pierce has written to John Gipp, deputy warden in Houghton county, to the effect that, because of the necessity of reducing the expenditures in his department, he is called upon to "lay off" several of the deputies under his direction, among them Mr. Gipp.

JUNE 2: The art collection in the Calumet high school is constantly growing and several excellent specimens of workmanship greeted the students upon their return to school yesterday morning. Among the new pieces placed in position during the recent holiday are bronze busts of Presidents Washington and Lincoln. These pieces are placed on the top of the book stacks and are strikingly attractive and impressive. There is also a three-quarter size statue of Moses which has been placed on the rostrum. This is a splendid piece of art. A bust of the noted scientist, Louis Agassiz, has also been received.

Probably the most striking of the entire collection is the statue of Sophocles, who is often spoken of as "the most perfect and next to Aeschylus the greatest of Greek tragic poets." This statue is about eight feet in height and displays the Grecian in his native dress.

JUNE 5: Lillian Russell, the American beauty, delighted a capacity audience at the Calumet theater last evening, in a racing comedy by George Broadhurst and George V. Hobart entitled "Wildfire."

JUNE 7: Arrangements have been completed for the engagement of the Finnish Humu and the South Range bands to take part in the grand parade on the morning of June 24, Finland's great national holiday.

JUNE 8: Prominent among the sights of interest in the copper country are the mines and mine buildings, manual training school, public library, shafthouses and engine houses, as well as the stamp mills, smelting plant, Houghton-Douglas Falls and Natural Wall.

Many other points of interest are located in and near Calumet, which are worthy of inspection. The "Palestra," one of the largest enclosed ice skating rinks in the United States, the armory, donated by the C.&H. Mining company, the broom factory where blind miners employ their energy with the skill which one would hardly expect blind people to develop.

The city beautiful has not been neglected, and in addition to well paved streets, Calumet has a large number of parks and beauty spots. The "C.&H." or "Tamarack" park has for years been a rendezvous for picnic parties, and gatherings of all kinds. The Electric park, owned by the Houghton County Traction company, is located near here and a few minutes street car ride will bring a sight seer to this attractive place where almost every convenience of the parks in the larger cities can be found. The Freda park of the Copper Range railroad is located but a short distance from Calumet, and can be reached by train at any time.

Calumet has thirty-eight churches, some of which represent the expenditure of large sums of money, and with few exceptions these edifices are out of debt.

JUNE 9: Peter A. Heikka of Pine street was arrested last evening, on complaint of his wife, charging him with non-support. The defendant is a "pasty vendor," and when arrested had a number of the Cornish brand with him. The wife tells a story in court to the effect that the man goes out with pasties for sale, and that the proceeds are spent for liquor.

JUNE 12: While engaged with his mate in rigging up a drilling machine between 9 and 10 o'clock last evening at the 64th level south of No. 4 shaft, Red Jacket shaft branch of the C.&H., a heavy fall of vein rock occurred, catching Tony Swetish in its embrace, and inflicting such injuries that he died in less than five minutes.

JUNE 14: A subscription list has been opened for the purpose of securing a suitable memorial to mark the Catholic portion of the burial ground at the Lake View cemetery. Already more than $600 has been promised to the fund, and it looks as if the memorial will be a beautiful one. It will consist of a large iron cross, at least ten feet in height, on which will hang a relief work in marble or some other suitable stone of the Savior nailed to the cross.

JUNE 15: Excursionists on the steamer Theodore Roosevelt, under the auspices of the Club D'Haberville, to Port Arthur, Canada, yesterday, were given a royal reception by their Canadian friends.

The thirteen months' old child of Mr. and Mrs. Waine Lehtola of Centennial Heights, was accidentally killed yesterday afternoon…According to the evidence of William J. Angove, who was proceeding towards the Lake View cemetery yesterday driving an automobile, the horse driven by the Lehtolas started rearing and plunging when the auto was within one hundred feet of it. Mr. Angove at once stopped his machine. In the meantime the animal kept on bucking and plunging, and eventually locked the wheels of the vehicle, at the same time endeavoring to turn around. The consequence was the occupants of the rig were thrown out, resulting in serious injuries to the face and head of the infant, from which it succumbed shortly after.

Game Warden John Gipp of Calumet went out Sunday in search of law violations in Keweenaw county. He spent the day at Thayer's Lake and reports that he found the shores of that "angler's paradise" strewn with bass, pickerel, trout and other beauties such as would delight the fishermen, indicating that the lake had been dynamited.

JUNE 17: The Finnish Temperance societies of copper and iron countries will hold a big re-union and temperance rally at the Tamarack Mills hall three days this week, the first session being held Friday Morning at 9 o'clock.

"Good roads for Calumet" is going to be the slogan, and the campaign has not come any too soon. With the proposed new sidewalks covering the principal parts of the C.&H. location, and better roads Calumet will soon have reason to be proud of the fact that it is the metropolis of the copper country.

CAUTION—Beware of imitations. There is only one Calumet. Only one 1909. Don't let some wise (?) guy tell you to stay away.

County Physician Jackson held a post mortem examination yesterday afternoon in the Olson morgue to determine the cause of death of the late Mrs. Ed Sorensen. Dr. Jackson found Paris Green in the stomach of the unfortunate woman, and came to the conclusion that she died from Paris green poisoning, self-administered.

JUNE 18: Calumet is to entertain a large number of Croatians a week from tomorrow, Saturday, June 26, Croatian day. All of the Croatian fraternal and other societies of the copper country will assemble here for the purpose of celebrating the Croatians' national day.

JUNE 19: Seventy-eight students, equipped with the liberal education afforded by the Calumet high school, launched their barks on the sea of life, with commencement exercises at the Calumet theater last evening. The class was the largest that has ever been graduated from the Calumet high school.

JUNE 24: Granite boulders, suitable for a hammer and drill contest, seem to be growing scarce in the vicinity of Calumet, and the committee entrusted with the task of providing granite for the contests to be held on July 4th is scouring the country far and near for such rock.

Cornish miners have always been prominent in hammer and drill contests, but this year Swedes, Finns, Austrians, Germans and Italians will appear against them.

JUNE 25: When all the world is serene, not a cloud in the clear sky, happily and comfortably situated for the summer, the coal bunkers filled for the comforts of next winter, health of self and family excellent, at peace with the world and himself, then the pesky mosquito ruffles a person's peace of mind these summer days. The long-billed, annoying insect has not as yet made its appearance, but a few more days of the present warm atmosphere and his specie by millions will manifest itself.

JUNE 30: Next month will occur the annual pilgrimage from this part of the country to the shrine of Ste. Anne de Beaupre, and hundreds from this section will make the trip.

This pilgrimage is confined largely to the French-Canadian people, although many of other nationalities are found among the journeyers to that quaint spot on the St. Lawrence river in the faraway Isle of Orleans, province of Quebec.

The drill boys employed by the C.&H. Mining company are planning for their annual picnic, which will be held at the C.&H. park., Monday, July 19.

JULY 1: In order to boost the copper country as a summer resort, the Chicago, Milwaukee & St. Paul railroad has gotten out an attractive little booklet setting forth the charms of Calumet, Houghton and the surrounding districts.

*Calumet, Mich.*

The northern terminus of the Mineral Range railway. Here is located the famous Calumet & Hecla mine, one of the largest copper mines in the world. Calumet has excellent schools, fine churches, a manual training school, a public library and an opera house. Good rock roads, "smooth as a floor" lead up Keweenaw Point to Eagle Harbor, 18 miles; Eagle River, 15 miles; Copper Harbor, 24 miles. This country attracts the automobilist, wheelman and kodak enthusiasts.

Ex-sheriff August Beck…is in the service of the C.&H. Mining company and is endeavoring to prevent the destruction of glass non-conductors used to fasten the electric wires to the poles, running from Calumet to the C.&H. pumping station at the lake shore.

For several months careless boys have been in the habit of shooting at the little glass globes which are used on the electric light poles to fasten the electric wires.

JULY 6: Thousands of people witnessed the hammer and drill contests in Red Jacket yesterday afternoon in connection with the Fourth of July celebration. The feature of the contest was the exhibition by R. Tucker, C. Seppala and M. Gemmell, the winners, who drilled clear through the rock, 39 inches in depth, before the expiration of the time allowance of fifteen minutes. Two of the members of the team are blacksmiths while the third is a miner.

Yesterday's two balloon ascensions were among the most attractive features of the day in Calumet. Prof. Bottriell and Prof. Martin, two daring aeronauts, amused the people at the risk of their lives. They made perfect ascents and descents.

Prof. Bottriell made the afternoon ascension, going up in a height of probably 2,000 feet, when he was suddenly shot out of a great wicker cannon and after falling through space at a terrific rate, Prof. Bottriell's great parachute opened out, and he descended gracefully. He alighted in the Y.M.C.A. park.

JULY 15: After cautioning his friends and companions and telling them that they were indiscreet to seek shelter beneath trees in a storm, such as that which visited the copper country yesterday, Emil Hulamaki, of Mohawk, cast his fears aside, and sought the same refuge from the violence of the elements, and he sooner had he done so than bolt of lightning struck the group, killing him and one other, and bringing serious injuries to the rest. The electrical storm which visited Calumet yesterday afternoon was one of the worst that has ever developed in the copper country.

JULY 19: High over tree top and hill, for over forty miles, from Bete Gris to Calumet, came a carrier pigeon yesterday bearing a letter from Will H. Faucett, who is spending a few days at the pretty summer resort, to Mrs. Faucett in Laurium. It was probably the most successful experiment with carrier or homing pigeons that has ever been made in the copper country, and will create considerable interest because of the fact that it offers an excellent means of communication between isolated summer resorts in Keweenaw county and Calumet people.

While the copper country berry pickers are waiting for the wild fruit to ripen, the harvesting of the home grown strawberry continues...The success of the strawberry cultivation in the copper country has caused a number of farmers to enter this field, and it is expected that in the future the strawberry crop will be one of the mainstays of the local tillers of the soil.

JULY 22: It was decided to install a drinking fountain outside the Red Jacket town hall.

The dials for the new Red Jacket town clock arrived this morning.

JULY 23: The Pabst Brewing company of Milwaukee is making extensive additions to its machinery and equipment at the local bottling works of the company in the Mineral Range yards. All of the company's beer for local consumption is shipped to Calumet in bulk from the Milwaukee plant, and bottled here.

JULY 24: The bath department of the library is more popular in the summer than in the winter. People frequently visit the bath department of the library two or three times per week during the summer months, and are refreshed by the cool water. The shower bath which is used infrequently during the winter months is much more popular during the summer.

It is very hard to get a good, capable girl these days for housework. The young women can earn a lot more working in the fields, and the majority of them seem to like it. Many have been used to farm work in the old country and are not averse to going into the local harvest fields.

JULY 26: A number of important improvements are being made at the plant of the Calumet brewery at Lake View location,

One of the most audacious bicycle thefts this summer was reported to Chief Trudell yesterday when the young brother of Nick F. Kaiser, village clerk of Red Jacket, left his wheel standing outside the Red Jacket post office for a few minutes while he went inside to get some mail. When he came out the machine had disappeared and the thief or thieves left not the slightest trace behind...It will be remembered that early this summer Chief Trudell actually had his own wheel stolen from him and he has never recovered the machine.

JULY 27: He only weighs about 130 pounds, but he is made up entirely of nerve and grit. And lucky for him that he is, as Jack Dillon of Mackinac island, performed a feat today on the flagpole attached to the dome of Red Jacket's town hall that caused many a passerby to stop, gaze and shudder.

This morning Dillon painted the flag pole attached to the dome of the town hall and also saw that the guy ropes and pulley at the top were in first-class condition.

JULY 28: Architect F.W. Hessenmueller of Calumet is authority for the statement that the building records for several years will be broken in Calumet during the present year.

Among the large buildings erected in Calumet are the Ulseth block on Sixth street, the Tambellini block on Portland, the Boone-Kohlhass block on Third street, Laurium, and the Elks' temple, which has been practically rebuilt.

JULY 30: The copper country has again become a Mecca for those of the hay fever district and by one and twos, they have wandered into this section until it is estimated that the hay fever colony in the copper country now numbers fifty...

The tourist season has also arrived in the copper country...Many of these visitors usually make a hasty trip through the town, get a glimpse of the big copper mining industry and hasten to the boats to visit Duluth, and the other cities in a like manner. Others, however, are more thorough in their sight-seeing and frequently remain several days in the city.

AUGUST 2: According to the story told the "News" by Officer Joseph MacNamara, he received a hurried telephone call Saturday night to proceed to Pine street immediately. On arriving there, he found officer Harry Hodge struggling with Kataja, whom he had under arrest, and surrounded by a yelling crowd estimated to be about 150 persons…

On reaching the Grand theater on Fifth street, MacNamara states that he saw Hodge go down after being struck from behind, and immediately the crowd closed on the officer, and trampled him under foot.

Officer MacNamara clung to his prisoner who was fighting desperately to effect his escape, and he had to club him into submission. While doing this, some of the crowd were hitting Officer MacNamara from behind, and one fellow sprang on his back, and endeavored to choke him. It was here that one man in the crowd came to the relief of the officer, and he states that if he meets the fellow he is going to thank him. He was a lumberjack, and somewhat crippled at that. He struck at the fellow clinging to MacNamara, and dropped him like a log.

Officer Hodge, himself a badly injured man, returned to aid his fellow guardian of the peace, but was roughly handled by the crowd. He remained in the fray, however, until the finish.

AUGUST 4: Bidding was warm at the auction conducted at Eagle River this week, to dispose of the old government lighthouse which has past its era of usefulness. John Vertin of Calumet was the final purchaser, paying $900 for the building.

AUGUST 27: Miss Maggie J. Walz, the Drummond island journalist and temperance worker, who has been in the city the last few days, is favorably considering the purchase of the Hotel Superior by public subscription, for the purpose of turning it into a girls' school.

SEPTEMBER 4: Work in the public schools of Calumet is progressing nicely, according to Supt. H.E. Kratz, and the superintendent and teaching corps are looking forward to a very successful year, having their daily duties so thoroughly systematized that good progress should be made.

There are 205 teachers on the pay rolls this term, and in addition there are a number of janitors, office assistants, truant officer, etc. At practically the last moment some of the teachers who had been engaged failed to report for duty, and the superintendent had to keep the wires hot in an endeavor to fill their places.

It is interesting to note that there was a total school attendance Monday, the first working day of the fall term, of 5,858. This was 194 in excess of the number that reported for school on the opening day of the fall term last year.

The total attendance in the high school the first day was 580, an increased enrollment of 119. In order to accommodate this large class of students it has been found necessary to utilize the large room formerly used as a woodshop on the second story of the building, and transfer the woodshop department to the basement, where are located the blacksmith and machine shops.

SEPTEMBER 7: F. Henry Heintze arrived in Calumet Sunday from Chicago to take charge of the new station of the United Wireless company at Tamarack Junior and will assume his new duties when that station is completed this afternoon. Although Foreman J.D. Fountain expected to have the installation complete by Sunday, the rain and high wind interfered with the work, and the last work is being done upon the station today.

In speaking of the local station, Mr. Heintze said, "It is a high power station and we expect to be able to talk to Chicago and Duluth without difficulty. The United Wireless company will soon have another operator in this city and a continuous service by day and night will be provided for commercial business. The station will be connected with the city by a telephone service and the office will be always open."

SEPTEMBER 8: Red Jacket will enforce the curfew law. It will go into effect this evening, action to this effect being taken at last night's regular monthly council meeting. With the chiming of the half hour after 8 o'clock each evening, the janitor of the Red Jacket townhall will ring the curfew bell, which is attached to the town clock. It is to be rung for two minutes. After the clanging of the last bell all boys and girls under 16 years of age must be at home, unless accompanied by parent or guardian, otherwise the officers have authority to place them under arrest.

SEPTEMBER 10: A telegram was received here this morning announcing the death in Astoria, Ore., yesterday afternoon of Fred Karinen, the well known Finnish editor and newspaper proprietor. The remains are to be shipped to Calumet for interment, and are expected here about Tuesday of next week.

For a number of years Mr. Karinen was engaged in the grocery business on Pine street. Later, he decided to enter the newspaper field. He owned and published for a number of years the *Finnish-American Utisett*, a periodical in the Finnish language, and in its day a power among the Finns of the copper country and elsewhere.

SEPTEMBER 15: Members of the investigating committee, appointed by the C.&H. miners' executive committee to look up deserving cases for the disposal of charity in Calumet, are telling some pitiful stories of some homes they have visited in Red Jacket and Laurium.

A member of the committee last evening visited a German woman in Laurium who has three small children. She was literally in a starving condition, and was scantily clothed. The children were in the same pitiable condition. There was nothing to eat in the home and the sight was such as to greatly affect this particular committeeman. The woman said she was left a widow seven years ago and that she is receiving some help from the county, but not enough to provide for herself and little ones. The miners' committee has taken the work of relieving her in hand, and has already provided her and the children with suitable clothing, as well as food.

There are other cases of a similar nature being unearthed by the committee daily, which tends to show there is a great deal of poverty existing in Calumet.

SEPTEMBER 18: The Calumet township authorities have been notified that there is indiscriminate shooting going on in the neighborhood of the Calumet dam, owned by the C.&H. Mining company. Spent bullets have entered homes in the Blue Jacket location and quite recently a gentleman walking along the banks of the dam heard the whistle of a bullet pass within a few feet of his head.

It is unlawful to shoot within the confines of a township or village, and any person caught doing so will be prosecuted. The township has an ordinance covering this, and it will be enforced.

A band of gypsies, comprising three women, two men and eleven children, of all ages, from an infant in arms up to 15 years of age, paid a visit to the South Shore depot this morning. They came in on this morning's South Shore train from Duluth and are now housed in the baggage department at the depot. The two men are out scouting around for a place to pitch their tents. Their effort will be vain as far as Red Jacket is concerned. Chief Trudell states that no gypsies will be allowed to locate in the village.

Hundreds of people visited the depot this morning to get a look at the dark-eyed, swarthy-skinned natives of southern Europe. One of the women, in particular, is a brunette of a striking appearance. The women and children do not talk English. All of the children, with the exception of the two oldest, are thinly clad. All appear healthy, however, and are apparently well fed.

SEPTEMBER 20: The Calumet Public hospital was placed under quarantine for a week yesterday because of the outbreak there of a case of smallpox. One of the patients was taken with the disease and when his malady was diagnosed as such he was removed to the county hospital. The nurses and others in the hospital were vaccinated and a strict quarantine will be kept until all danger is passed.

The season for roller skating opened at the Palestra on Saturday evening, with a large crowd in attendance. The floor is in excellent condition, and since the popular pastime was discontinued in the spring the skates have been overhauled and placed in good condition.

SEPTEMBER 21: The announcement has been made that the C.&H. Mining company has consented to donate to the community, for public park purposes, the large field between Calumet location and the Red Jacket village. The action on the part of the mining company has been

entirely voluntary, and will provide an opportunity for the most important civic improvement that Calumet has ever enjoyed.

The announcement, which was made yesterday, was to some extent an advance notice, the object of which was to assure the Italians of this community that they will have a place for the new Columbus statue.

SEPTEMBER 27: This morning, a representative of one of the old line insurance companies paid a visit to the township clerk's office for the purpose of securing data concerning the different nationalities of the inhabitants of Calumet, and the numerical strength of each.

The only authentic information was obtainable through the birth records, which disclosed the fact that the Finns were in the lead, with the Austrians second, and the English and Italians about tied for third place. Not long ago, the English held the lead by a large majority, but they seem to be gradually giving way to other nationalities, particularly the Finnish. There is hardly any reason to doubt that the Finnish residents in Calumet township outnumber any other nationality at a ratio of almost two to one.

SEPTEMBER 30: Today is known as "Memory" day, a day on which all who have loved ones in the city of the dead are supposed to visit the cemeteries, decorate the graves and fix them up for the coming winter. It is likely that a number of Calumet residents will take advantage of the occasion and visit Lake View with this purpose in view. "Memory" day had its origin during the past legislature, an act being passed to memorize the day. It is not a legal holiday.

OCTOBER 4: The All-Star cricket team, selected from the best players of the teams in the copper country, won the match from the C.&H. team.

OCTOBER 5: A conservative estimate places the total amount of ice cream consumed in Calumet during the past summer at 30,000 gallons...Although it seems almost impossible to believe, the citizens of Calumet, young and old, have spent about $40,000 in cold cash to appease that tickling appetite for something cool in the warm days of the summer...the majority of the small retailers have dismantled their fountains and ice cream parlors for the season.

OCTOBER 8: Owing to the prevalence of typhoid fever in Red Jacket, and the fact that the disease is making headway, Health Officer P.D. MacNaughton has ordered a sample of Red Jacket's drinking water to be sent to Dr. V. Vaughn of Ann Arbor, for analysis.

OCTOBER 12: Gone is the balmy autumn weather which has prevailed almost uninterruptedly for the last few weeks in Calumet. Gone are the thoughts of summer and the cozy ice cream parlor. These were ushered out with the downpour of rain and snow accompanied by a northeaster of arctic proportions last night…Steeples and housetops presented a wintry appearance this morning and through the day thoughts of winter prevailed.

OCTOBER 27: Marshal Trudell…often acts in the role of a domestic peacemaker without recourse to law…One of the means employed to smooth things over and get the couple in good humor was the telling of stories, in which the chief takes the palm. One of the stories he told the reunited couple is a "Cousin Jack" story, dating back to the jungle show which visited Calumet this summer. A Cornishman and his wife entered the show, and started to inspect the cages where the animals were confined. Not being able to read English very well the Cornishman, pointing to an animal with a long snout, said to his wife:

"'Ere Mary Ann, cus tha tell me what thet theer thing theer es, weth the long snoot?"

"Sure," said his better half, "that's a hant-eater."

"A hant-aiter," said Jack, "ef 'twas a mather-in-law aiter, I'd taake un 'ome."

During the past few weeks, since the adoption of mine time in Calumet, several patrons of the Calumet theater and other local places have requested *The News* to call attention to the fact that it would be much more satisfactory to them if such places should use standard time, instead of adopting mine time.

OCTOBER 28: Red Jacket is likely to have another moving picture house in the near future…This will make three moving picture houses for Calumet, including the Grand and the C.S. Sullivan theater.

OCTOBER 30: "Men are scarce," said Employment Agent G.L. Perrault this morning, in response to a question concerning the labor market. "Without exaggeration," said Mr. Perrault, "I could place 400 men right now into jobs in the copper country. I only wish I could get that many. But I can't."

NOVEMBER 12: Evangelist Herbert C. Hart fearlessly denounced the dance, the theater, and cards last evening at the revival meeting conducted at the Calumet M.E. church…"Ninety per cent of the divorces of this country have their origin in the dancing parlor and the low-down theater."

NOVEMBER 17: The heavy snowfall of the past few days caused the "beautiful" to accumulate in deep banks upon the railroad tracks and the plows were kept busy for several hours both yesterday and today. Almost all of the locomotives which operate in the copper country have been equipped with steel plows, and the larger plows have also been prepared for the future battles with the snow.

Sleighs were placed in general use in Calumet yesterday and today, and they are now much more numerous than wheeled vehicles.

Miss Maggie Walz, whose work among the Finnish people as editor, financier and practical philanthropist has made her one of the best known women in upper Michigan has been engaged by the Marquette Woman's Home Missionary society of the Methodist church to deliver a lecture on Wednesday of this week, says the Marquette Mining Journal.

NOVEMBER 27: The village of Red Jacket and the Red Jacket mine or shaft were named after the famous Indian, a Seneca, Red Jacket, whose real name was Sagoyewatha…the fleetest runner among the Indian scouts employed by the British in the revolutionary war. …A British officer toward the end of the revolution gave Sagoyewatha a cast-off uniform jacket, brilliant scarlet and faced with gold braid. And thereby he won for himself the nickname by which he is best known to history—"Red Jacket."

DECEMBER 1: Miss Maggie Walz of this city has been selected as the delegate to represent the Houghton County Suffragists at the state convention to be held at Grand Rapids on December 7 and 8. Miss Walz was named at a meeting of suffragists held in Miss Walz's office in the Walz building on Monday evening.

DECEMBER 4: In a short paper which he gave before the Italian-Literary club of Calumet this week on "The History of Calumet," Dominic Suino, one of the old pioneers, made a few interesting statements. One of these was that while on a visit to Rome about eight years ago, he visited the bedside of Ed. J. Hulbert, the discoverer of the Calumet & Hecla mine. He told the members of the club that Mr. Hulbert discussed the finding of the Calumet lode in company with a Mr. Johnson and three or four Indians.

…Mr. Suino spoke of the railroad that once ran through Fifth street, Red Jacket, carrying ore to the smelter, which was at that time located on Waterworks street, near the Calumet dam. Soon after the railroad passed through Fifth street, the mining company put up a few small cottages on either side of the street for the use of the workmen. Mr. Suino said that the presence of the railroad on Fifth street accounted for the narrowness of the street as compared with the other streets in the village.

DECEMBER 10: Arthur Boase of the People's Fuel company, of Calumet, this week killed a snow owl, measuring four feet, eight inches from tip to tip. The bird has been taken to a taxidermist to be mounted.

Mr. Barnham has issued invitations to the carrier boys of *The Calumet News, Mining Gazette, Copper Journal, Paivelehti, Glasnik, Hrvatski* and *Italian Miner*, to be his guests for the evening, and the boys are promised a real good time.

DECEMBER 13: Foreigners living in this city are beginning to send their usual Christmas offerings home and money order checks are rushed…Austrians, Finns, Italians, Greeks, Syrians, Belgians, Germans, Scandinavians and other nationalities shoulder each other at the money order window, waiting to be instructed, and this is the hardest part of the clerk's work, taking much time and a lot of patience.

DECEMBER 14: The management of the Glass Block store has made arrangements to install a new feature at this big department store on Fifth street, for the benefit of the holiday shoppers, particularly those from out of town. A tea room will be opened by the management and tea served to shoppers during business hours.

DECEMBER 15: To help the Salvation Army increase its funds for the Christmas dinner baskets for the poor of this community Adjutant Parkhouse has made arrangements to place three "kettles," suspended on tripods, at prominent street corners on Fifth street on Saturday.

DECEMBER 16: One of the most attractive Christmas windows in Calumet is to be seen at the Glass Block store. A Santa Claus scene is presented. It shows a sled containing Santa Claus and a load of toys drawn by four reindeer. A label bears the words, "On the way to the Glass Block store." In the background is moving scenery, operated by a motor, which gives the impression that the reindeer and sled is passing through miles of country.

DECEMBER 18: United States immigration officers were in Calumet last evening and effected the arrests of three Chinamen, who are believed to have been brought into the upper peninsula since the passage of the Chinese exclusion act.

The Chinamen were taken from the Willie Lee laundry, near the Mineral Range depot. Each asserted that he has his "choc tee" which is a certification of residence, and in effect previous to the Chinese exclusion act.

One of the three men arrested last evening has a wife in Calumet, the only Chinese woman, it is believed, in the copper country.

DECEMBER 27: Christmas has come and gone, but it has left many pleasant memories.

Every church, both Protestant and Catholic, observed both Christmas day and yesterday with appropriate music and other features. The poor of this district were looked after as never before, thanks to the Associated Charities, the Salvation Army and a number of societies and other agencies engaged in the work of relieving the needy. More than one choir of carol singers were on the streets of Red Jacket and Laurium Christmas eve.

DECEMBER 28: It is believed by immigration men that the coming spring will witness a large exodus of Finn laborers from the land that is being ruled with an iron hand by Russia. Letters are being written to friends for aid in leaving the country.

It was decided to erect the ski jump on the Swedetown hill, provided the C.&H. Mining company is willing to grant permission. It is proposed to hold a ski jumping competition on Washington's birthday, February 22, and also to arrange for a race on skis, probably as far as the Franklin location and return. Ski riding and jumping is becoming a very popular pastime locally.

A serious fire broke out about 5:30 o'clock yesterday afternoon in the Hutchins building, on Sixth street, and before the flames were gotten under control the interior of the second and third floors were gutted and the rest of the building more or less damaged by fire and water.

It was one of the fiercest fires that has occurred in Red Jacket in some time.

---

**Photos, pages 157-158**

Page 157: Top: Looking west on Oak Street. St. Joseph's Austrian Catholic church background (now St. Paul's). *Voelker*
     Bottom: Michigan House, left. Looking east on Oak Street. April 1909. *Agnich*
Page 158: Top: 8th Street?, Red Jacket. *RCM/Mantel*
     Bottom: "Red Jacket from new depot." Looking east on Oak Street. *MTU-Copper Country Historical Collections*

ak Street, Calumet, Mich.

# *Calumet* **1910** *News*

*Shattering all scientific calculations and completely puzzling learned astronomers, who declare they made sure of the unprecedented phenomena with repeated observations here before daybreak this morning, the glowing tail of Halley's comet appeared in the eastern sky today at a time when the world's comet authorities had agreed it would be in the west.*

JANUARY 1: It is the first time in the history of the village of Red Jacket that the boys connected with the local papers have been banqueted and they are going to show the host how well they appreciate his kindness by cleaning up everything on sight.

JANUARY 3: Colder tonight. That's what the weather man says. Residents of Calumet who have shivered during the intense cold of the past twenty-four hours find no relief by consulting Forecaster A. Wiesner, in charge of the weather bureau at Houghton, who predicts that the severe storm which has enwrapped the upper lake region today is to continue tomorrow.

JANUARY 7: About 40 single men, all employees of the Tamarack Mining company, were laid off yesterday from No. 2 shaft. A temporary stoppage of operations on the Osceola amygdaloid is given as the cause.

JANUARY 19: Gust Mattson was found guilty in Justice Jackola's court last evening of breaking into a Finnish bath house early Sunday morning. Mattson is alleged to have wrenched the bath house door from its hinges, and finding the place warm and comfortable passed the remainder of the night there. He was fined $5 and costs, and ordered to make good the damage he had committed.

JANUARY 22: The Slovenian Young Men's union will give a masquerade dancing party at the Italian hall of Red Jacket, this evening, for the benefit of the Cherry mine widows and orphans. The event will be a very pleasant one, and music will be furnished by the Red Jacket orchestra. Prizes amounting to $30 will be awarded to the best maskers.

JANUARY 25: Automobilists are planning a campaign in hopes of having a law passed that will make it obligatory for persons driving carriages of any kind during the night to have them equipped with lights of sufficient power so that they can be easily discerned at a reasonable distance.

A large number of accidents are caused by the control of the machines being lost by broken brakes. This may occur when an auto is going along a dark place in the road at a fair rate of speed and the chauffeur suddenly sees a carriage loom up directly ahead. He then throws on the emergency brakes and in many cases the sudden impact of the brakes and the sudden stopping of the car causes something to snap and then everything is over except the call to be sent in for doctors and help.

Will the Calumet indoor baseball league, which started off with such a flourish of trumpets, and which promised

to be such a success, be disbanded? This is the question that is agitating the minds of the managers and members of the respective teams.

JANUARY 28: Frank Talentine, of Osceola, is the possessor of a family heirloom, which he values as highly as all other worldly possessions. The article in question is a sword which once flashed in the army of Napoleon Bonaparte in his famous European military campaigns.

JANUARY 30: Calumet ski jumpers have shown much more consistent form in their practice work this year than last…If the showing is satisfactory, it is likely that some of the local jumpers will enter the tournaments to be conducted by the Ishpeming, Norway, Scandia and Munising clubs later in the month.

FEBRUARY 7: There are more men out of work just now in and around Calumet than I ever saw before in all my life," was the startling statement made to the *News* this morning by G.L. Perreault, the well known employment agent of Pine street.

FEBRUARY 8: As the result of a very serious accident in No. 1 shaft, South Kearsarge mine, shortly after 3 o'clock yesterday afternoon, two miners, Joseph Teddy and James Ratz, were killed and four others slightly injured.

The victims…were working at the 21$^{st}$ level, beneath a heavy wooden covering which had been erected to protect them from falling rocks and other material. They had no admonition of their impending fate. The heavy skip, weighing about nine tons, dropped in an instant to the bottom of the shaft where it crashed through the timber framework erected and pinned the men beneath it.

FEBRUARY 11: Calumet's growth has been manifested more in the outlying locations than in the town proper. It is doubted if the population of Red Jacket is as large now as in 1904 when the census enumerators found 3,784 people here. Laurium, however, has shown a big increase and although the population in 1904 was 7,653, it is thought that the 11,000 mark will be approached this year.

FEBRUARY 16: During early March it may be possible to observe the comet with the naked eye, and it will be plainly visible with a three-inch telescope.

Halley's comet is the first that has been visible from the earth since the perfection of the spectroscope, by means of which the chemical composition of luminous bodies is determined by analysis of the rays of light they give off,

and the study of the new celestial visitor is expected to clear up many disputed points abut the tails of comets.

FEBRUARY 19: The ice harvest is on in Calumet. The Calumet Ice company, owned by the Demarois Bros., has a large force of men employed at the Beaver dam, and the ice is being stored in the company's local ice houses. The ice at Beaver dam is quite-thick and of good quality. The frozen water is as clear as crystal, according to the members of the firm.

While lying asleep on the tracks of the Mineral Range railroad between 12 and 1 o'clock yesterday morning, Jacob Kokonen, aged 30, of Swedetown, was struck by Engine No. 161 and carried a distance of 290 feet before the locomotive could be stopped.

FEBRUARY 24: Roy Rosskilley, a pump boy, employed at the No. 21 shaft of the C.&H. mine, had a remarkable escape from death last evening. Rosskilley fell down the shaft about 100 feet from the 15th to the 16th level, and was practically uninjured.

The recently organized Calumet Curling club will give a skating party this evening, the proceeds of which will be a nucleus for a fund with which a new curling rink in Calumet next year.

FEBRUARY 25: Copper country Italians have contributed to a fund of $1,000 which was deposited this morning in the First National bank of Hancock, to serve as a purse for a band contest between D'Urbano's crack Italian band and the famous Calumet & Hecla band of Calumet.

It is believed that the challenge is the result of a recent criticism of the D'Urbano band, which appeared in an Eastern musical paper, over the signature of George D. Barnard, director of the C.&H. band.

FEBRUARY 26: Stephan Volch, a miner, employed at the No. 5 shaft of the Tamarack, was instantly killed about 3 o'clock yesterday afternoon, by being struck by a fall of rock. Volch was working at the 34th level south, when a rock measuring about five feet in length, four in width and one in thickness fell upon him, inflicting injuries from which he died shortly afterward.

Manager Fred Cowley of the C.&H. band refused to be quoted when asked last evening concerning what action the members would take upon the challenge given yesterday by the D'Urbano band. From the way Mr. Cowley spoke, it does not appear likely that the local musical organization will accept the challenge, choosing rather to ignore it.

FEBRUARY 28: Alleging that his wife started after him with a large knife, Joe Acotto, residing in the Lambert building on Sixth street, last night fired two revolver shots at her, both of which took effect, one lodging in the woman's right breast and the other in her hip. After the shooting, the woman walked to the home of a friend on Pine street, while Acotto went to the Red Jacket fire hall, and gave himself up.

MARCH 2: "I would like to train him and make a 'world beater' out of him," said Stanislaus Zbyszko, the champion Polish wrestler, referring to Karl Lehto, the copper country Finnish champion, after the latter had won the handicap wrestling match at the Palestra last evening.

Acting on the basis that he has to throw every competitor he meets before he can get a match with Frank Gotch, the world's champion, Zbyszko, the Polish champion catch-as-catch-can wrestler, this morning issued a challenge to wrestle Lehto, either in or out of the copper country, in any city the Finnish champion may name, for a straight catch-as-catch-can match.

MARCH 5: Tomorrow is the one day in all the year when particular significance is placed on thoughts of mother. Several years ago, "Mother's Sunday" sprang into existence, a day set aside as a sort of memorial to the American mother, when all men and women are expected to pause and think of those who gave them birth and who suffered and struggled so that the present day men and women might have modern advantages.

MARCH 8: The fact that two shafts of the Osceola mine have been closed down has resulted in the departure of a large number of miners from that location for other mining camps. The exodus has been very noticeable during the last few days, it being estimated that no less than fifty miners from Osceola and Calumet have left for other fields where they have secured or will secure positions.

MARCH 10: They stated that Jilbert ordered Andrew to pry down a loose piece of rock, while the two unfortunate men stood on one side and directly underneath a larger piece of rock. Through some means, the heavier piece of rock fell just as Andrew released the smaller piece. The men's lives were instantly crushed out, several tons of rock falling on them. Andrew was also caught in the fall of ground, and dangerously injured. He was removed to the C.&H. hospital.

MARCH 17: The Calumet Brewery company has placed an order for a power or automobile truck to be used for delivery purposes in Calumet this summer. With the exception of the C.&H. Mining company the firm will be the first to introduce this class of conveyance locally.

MARCH 21: The Copper Range Railroad Co. yesterday inaugurated its new sleeper and dining car service, "The Copper Range Limited," pulling into Calumet at 1 p.m. and departing, southbound, at 3:30 o'clock.

Members of the Slovenian-Croatian colony in Calumet numbering about 100 will locate during the coming spring and summer in the White River Valley district, Oceana county, Southern Michigan.

The Houghton-Douglas falls, located about half way between Calumet and Lake Linden was a big attraction for Calumet people yesterday. The Houghton County

Street Railway company provided a special street car service between this city and the falls, and the cars were crowded throughout the entire afternoon.

MARCH 22: Two more victims, the result of mine accidents, have passed away in Calumet during the past few hours. John E. Wahlgren, blasted on March 17, died last evening about 10:30 o'clock, and Albert Andrews, who sustained a broken back on March 9, by a fall of rock, passed away at the C.&H. hospital about 6:30 a.m.

MARCH 26: Harvey Cornelier, manager of the Eagle Drug store of Calumet is one of the happiest men in Calumet today. Harvey is captain of the Red Jacket Elks' bowling team, and last evening he attained the goal to which all bowlers strive, a perfect score. The score was made on the Elk's alleys, and it is the first time any copper country bowler has made twelve "strikes" or a score of 300 in any one game.

MARCH 29: Cambridge, Mass., March 29.—Alexander Agassiz, the eminent naturalist and president of the Calumet & Hecla Mining company, died yesterday on the steamer Adriatic, bound from Southampton for New York.

Agassiz was a director of several copper companies and a son to the famous naturalist, Jean Paul Louis Rudolphe Agassiz and was engaged in scientific researches for over fifty years.

Alexander Agassiz was born in Neuchatel, Switzerland, December 17, 1835. His mother, Cecile Braun, as well as his father, Professor Louis Agassiz, the eminent Harvard naturalist were Swiss. He came to the United States when eleven years of age, and at sixteen entered the Harvard University.

As president of the C.&H. mine, Mr. Agassiz was well known in the copper country. It was his custom for years to visit this section twice each year, in the spring and the fall, and he had many friends here, some of whom remembered him from the time he developed and superintended the mine in the sixties.

Calumet generally learned to look upon Mr. Agassiz with the greatest of respect. He contributed largely to the betterment of the social and educational conditions of the community and has given many benefactions. Among these may be mentioned the C.&H. public library, and the Calumet Light Guard armory. The introduction of manual training into the Calumet public schools was also largely due to Mr. Agassiz's assistance, and the erection of the most modernly equipped manual training school in the state was made possible through his friendship for the community.

He provided the most ideal working conditions possible for the men employed in the C.&H. mines while superintendent and president of that company. Commodious residences were built for the workmen and their families and other conveniences supplied. Every employee of the mine felt that he had a personal friend in Mr. Agassiz, and during times when financial panics made it seem advisable to suspend operations here, he did his utmost to keep the mines working, and provide employment for the men, so that they need feel no hardship.

MARCH 31: Announcement was made this morning that the Calumet & Hecla and subsidiary mines will close at noon Saturday out of respect for the memory of late President Agassiz. The mines affected are the C.&H., Tamarack, Osceola, North and South Kearsarge, Ahmeek, Seneca, LaSalle, Tecumseh, Allouez, Centennial, Superior, Isle Royale and Laurium. Mr. Agassiz was a director of all these properties.

APRIL 4: The memorial services held yesterday afternoon in the Calumet Light Guard Armory, in honor of the late Alexander Agassiz…

"He was one of the best known men throughout the civilized world," said Judge Streeter. "Perhaps there was no scientific society of note in the world with which he was not connected as an honorary, active, or corresponding member. He was distinguished as a citizen, as a financier, as a scientist, and in many other ways, but through it all his aims and regards were closely allied with Calumet and the people residing here."

"The schools were particularly the delight of this man," said the speaker. "There could not be too many school houses for Mr. Agassiz. Never during any depression in copper were the schools or the property affected. I never knew Agassiz to do an unjust thing…"

"Alexander Agassiz did not believe there could be any conflict between capital and labor. He knew that either without the aid of the other was absolutely worthless."

A prominent local architect informed *The News* this morning that there will be no building boom in Calumet this summer. Plans for several large buildings have been drawn, but it is unlikely the proposed work will be done this summer. Money is not plentiful and this is the chief reason for the present outlook.

APRIL 19: There is a big exodus out of Calumet almost daily for farming and fruit districts. The middle west is receiving some of this emigration, while others are going south, and not a few to the great north-western districts. A large number of Finnish people have gone to the state of Washington during the past two months, to engage in farming or mining.

It is interesting to note that the Italians leaving here are making for the fruit farms, while the Finns are interested more in agricultural farming.

It is believed that this spring has witnessed the biggest emigration out of the copper country than ever before in its history. Certain it is that the local railroad travel has been the biggest in several years. A considerable number of men have been thrown out of work—temporarily at least—and as the greater majority of these do not wish to remain idle, they are going to other points.

APRIL 22:…It appears that the young people's parents died when both were young, and the young woman was sent to a relative in the northern part of Sweden, while the boy was brought up by a relative in the northern part of Finland…

As bit by bit the tale of being left an orphan was unfolded by the young man, the young woman plied her lover with questions with the result that no doubt was left in the mind of the young woman that her lover was her own brother.

John Nowak, a timberman, was instantly killed yesterday about the noon hour by being struck with a falling piece of timber at the 59th level of No. 5 shaft, Calumet branch of the C.&H. mine. The timber fell from the 51st level, and had thus fallen a distance of 800 feet before it struck the unfortunate man, crushing his head to a pulp.

APRIL 23: The copper country and Lake Superior in common with a great stretch of country is now in the midst of a terrible blizzard that bids fair to exceed any storm ever before recorded in his part of the country.

George Madurich, a trammer, died about 8 o'clock last evening in the C.&H. hospital from injuries received earlier in the afternoon while at work in the Hecla branch of the C.&H. mine. He was prying out some loose rock when a large quantity of rock fell away, pinning Madurich between the wall and the side of the car.

APRIL 25: "They say we suffragists are not domestic and not practical," said Miss Walz. "Consider this matter as an illustration. It is our purpose to teach the girls how to become good homemakers; how to become domestic. Just as truly we propose to shelter them from foolish marriages.

"Some of the foreign girls, coming to this country without experience and fearful for the future, marry men whom they do not love at all. They accept faulty men unconditionally for the sake of a home which, in many instances, they are not able to care for.

"We propose that these girls and American girls, too, shall have a chance to learn to care for themselves. Then they have a real choice when an offer of marriage is made them. If they really want to marry they are ready to take good care of a home."

APRIL 27: One of the biggest real estate deals that has been consummated in Red Jacket in some time took place this morning, when the Calumet Brewing Company purchased the Copper Range hotel building on Sixth street, from John Schroeder. The purchase price was $18,000.

The Calumet Brewing company is a local concern, with a modern plant located in the Lake View district. Practically all of the stock is owned by local business people.

MAY 5: Calumet Poles will observe the 119th anniversary of the adoption of the Polish constitution next Saturday. The constitution of Poland and the declaration of independence was signed May 8, 1791.

MAY 7: Thursday, May 5, without especial notice, except to a party of local miners, who will ever remember the date, as it marks a day when they were miraculously saved from what probably would have been an awful death.

On May 5, 1905, a party of 32 miners were being lowered in the Red Jacket shaft. Just as they reached the 1,500-foot level, the steel wire rope attached to the cage broke, and the men expected to be hurled immediately to their death. They started to fall but the safety catches with which every cage is equipped in the perpendicular shaft, acted splendidly, and the men's lives were saved.

MAY 13: The Red Jacket village council, at a special meeting last evening, decided to re-decorate the interior of the Calumet theater, the work to be done probably during the month of July. It was also decided to have the old fire hall on Fifth street inspected and if considered unsafe to have it torn down.

MAY 16: Drawn by engine No. 500, one of the best on the road, with engineer Fred Reinhardt at the throttle, the new Northwestern passenger train arrived in Calumet at 10 o'clock this morning, almost on schedule time. Dan Vaughan of Marquette was the conductor. The train is one of the finest that has ever pulled into this city.

MAY 17: Just as sure as May 18 rolls around, the older residents of Calumet will get their heads together and talk about the disastrous fire that swept the village of Red Jacket practically from end to end on that date just 40 years ago. Heroic attempts are told of the efforts to fight the fire, but all proved futile, and it was not until three business and residence blocks of the village, bounded on one side by Elm street and on the other by Portland street had been wiped entirely out of existence, that the fire subsided.

Copper country fruit growers anticipate that the strawberry crop this year will be one of the largest on record. The plants are now in blossom and if the conditions continue to be as favorable as they have been, Houghton county will undoubtedly rival Ontonagon county as a producer of this luscious fruit.

MAY 19: Shattering all scientific calculations and completely puzzling learned astronomers, who declare they made sure of the unprecedented phenomena with repeated observations here before daybreak this morning, the glowing tail of Halley's comet appeared in the eastern sky today at a time when the world's comet authorities had agreed it would be in the west.

Francis De Lemorande (Frank Lovejoy) died in Calumet yesterday after a two weeks' illness with erysipelas and dropsy. Lemorande was a well known figure about Calumet, he having lived here for more than fifty years.

The decedent was born at Sault Ste. Marie, 68 years ago, of French parentage. Throughout his life he was always proud to assert that he was a descendent of the court of France at the time of Napoleon Bonaparte.

MAY 23: A three-year-old Laurium tot, having shared in the nightly observations for the comet, startled her mother this morning by screaming: "Mamma, the tomet, oh mamma, see the tomet with a tail." Investigation showed a large yellow kite with a long rag tail in the heavens. At least one young person is now satisfied there is a Halley's comet.

MAY 26: A boys' band, known as the Finnish Cadets' band, numbering 50 pieces, has been organized in Calumet. Prof. Jacobson, leader of the Finnish Humu band, is in charge.

MAY 28: On going out early this morning to drive their cows in from pasture, back of Centennial Heights, Mesdames Hautivitta and Toppila discovered the body of Herman Wiedelmann, suspended from a tree. The women ran screaming back to the location and Marshal Trudell was summoned to the scene. When the body was cut down life was found to be extinct, and a medical examination showed that Wiedelmann had been dead some time.

The decedent, who was about 60 years of age, and the father of "Big Lydia," had been despondent for some time, although it was not feared he would take any steps to destroy himself.

MAY 30: Because of the cold weather and snow today, plans for the observance of Memorial day in this city were considerably altered.

JUNE 6: Thousands of people lined the streets of Red Jacket to witness the parade of the many Catholic societies, that took part. The parade was one of the largest ever witnessed in this city, it taking 30 minutes to pass a given point. The parade was headed by Chief Trudell who acted as grand marshal, assisted by Homer Beauchaine and others.

JUNE 8: Next to Christmas, and possibly the annual Sunday school picnic day, the children of the churches look forward to the observance of "Children's day" with the most pleasure. The celebration, which is used for different purposes in the various denominations, always takes the nature of a program made up entirely of numbers given by the young folks.

JUNE 18: The last scene in the four years' high school life of seventy-seven students of the Calumet high school was witnessed last night in the Calumet theater when the graduates marched to the stage and took their places on the platform.

James Olds, a Tamarack miner, was instantly killed about 4 o'clock this morning through a fall of rock. The accident happened between the 28th and 29th level of No. 2 shaft of the Tamarack mine.

JUNE 22: Red Jacket will expend at least $1,200 in its Fourth of July celebration.

JUNE 23: Today marks the celebration of the 25th anniversary of the organization of St. Jean Baptiste society and in connection with the observance, occasion was taken to dedicate the parsonage of St. Anne's French church.

JUNE 25: Almost all of the summer cottages at Bete Gris are now occupied and it is thought that by the middle of next month, the season will be in full swing. There are now about 18 cottages at this pretty little resort, which is said to be one of the best in the upper peninsula. It is expected that the season will be one of the best in its history. Contractor Edward Ulseth of Calumet has a force of men making alterations and improvements on his summer cottage at Bete Gris and it is thought these will be completed early next week.

JUNE 27: At a meeting of the members of the Knights of King Arthur, held Saturday evening in the Y.M.C.A., it was decided to organize a "hiking" club, and commencing with tomorrow, hikes will be enjoyed each Tuesday between now and the date set for the local camp, which will probably be held at Eagle Harbor, commencing August 2. Some of the hikes will be for long distances, and will extend over night, the boys taking along blankets and food strapped to their shoulders.

Marcus Stanfel, a trammer, was killed Saturday evening by a fall of vein rock at the 59th level, north side of the Red Jacket shaft branch of the C.&H. mine. The decedent was aged 25 years, and a single man.

JULY 5: One of the first Fourth of July accidents of yesterday, occurred early yesterday morning on the Ahmeek switch of the Houghton County Traction company when one of the Mohawk cars was damaged as a result of running over some dynamite which had been left on the rails. It is thought that the dynamite was placed on the rails merely as a prank, but it came near resulting in severe injuries for those involved.

JULY 7: Plans are being made by a party of well known automobile enthusiasts in Calumet and Laurium to undertake an unusual trip some time next month. According to one of the members of the party who was seen yesterday, an attempt will be made to go from Calumet to Chicago without resorting to any means of transportation than their machines.

JULY 12: A miners' band is being organized by John Glasson, a well known musician and an employee of the C.&H. Mining company, to take part in the big C.&H. miners' parade, which will be held in connection with the annual charity picnic on Saturday, July 30, at the C.&H. park.

The celebration of July Fourth in Calumet and vicinity claimed two more victims yesterday, when John Torvu, aged 56 years, passed away at the Calumet hospital from tetanus poisoning, and Oscar Edward Soronen, the eleven-year-old son of Mr. and Mrs. Alex Soronen, of Swedetown, died from the same cause at the home of his parents. Both were victims of toy pistols, the wounds they received having been in the hands.

Torvu received his wound while endeavoring to explain the danger of toy pistols to his nine-year-old son.

JULY 14: It will be remembered that when William Wesslund, or Granroth, was killed at the North Kearsarge branch of the Osceola Consolidated on April 13 of this year, through an explosion of dynamite, there was found wrapped up in a cloth in the man's digging clothes' pockets, $1,010 in bills.

On going through the decedent's trunk in his boarding house recently, a large glass jar was discovered. Inside the jar was a ball of yarn tightly wound, and when this was unrolled a further sum of $1,013 was revealed.

JULY 18: Calumet & Hecla still holds the distinction of being the only copper mine working at a profit on a conglomerate belt, or lode. Other mines have been started on the same formation, and millions of dollars have been expended in trying to develop profitable ground, but upon either end of the mass of water-worn pebbles (the remnant of an old beach), there is not copper enough to pay for the extraction.

James L. Malone, expert billiardist and former champion pool player of the world, who is giving exhibitions in the copper country, speaks very highly of the talent shown by Wilfred Wilmey, a well known local billiard player. Although Wilmey has been playing billiards but a few months he has become very expert with the ivories.

JULY 19: Copper country farmers have given up all hopes of harvesting anywhere near normal crops this season. It has been the driest season in many years, and in addition to this handicap grasshoppers are numerous and are doing great damage.

JULY 22: The management of the Copper Range railroad has installed electric fans and screen doors on their new Limited train and the train is now practically free from dust. It is the aim of the management to make this run as free from dust as possible, and to this end they have graded the railroad with stamp-sand.

JULY 29: The popularity of the copper country as a hay fever resort is increasing every year. The fresh breezes of Lake Superior afford the surest and speediest relief known for this ailment. Hundreds of people come here to find relief and few, if any, have been disappointed.

JULY 30: Today is miners' day in Calumet. The big annual picnic of the Calumet & Hecla miners is being held and it promises to be an unqualified success. Fine weather is favoring the affair, and thousands of visitors are in Calumet today from all parts of the copper country.

AUGUST 1: The hammer and drill contest between the Calumet and Butte teams for the national championship Saturday afternoon at the Athletic park, in connection with the annual picnic of the C.&H. miners, was won by Butte…

It was one of the greatest hammer and drill contests this country has ever witnessed. The Butte team was composed of more robust and sturdy men than the locals, and the "twisting" of McClain was a feature. Within the first two or three strikes of the hammer McClain was hit on the hand with a hammer, blood flowing freely. He worked gamely, however, despite his injury, and was frequently applauded for the remarkable way in which he changed drills. Becker, who "twisted" for the locals, also came in for much applause for his work in changing and handling the drills.

AUGUST 3: In comparing conditions in the two mining camps, the men from Butte expressed the sentiment that conditions on whole here are superior to those at Butte. They noted the absence here of the dreaded copper water, found at Butte, which destroys the clothing and shoes of the miners in a very short time. Although wages at Butte are higher, living expenses are higher. The men were delighted with the cozy homes of the Calumet miners and general surroundings.

AUGUST 9: George Malovich, a timberman in the employ of the C.&H. Mining company, was killed yesterday while at work in the 57th level, No. 6 shaft, Hecla branch of the C.&H. mine, through being struck on the head with a piece of falling timber.

A skip was being lowered at the time the accident occurred, and the evidence was to the effect that it jumped the track at the 44th level, and that a piece of timber on the skip was dislodged and fell to the 57th level, about 1,300 feet, striking Malovich in its descent.

AUGUST 10: Shrubs and trees in Red Jacket are being destroyed by the codling moth. Especially is this noticeable on Eighth street. Practically all of the trees there are showing signs of damage by caterpillars and the matter is to be brought to the attention of the authorities with a view to stamping out the plague.

It is also said that fires are destroying trees and other vegetation between Tamarack No. 5 and the Lake View cemetery. This is one of the prettiest driveways in this district, and active steps are about to be taken to stop this destruction.

AUGUST 13: Calumet was visited last evening by one of the most severe electrical storms of the season. A fire alarm was turned in from Box 13, a small blaze having been caused by the lightning at the Calumet blacksmith shop but no serious damage resulted.

AUGUST 17: "Maggie Walz, 'Maggie the Finn,' as she is referred to often, is a famous personage throughout the upper peninsula and she is regarded as a saint by the Finns. She came to the Calumet region years ago, a poor girl from the old country. She saved a little money, bought a piece of land and one day a find of ore was made on it. Now she enjoys the royalties from this and also has other good investments in the north country, and all her income is spent in helping her countrymen.

"She has educated them, nursed them and taught them how to make the most of the life in this country. She is a worker for temperance and it was largely her labor that made the town of Detour dry. She is also a worker for women's suffrage."

Norland, the pretty little resort of J.P. North of Calumet, at Copper Harbor is very popular this year despite the fact that it is harder to reach than other points in Keweenaw…Railroad accommodations are available as far as Mandan, via the Keweenaw Central road, from which point Copper Harbor can easily be reached by stage. The many historic associations clustered around Copper Harbor as well as the pretty scenery on every hand make it a favorite with local people.

The older resorts, Eagle Harbor and Eagle River have not suffered in popularity, and have entertained large crowds this summer. The proximity of the Crestview park and the many improvements which have been made have proved a big help to Eagle River and the campers have been numerous at all times.

AUGUST 22: What is believed to have been the first death of a Chinaman in Calumet township, occurred late Saturday night, when Charlie Wong, formerly in the employ of Willie Lee, of Fifth street, passed away after a short illness…

The remains of Wong were shipped to Chicago yesterday for interment, there being a Chinese cemetery in that city.

The bodies of departed Chinamen are not, as is generally supposed, shipped direct to China for burial. In various parts of this country cemeteries are located, where the bodies are interred until a period of time—usually five years or more—has elapsed, when the bones are dug up and shipped with numerous others to China for interment.

AUGUST 29: Mike B. Sunich, a timberman, had a miraculous escape from death this morning when he mis-stepped from "the transfer cage" to the "repair cage" in the Red Jacket shaft branch of the mine, where he was working. After dropping 150 feet he clutched the skip rope and saved himself. His hands were badly burned from the rope, but otherwise he was unhurt, and is being congratulated by his many friends on his providential escape. Had he not clutched the steel rope in his fall through space he would have dropped to the bottom of the shaft, more than a mile deep, and been instantly killed.

While the Keweenaw Central passenger train was pulling into the yards of the Copper Range road in Calumet this morning, some boys threw a rock through one of the windows, striking a woman passenger in the face, cutting her severely.

AUGUST 30: When the last state census was taken, six years ago, there were 28,587 people in Calumet township proper and 70,625 in Houghton county, or Calumet had 40.5 per cent of the total population of the county. If Calumet has grown as rapidly as other parts of the county and there seems every reason to believe it has the same percentage of Houghton county's 88,098 people, would give Calumet township a population of 35,680. Osceola and Tamarack locations, which are really a part of Calumet, although Osceola people receive their mail at a different postoffice, comprise about one half of the total population of Osceola township, and the population of these localities might reasonably be included with that of Calumet. By combining the estimated population of Osceola and Tamarack locations, one half of the Osceola township total, with that of Calumet, it will be found that Calumet has 40,332 (estimated) people.

SEPTEMBER 19: Richard Thomas, one of the oldest miners in the employ of the Calumet & Hecla Mining Co., was killed while at work this morning at the thirty-seventh level pump station, No. 5 shaft, Calumet branch of the C.&H. It is said that while the deceased was "pinching out" some rock, a mass broke away and fell upon him, killing him instantly.

SEPTEMBER 26: The management of the Houghton County Traction Co. has decided to close Electric Park for the season of 1910. The season has been a very busy one, enormous crowds being entertained without accident or disorder.

There were nine open air band concerts, forty-one free dances and fifteen private parties beside many public and private picnics. During the season, the attendance was 46,297 adults and over 4,000 children.

SEPTEMBER 27: One of the most important questions to be taken up at the next regular meeting of the Calumet township board, to be held Tuesday morning of next week, is that of erecting "sign" or "guide" posts at certain cross-roads in the township, denoting the proper side of the road to take in making turns.

These guide posts are being introduced mainly for drivers of automobiles, as well as persons driving teams. It is probable that the board will order the erection of at least two sign posts this year, one at the corner of Red

Jacket road and Calumet avenue just outside the Calumet Congregational church, and the other at the corner of Depot and Calumet avenue.

Both these corners are conceded to be dangerous spots, not only to the drivers of autos and vehicles, but to pedestrians as well. It is believed that with the erection of sign posts, drivers will slow up on approaching and also take the right side of the road.

SEPTEMBER 28: A peculiar malady had taken hold of Alex Gillette, of 3946 Temple street, Newtown. He is suffering from a sort of weakness, which has developed into lassitude, and unless someone is with him all the time, and engaging his attention, he drops off into a heavy slumber, from which he has to be awakened to partake of his meals.

SEPTEMBER 29: With practically all the counties in the upper peninsula busy with highway improvements, it is a question of but a short time when motor cars can be driven all over this region. Ultimately the upper peninsula will have as fine roads as any part of the country.

OCTOBER 7: An interesting visitor to Detroit the past few days was Miss Maggie Walz, of Calumet, Mich., who has just returned from several month's travel in Europe and who came to Detroit for the purpose of interesting local club and fraternal society women in the Woman's Home, College and Sanitarium in Marquette, says the *Detroit Times*.

"I want to have a home for friendless women, old and young, and a place where they may be taught domestic science in all its phases. I hope some day to be able to say the home has solved the 'servant girl problem' in Michigan by supplying first-class maids for housework.

"I went to Europe this summer as a delegate to the world's W.C.T.U. congress and the World's Missionary congress, and after those gatherings went to London, where I fell into a big woman's suffrage convention, and as I am a strong equal righter I took a hand in that," said Miss Walz. "Then I went to my old home in Tornea, Sweden, to see my mother, the only member of my family who has not left the old home to make a new one in America."

OCTOBER 11: Commencing at sunset tomorrow evening and continuing until sunset Thursday evening, the Jewish stores of Calumet will be closed so that Yom Kippur, the Jewish Day of Atonement, may be observed. Preparations have been made for services to be held in the Odd Fellows' hall in the Union building on this occasion, the services being similar to those held in honor of the Jewish New Year about ten days ago.

OCTOBER 20: To be precipitated from midsummer into the dead of winter in the brief space of twenty-four hours is the rather trying experience which has just fallen the lot of the copper country. From the balmy days of the first part of the week, with the thermometer hovering around the 80 mark, it was a rather sudden jar for local residents to wake up this morning to find the housetops covered with snow, and more of "the beautiful" falling.

OCTOBER 26: The girls of Calumet are to have a club room. This announcement was made to a representative of *The News* this morning by Miss Winnifred Salisbury, secretary of the Calumet Associated Charities who has been proffered the use of the rooms over Bear Brothers meat market on Fifth street without charge as a place where Calumet girls, particularly working girls, may gather and spend their evenings. The rooms will be kept open at all hours and undoubtedly will attract girls and provide a place where they may read, enjoy various games and amusements, and cultivate the social side of their natures.

OCTOBER 27:
CALUMET & HECLA PUBLIC LIBRARY REPORT BEST YET SUBMITTED

Circulation of Foreign Books

| | |
|---|---|
| German ................ | 1,203 |
| French ................. | 926 |
| Italian .................. | 1,417 |
| Swedish .............. | 1,215 |
| Norwegian ........... | 519 |
| Finnish ............... | 2,948 |
| Polish ................. | 862 |
| Slovenian ............. | 956 |
| Croatian .............. | 941 |
| | |
| Total ................. | 10,987 |

NOVEMBER 5: Dominic Miglio, residing at 4032 Elm street, has just received a patent from the U.S. patents office, for an attachment for miner's lamps, which Mr. Miglio claims will increase the life of the lamps and add to their usefulness.

NOVEMBER 15: Word has been received in Calumet announcing the death of Edwin J. Hulbert, explorer, which occurred at Rome, Italy, where he had been located during the later years of his life, on October 20. Mr. Hulbert was the discoverer of the Calumet conglomerate copper lode, and the man who made Calumet possible.

Mr. Hulbert was the first white child born in the Lake Superior region, and the oldest pioneer of Upper Michigan. After spending his boyhood at the Soo and at Detroit, he came to the Keweenaw peninsula in 1852, when 23 years of age.

In August 1864, Hulbert employed his brother, John Hulbert and his old associate, Capt. Amos Scott, to open up the lode he had discovered, the first pit being sunk at a spot close to the site of the present No. 4 shaft, Calumet.

Mr. Hulbert surveyed the streets of the village of Red Jacket and made his residence here for a number of years. When the town was originally platted, what is now Fifth street was intended only for an alley, and Sixth street was to have been the main business thoroughfare of the town.

DECEMBER 20: "I do not remember the time when more cases of poverty were reported to the Salvation Army, in proportion to the size of the community, as there have been in Calumet this year," said Adjutant Symmonds of the Calumet corps this morning when discussing the Christmas effort of the army workers.

### Photos, pages 167-170

Page 167: Downtown, Red Jacket. *Dave Tinder*
Page 168: Top: Red Jacket baseball ground (Agassiz Park). Isler. *Keweenaw National Historic Park*
   Bottom: Baseball team. George Gipp, fourth from right, standing. *Superior View*
Page 169: Top: "Karl Lehto ja Karl Virtanen vapaapainissa 1910." *Finlandia*
   Bottom: Boxers in Calumet area. *Superior View*
Page 170: Top: Skiers along Mine Street. *MTU-Copper Country Historical Collections*
   Bottom: Calumet & Hecla Bath House, 1913. *Keweenaw National Historic Park*

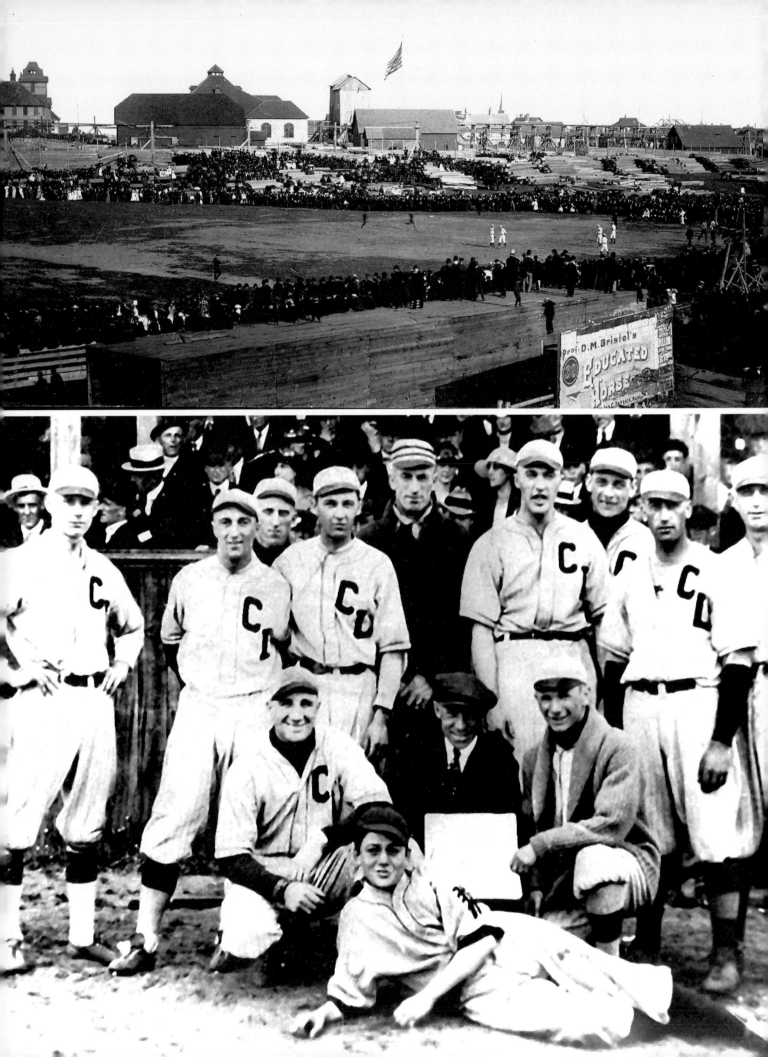

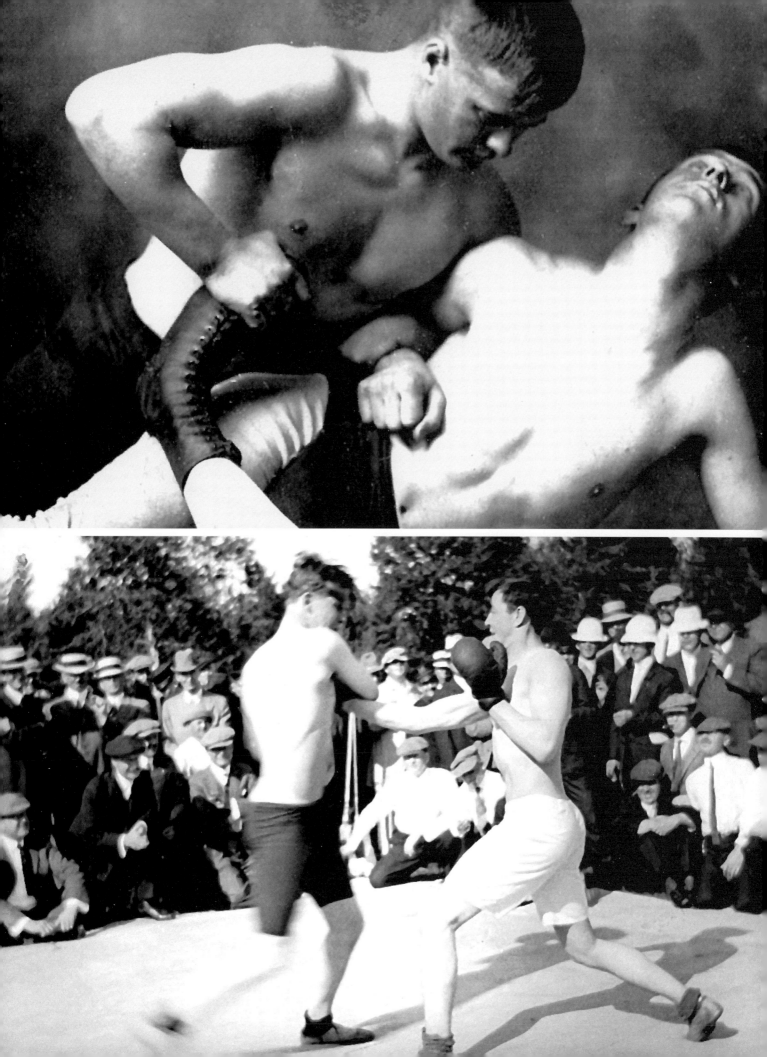

# *Calumet* **1911** *News*

*Mme. Bernhardt…spent the afternoon yesterday in a trip down the No. 2 shaft of the Hancock mine,
the descent and the journey through the interior underground workings being accomplished in safety
and comfort by the celebrated French woman and those in her party.*

JANUARY 3: The directors of the Calumet & Hecla company have mailed to the shareholders of that company and the various constituent or subsidiaries the proposal for consolidation…of following-named corporations:

SENECA MINING COMPANY
AHMEEK MINING COMPANY
ALLOUEZ MINING COMPANY
OSCEOLA CONSOLIDATED MINING COMPANY
CENTENNIAL COPPER MINING COMPANY
TAMARACK MINING COMPANY
LAURIUM MINING COMPANY
LA SALLE COPPER COMPANY
SUPERIOR COPPER COMPANY
CALUMET AND HECLA MINING COMPANY

JANUARY 4: In an editorial entitled "The Top of Michigan," which appears in the current number of the *Journal of Education*, A.E. Winship of Boston, the editor of that publication, describes the schools of the copper country and the conditions under which they are managed…

"The Calumet building cost about a quarter of a million dollars, and has every conceivable appointment and equipment for a nobly modernized secondary school, from the library and laboratories on the scholarship side to all-around shop work on the other.

"Calumet has demonstrated that boys as well as girls can be tempted to the high school, as there are twenty nationalities enrolled in the high school. This is probably the record. Despite the fact that it is a purely mining community, it is the third largest high school in the state. The enrollment is 775 in a mining population of 50,000.

"The public library is so near the high school that it can be used as freely as though it were literally in the building. There are in the library 35,000 volumes, and the librarian could not be more efficiently devoted to the school use of the books if she were simply a high school librarian."

The forty-mile blizzard which raged Sunday afternoon claimed one victim in the copper country, George Law, aged 60 years, proprietor of the boarding house at Mandan, who was frozen to death while driving home from Copper Harbor. The body was found frozen in an upright position in his cutter, yesterday afternoon by a searching party. Law probably had been dead a couple of days.

JANUARY 5: Archie Neubigan, aged about 50, attempted to commit suicide this morning by cutting his throat with a large jack knife, severing his windpipe, the blade passing through and entering the mouth. Dr. C.H. Rodi, who was called, stopped the hemorrhage, later taking the man to the Calumet Public hospital.

JANUARY 16: Ex-Sheriff August Beck, now a special officer in the employ of the Calumet & Hecla Mining company, was pleasantly surprised yesterday when he was visited at his home at 200 Rockland street by a large party of friends from Houghton and other points in the copper country.

JANUARY 19: "My dear, I won't cause you any more trouble," said Mrs. Hilda Olson to her husband, Hjalmar Olson, in Prosecuting Attorney W.J. MacDonald's office last evening, and with the utterance of these words, she fell to the floor of the room unconscious. Realizing that her actions indicated she had taken poison Attorney John D. Kerr, who was present in the room at the time, summoned physicians, who had the woman removed to the Calumet Public hospital, where they worked for three hours in an attempt to save her life. Carbolic acid was the poison used and the woman died at about 11 o'clock.

JANUARY 20: At a well-attended meeting of the members of the Calumet Ski club, held in the Ulseth offices on Fifth street, last evening, it was decided to act on the offer of several business men who are prepared to donate handsomely towards the erection of a big ski slide, provided the members of the club abandon their present hill in the Old Colony district and select a hill closer to Calumet.

JANUARY 27: John Gipp, deputy state game, fish and fire warden, died at 8:30 o'clock this morning at the family residence on Fourth and Hecla streets, Laurium, after suffering from a complication of diseases for several weeks. He is survived by a wife and ten children, as well as two brothers and two sisters. The sons are George, John, Fred, Lewis, Albert, Jacob, Walter and Gilbert.

JANUARY 30: It is estimated that more than 2,000 Calumet people braved the elements yesterday afternoon to witness the ski runners start on their race from Calumet to Houghton.

JANUARY 31: Clerk George Martin of the township, has issued bounties for 2,146 sparrows, Clerk Ellis of Red Jacket for 1,254 and Clerk Martin Prisk of Laurium for 559.

FEBRUARY 1: A movement has been launched by the mail carriers of Calumet, the aim of which is to bring about the abolishment of all Sunday work in the postoffice.

FEBRUARY 2: Old residents are recalling the early days, when snow storms brought with them as much as twelve feet of snow. Those days seem to have passed, but the present snow fall is conceded to have occasional drifts in some places fully ten feet in height.

FEBRUARY 4: "Where hae I ben?" repeated Donald as he came in after one o'clock this morning. "Weel lass, I hae ben oot."

"Where aboot oot?" snapped his wife, "Oot wi' that ramblin, guid-for-naethin' Sandy, eh? I thocht I told ye."

"Wull ye gi' me a chance t' explain masel'? roared Donald.

"I was sayin' I'd ben cot at the St. Andra's concert, wi' the biggest crowd o' Scotch iver gathered under one roof in Calumet…"

FEBRUARY 6: The snow problem is proving a difficult one in the copper country, and in Calumet in particular, where large quantities of "the beautiful" have fallen during the past few days, Street Commissioner Jacka is ably coping with the difficulties as they arise, but finds that in order to make more rapid progress he will have to take on more men. He has decided that he will handle the snow at night as well as during the day, and is engaging more men to work night shift.

MARCH 2: Children should be taught that snow is unclean and, therefore, dangerous to eat, says a medical authority. The pretty white substance is certainly tempting, and the child on its way to school catches from a fence post a delightful handful and eats it. Or some more enterprising youngster mixes a glass of "snow ice cream" and enjoys the pleasure of the soda fountain without the need of a nickel.

A bit later, perhaps, the child "comes down" with diphtheria, tonsillitis or some other disease, although it has not been, apparently, exposed in any way to contagion…

Choose the whitest snow, then let it melt, closely covered, in a perfectly clean tumbler. If you examine this dirty snow water and observe the sand, cinders, hairs and so on you will not again wish to eat even the most attractive snow. The microscopic dust plants, which surely accompany them, are the real sources of trouble.

Can Gotch throw Karl Lehto three times in an hour? That's a question that will be answered at the Lyceum next Monday evening.

It is probable that Lehto will learn more wrestling in his bout with Gotch than in any other contest in which he has taken part. Ever since he landed in this country Lehto has looked forward to a meeting with the champion of all champions, not because he ever dreamed he could defeat Gotch, but because this match will be the greatest in the career of the young Finn, and also because he hopes to make a showing that will surprise his staunchest friends.

Karl Lehto will leave for Finland after the match with Gotch and will defend his title in several of the big tournaments on the other side of the water. He expects to take on twenty pounds in weight before he returns to the United States.

MARCH 4: The following dance program has been prepared by the Calumet orchestra for the party to be given at the Italian hall this evening by the Red Jacket shaft drill boys:

Waltz, "Sweet Memories."
Two-step, "Miss Liberty."
Waltz, "Queen of Beauty."
Two-step, "William Tell."
Waltz, "The Stranger's Story."
Two-step, "Motor King."
Waltz, "Garden of Love."
Two-step, "Jungle Queen."
Waltz, "The Third Degree."
Two-step, "Great Divide."
Waltz, "Poet and Peasant."
Two-step, "Monstrat Viam."
Waltz, "Dollar Princess."
Two-step, "That Mesmerizing Mendelsohn Tune."
Waltz, "A Waltz Dream."
Two-step, "Sweet Italian Love."
Four extras.

MARCH 7: *Informal Vote Favors C.&H. Consolidation*
Calumet & Hecla, Allouez and Tamarack Stockholders Vote on Merger Plan at Annual Meetings
Outcome is Only Expression of Opinion in Regard to Project—Formal Vote to be Taken Later—Osceola Meets Thursday.

Corporal Cowley was working for the village of Red Jacket yesterday at the snow dump in the field between Red Jacket shaft location and the village. He noticed a number of boys playing on the snow banks on the sides of this stream, and while watching them saw one of the number slip over the bank and roll into the mud and water. Mr. Crowley hurried to the spot and pulled him out by the feet.

The boy's head and shoulders had stuck in the mud at the bottom and but for the prompt action on the part of the rescuer, he would surely have suffocated.

MARCH 8: A burglary was committed in Red Jacket last night, the warehouses of the Haas Brewing company and the Ziegler Bedding company, situated side by side in the Red Jacket yards of the Copper Range railroad, being broken into.

MARCH 10: That very natural desire on the part of some business men and others to hasten spring along a little by removing the snow and ice from the sidewalks before their business places was discouraged by Marshal Joseph Trudell today.

So that all may act in unison, Marshal Trudell issued an order requesting everyone to refrain from cutting the ice until a formal notice is given.

Trenches to care for the water have not been entirely completed yet and the village is not quite prepared to remove the snow. The sidewalks are now covered with from twelve to sixteen inches of snow and ice, which, if thrown up on the street, would necessitate a big expenditure for removal, whereas if the sidewalks are left as they are for another week or possibly ten days, the expense would not be nearly as great.

MARCH 11: An explosion in a coal stove, which alarmed the vicinity for a radius of several hundred yards, occurred about 7:30 o'clock last evening in the home of Emil Kokotovich, in the alley way between Seventh and Eighth streets, just back of the residence of Edward F. Cuddihy, who owns the building in which the accident happened.

The theory is advanced that dynamite may have been brought into the home with some kindling wood.

The C.&H. matter now rests pending the action of the court at Grand Rapids, Mich. Street opinion is that Calumet has scored a big victory and has come out of the contest with flying colors. It seems now only a question of time until the consolidation becomes an accomplished fact.

MARCH 14: Yesterday's annual election in the village of Red Jacket was a quiet one. Out of a total of some 600 votes only 163 were cast. Scores of voters, many of them business men, did not take the trouble to vote, because of the fact that there was no opposition to the regular nomination ticket.

The nomination ticket elected is as follows:—

President—Frank H. Schumaker.

Trustees—James McClure, Michael Sunich, and Frank M. Kinsman.

Clerk—John J. Ellis, Jr.

Treasurer—Patrick J. Ryan

Assessor—Joseph Wilmers.

MARCH 16: The five Hungarian societies of Houghton county will gather at Kearsarge on Sunday afternoon to celebrate the anniversary of Hungarian Independence. The anniversary which is to be celebrated is one dear to every Hungarian and it is expected that a large percentage of the Hungarian population of the county will participate.

MARCH 21: Health Officer Robert M. Wetzel's annual report, presented at the annual meeting of the Calumet township board this morning, shows the following:

Scarlet fever cases during the fiscal year, ending February 28, 124; smallpox, 69; measles, 444; diphtheria, 164; whooping cough, 49; typhoid, 13; pneumonia, 81; lockjaw, 3. In addition there were 35 cases of tuberculosis.

MARCH 24: According to the bi-ennial report of the Upper Peninsula Hospital for the Insane, which has just been issued, the percentage of insanity in Houghton county is very small when compared with that of some of the other counties in this section. A total of 113 patients were sent to the hospital from this county from July 1, 1908 to July 1, 1910, or an average of 1.28, for every 1,000 inhabitants.

It is here! No longer need the fair sex of Calumet worry about the style of their Easter gowns, for the harem skirt, the very latest, has arrived. Two of those bewitching creations have made their appearance in Calumet and now that the way is clear others may be expected. Both the Red Front Store and Gately Wiggins company have received 'em and while so far as can be ascertained, this particular style of skirt has not yet been seen on the streets, it is said it soon will be. Whether the latest creation will prove as popular in this city is not for mere man to predict. At any rate, Chief Trudell is not worrying about having any riots to quell in the near future.

APRIL 10: Evidence of what is believed to be a case of infanticide was discovered by employees of the Chicago and Northwestern passenger train which reached this city today, when the burned and badly decomposed body of an infant child was found in a suit case which had been left on the train by unknown persons.

APRIL 13: A notable theatrical attraction has been booked by Manager Cuddihy of the Calumet theater for the evening of April 30, when Madame Sarah Bernhardt, the famous French actress, who is making another tour of this country, will be seen here.

Her first "farewell" tour brought her in 1887. Farewelling was one of the specialties of the man who managed her in those days. But, to be just to his memory and his genius, we should add that Mme. Bernhardt was then in frail health. Now, in her sixty-seventh year, she is in vigorous health.

APRIL 14: August Niemi, John Sarvala, Vertte Juoppa, George Haipinen and Erick Antonen were arrested late last night, following a raid by Marshal Joe Trudell and Nightwatchmen MacNamara and Spehar. The charge is that of creating a noise and disturbance on the North end of Fifth street about 11 o'clock last night. During the mix-up Officer MacNamara was struck over the forehead by Niemi with some blunt instrument, suffering a severe contusion.

APRIL 21: Calumet is to have a Chinese wedding. John Sing, a Fifth street laundryman, appeared in Justice Fisher's court yesterday afternoon, and applied for a marriage license, to wed an East St. Louis, Ill., young woman, who arrived here yesterday to become the wife of Sing. She is not the first white girl to wed a Calumet Chinaman, but such occasions are rare.

Through the efforts of the Calumet Branch of the French Naturalization club it has been ascertained that there are about 1,500 French residents in Calumet township, comprising both sexes.

APRIL 24: John Lee of Kearsarge, known generally to residents of the copper country as the man England could not hang, told a simple yet pathetic story of his life, with incidents connected with the three attempts to hang him and his subsequent life in prison, covering a period of twenty-three years, to a fair-sized audience in the Calumet theater yesterday afternoon.

MAY 2: Calumet will be included in the itinerary of at least three circuses this summer. Announcement has already been received that the big Yankee Robinson show has been booked to appear in this city on June 20 and that two others, the Sun Brothers and the W.H. Coulter shows, will be here on July 23 and 25, respectively.

MAY 22: Prompt action on the part of Otto Decker of the firm of Decker Bros. and John Kivela, manager of the Metropolitan Pharmacy of Calumet, probably will save the life of a man who gives his name as Oscar Koski and his residence as Hancock, who drank about two ounces of nitric acid in Decker Bros.' saloon this morning.

MAY 29: The formal opening of the Crestview park for the season will occur tomorrow. The management of the Keweenaw Central railroad has arranged to run the first excursion trains of the season tomorrow and there will be dancing at the popular amusement place both afternoon and evening.

Electric park, the Houghton County Traction company's delightful resort, was opened for the season yesterday, the concert by the Calumet & Hecla band in the afternoon being the feature.

JUNE 1: Mme. Bernhardt, in company with President John D. Cuddihy of the Hancock mine, General Manager John L. Harris, Dr. J.E. Scallon, who acted as interpreter, and several members of Mme. Bernhardt's company, spent the afternoon yesterday in a trip down the No. 2 shaft of the Hancock mine, the descent and the journey through the interior underground workings being accomplished in safety and comfort by the celebrated French woman and those in her party.

The descent into the mine shaft was made in the big Kimberly skip, which had been specially upholstered and cushioned for the occasion.

JUNE 6: The streets of Red Jacket are being utilized by boys these days as baseball grounds, much to the annoyance of pedestrians who are fearful of being hit by batted or wildly thrown balls.

JUNE 10: Calumet and Osceola townships, the villages of Hubbell and Lake Linden and Keweenaw county have 140 automobiles, costing the owners a total of $247,000, or an average of $1,700 per car. Calumet township has nearly all of the automobiles, there being only a comparative few in Hubbell and Lake Linden, and Keweenaw county.

JUNE 15: With his day's work about completed, and in the act of placing the last piece of timber in position, Alex Ikonen, a single man, aged twenty-five was struck over the head with a large piece of rock yesterday afternoon, in the south branch of the C.&H. mine, and died from his injuries about 7:30 last evening.

JUNE 19: Through the accidental discharge of a 38-calibre revolver, in the hands of Anton Ozich, aged 17, Louis Golop, aged 24, is dead.

JUNE 21: Anton Kowalski, aged 55, a sprinkler in the employ of the C.&H. Mining company, was killed at noon by falling down several levels in No. 6 shaft, Hecla branch of the mine, and Joseph Gonetro, a roller fixer, received serious injuries through being struck by Kowalski's body in its downward flight, he sustaining a fractured skull and severe scalp wounds.

The international convention of the Finnish Lutheran Apostolic churches is being held in Calumet this week, the delegates meeting daily in the Finnish Apostolic Lutheran church, on Pine street, of which Rev. A.L. Heidemann is the pastor.

As a feature of his natatorial exhibition last evening, in the Y.M.C.A. swimming pool, Prof. Callis, who is conducting swimming lessons at the Y.M.C.A. this week, attempted to lower the national Y.M.C.A. record for 25 yards, with one turn. He failed to knock any time off the record established, but swam the distance in 13 3-5 seconds, just 2-5th of a second longer than the record, which is 13 1-5.

JULY 5: One fatality and several minor accidents marred Calumet's celebration of the Fourth yesterday, although the intermittent showers probably prevented a heavier list of casualties.

JULY 15: Through the falling of a pulley block, while hoisting a piece of timber in position yesterday afternoon in the Red Jacket shaft of the C.&H. mine, Jacob Puhek, aged 20, was instantly killed.

JULY 21: Mangled almost beyond recognition, the body of John Bruno, a sprinkler in the employ of the C.&H. Mining company, was picked up at an early hour this morning on the 39th level of No. 9 shaft, South Hecla branch of the mine. It is supposed through some means he was struck by a descending skip, and fell two levels below.

George W. Wickersham, Attorney General of the United States, spent several hours as Calumet's guest this morning. He conversed freely with a representative of *The News*, and manifested the greatest interest in the affairs of the copper country, particularly in the cosmopolitan nature of this community, when told there were about thirty-five nationalities here. He seemed greatly pleased with the fact that so many nationalities live peacefully together here.

AUGUST 1: That one-third of the copper mined in Michigan's copper fields is mined at a loss, is the claim of State Geologist R.C. Allen...

"The question in Michigan is not how much copper have we left, but how long will we be able to mine copper in competition with other districts having large reserves of high-grade ore from which copper can be made at six and seven cents a ton."

AUGUST 9: Hammer and drill teams are being organized by Calumet high school students, and soon after school starts the students will issue challenges to other high school teams in the copper country.

Anton Boggio, a timber boss, aged 47, was instantly killed at 9 o'clock this morning, by being struck on the head with a piece of timber that he and the other members of the timber gang were hoisting into position at the 68th level south of No. 4 shaft, Red Jacket branch of the C.&H. mine.

AUGUST 17: While walking along the eastern bank of the Calumet dam about 6 o'clock last evening, Hjelmar Poikala of Centennial Heights, noticed the clothing of a boy. Surmising that something was wrong, Poikala promptly divested himself of his clothing, and started to investigate the bottom of the dam, which was about five feet deep at this point. After walking around for some time he stumbled over the body of a boy who proved to be Arvid Beck, the eleven-year-old son of Mrs. Julia Beck of Laurium. No one witnessed the drowning.

AUGUST 23: S.F. Loch, proprietor of the Central hotel...arrived home yesterday after completing a 2,500 mile automobile trip through Minnesota, South Dakota, Nebraska, Iowa, Wisconsin and Michigan.

AUGUST 31: Edward Moss, colored, aged about 50, was found dead in a downstairs room in an unoccupied house on the Hutchinson property, Sixth street...He came to Calumet from some city in Georgia about fifteen years ago, and held several positions as barber, chef in local restaurants, acting as cook for Y.M.C.A. campers and local parties of fisherman and hunters.

SEPTEMBER 1: Girls and women must be kept out of saloons in Calumet, according to Miss Luella Burton, of Detroit, a special deputy in the employ of the state labor department. Miss Burton has been here for several days investigating conditions in the stores and saloons, and although she found the majority of the merchants living up to the labor laws regarding the employment of women, and only minor violations in stores not strictly up to the mark, she declares she was inexpressibly shocked at the conditions in some of the saloons conducted by proprietors accustomed to the employment of girls and women, or to girls and women frequenting such places.

SEPTEMBER 5: At the inquest this morning, held by Coroner William Fisher, to inquire into the circumstances surrounding the deaths of William Chinn, aged 43, and John Kurtti, aged 25, who met death in the Red Jacket shaft about 4:30 p.m. yesterday, the jury returned a verdict to the effect that death was due to the men being thrown from the cage in which they were ascending to surface.

SEPTEMBER 9: The following list shows the attendance in the various schools of the district:

|  |  |
| --- | --- |
| High School | 670 |
| Washington | 855 |
| Albion | 227 |
| C. Briggs | 253 |
| E.Field | 170 |
| Florida | 133 |
| Franklin | 324 |
| Garfield | 138 |
| Grant | 316 |
| Hamilton | 216 |
| Holmes | 277 |
| H. Mann | 199 |
| Irving | 285 |
| Jefferson | 160 |
| J. Duncan | 256 |
| Lincoln | 309 |
| Longfellow | 195 |
| Webster | 216 |
| Whittier | 59 |
| Lake Shore | 24 |
| Total | 5,624 |

OCTOBER 6: It is officially announced that the proposed Calumet & Hecla merger is abandoned. The stockholders of the companies involved are notified to this effect by a circular signed by the directors of C.&H., the reasons assigned being uncertainty as to when final decision may be had in the various suits now pending with respect to the merger; and the sacrifice of time which the officials would be obliged to make if litigation were further continued, which time should be devoted to the operation of the properties.

OCTOBER 11: Supt. Edward J. Hall, of the Calumet public schools, has completed the compilation of the attendance for the opening month of the second year, September, showing there was a total enrollment of 5,780 pupils in all grades.

It is interesting to note, according to Supt. Hall's figures, that 180 girl students in the high school have taken up the study of physical culture, while the seventh and eighth grade pupils in school District No. 1, to the number of approximately 400, also are taking the physical culture course. This department is in charge of Miss Judith Botvidson.

OCTOBER 14: Fire, believed to have been the work of incendiaries, broke out yesterday on Peter Coppo's farm, Section 30, and before it was overcome had caused damage estimated at about $3,000. A large hennery, incubators and other poultry equipment, were destroyed. The chicken ranch is a complete loss.

OCTOBER 16: John Harrington, charged with being a common drunkard, was given a jail sentence of thirty days this morning by Justice Jackola without the option of a fine. During his thirty days' incarceration in the county jail, the sheriff will take steps with the U.S. authorities to have Harrington deported.

OCTOBER 17: At a statutory meeting of the Houghton county board of supervisors this morning, the report of the late Mine Inspector Peter Dawe was read. It showed a total of 51 fatalities up to and including September 30.

The fatalities occurred at the following mines and branches: Amygdaloid, C.&H., 4; Baltic, 2; Calumet branch, C.&H., 1; Centennial, 1; Champion, 2; Hecla branch, C.&H., 3; Isle Royale, 1; North Kearsarge, 1; North Tamarack, 2; North Quincy, 2; Red Jacket Shaft, 7; South Hecla, 4; South Kearsarge, 3; South Quincy, 8; Superior, 5; Tamarack No. 5, 3; Winona, 1; Wolverine, 1.

The deaths by nationalities are as follows: American, 1; Austrian, 15; English, 9; Finnish, 11; French, 1; Italian, 10; Norwegian, 1; Polish, 1; Swedish, 2.

The following are the months in which the deaths occurred and number: May, 7; August, 7; February, 6; April, June and July, 5 each; March and October, 4 each; September, 3; January and December, 2 each; November, 1.

OCTOBER 20: The Elks' minstrel show, the initial performance of which was given at the Calumet theater last evening, met the anticipations of the most critical.

OCTOBER 31: The modern Hallowe'en has become a conglomeration of noise and nonsense. It can be readily distinguished by the shriek of whistles, the ringing of door-bells, the buzzing noise of tic-tacks, the blowing of horns, the irate yells of some weary householder as he runs amuck into some wire stretched across the sidewalk, and the screams of youthful marauders as they flee from the grasp of the severely angry taxpayer.

Ingenuity is often used in the construction of devices to make the night air hideous with noise. On Hallowe'en night nerves should be carefully packed between two thicknesses of quilts and tickled with some soothing sleep producer. Pieces of tin, old horns, steam whistles, cow bells and broken glass thrown on the front porch, are some of the devilish devices employed by boys and young men in the full flush of youthful spirits.

NOVEMBER 6: Andrew, the eight-year-old son of Mr. and Mrs. James Ednie, of 63 Mine street, met with a shocking accident yesterday afternoon, while riding behind one of the hacks of the Jacka livery: The boy had his left leg caught in one of the wheels, and before the hack could be brought to a stop, the leg had been practically torn off.

NOVEMBER 13: "You have one of the finest Y.M.C.A.'s from an equipment and architectural point of view that I have seen in this country," said Rev. J.E. Rarrow, of Brooklyn, N.Y., to a *News* reporter this morning.

"There is only one other building that I can liken to it," said Dr. Farrow, "and that is situated in a residential town close to Philadelphia, where the inhabitants are quite wealthy."

NOVEMBER 17: Several inches of snow fell in the copper country last night, adding to the wintry conditions already prevailing and giving convincing proof that winter is here to stay. The last wheeled vehicles have disappeared from the streets and the fire apparatus has been placed on runners, with the expectation that they will be required continuously from now on, the probabilities being very slight that wheels will be used again before next spring.

NOVEMBER 18: Henry Grimmer, aged 49, employed in the H.&P. engine house, of the C.&H. Mining company, fell from a small stool on which he was standing about 7 o'clock this morning. He was rendered unconscious by striking his head on the cement floor, and died about two hours later.

DECEMBER 11: Peter Martin, a teamster in the employ of the Jacka livery, and who also takes charge of the barn at night, was shot at about 12:30 o'clock last night. Fortunately the bullets were deflected from their course by striking the iron bars guarding the windows of the office.

DECEMBER 13: Although it has been frequently stated that Calumet's poor are more numerous this season than for several years, the relief campaign is correspondingly large and if the response is in proportion, there will be no need for any child to face that tragedy of an empty stocking or for any poor mother to explain to her little ones why Santa Claus has forgotten them.

DECEMBER 26: Christmas passed quietly in Calumet. The weather was blustry, but not so much so as to interfere to any great extent with the pleasure of the day, which for the most part was observed as a home holiday with numerous family reunions. In the churches likewise the day was marked as one of the most notable of the year, with special music and services, and exercises for the children.

Early Christmas eve and on Saturday evening also, several companies of carol singers appeared on the streets of Calumet, and carried out the quaint old Cornish custom.

Miss Mary, daughter of Mr. and Mrs. M.M. Morrison, Depot street and Calumet avenue, sustained shocking injuries to her face and body in Chicago, through being burned while playing the part of Santa Claus at a Christmas entertainment. Mrs. James MacNaughton, who was in Chicago, accompanied the unfortunate young lady.

DECEMBER 28: Announcement is made of the formation of the Northland Shoe Manufacturing Co. in Calumet…The company expects to make a specialty of miner's boots and heavy working shoes.

DECEMBER 29: One of the largest iron castings yet turned out at the C.&H. foundry was perfected yesterday when a 15-ton piece of metal to be used in one of the rock houses was completed. Casting the piece was witnessed by a large crowd of interested onlookers.

---

**Photos, pages 177-180**

Page 177: Looking north at the 100 block, Fifth Street, Red Jacket. *MTU-Copper Country Historical Collections*
Page 178: Top: Red Jacket suburb. *RCM/Mantel*
　　　　　Bottom: National Lutheran Church, 8th Street and Elm Street. *Finlandia*
Page 179: Top: Fifth Street parade. *MTU-Copper Country Historical Collections*
　　　　　Bottom: St. John Baptiste parade, Scott Street, 1909. *MTU-Copper Country Historical Collections*
Page 180: Miners going home for pasties, 1912. *Agnich*

---

# Calumet 1912 News

### 1,350 ARE LOST
ONLY 868 SOULS ARE SAVED FROM THE TITANIC
GRIEF OF RELATIVES OF DEAD IS DISTRESSING

JANUARY 23: Word was received in Calumet today announcing the death...at the University of Michigan hospital at Ann Arbor, of Adolph F. Isler, one of the real old pioneers of the copper country.

Cancer of the bladder was the cause of Mr. Isler's death, he having been ill but a few weeks. About ten days ago, upon the advice of local physicians, he went to Ann Arbor to undergo an operation...

He established a drug business in Calumet after closing out his L'Anse store and conducted it for several years, finally disposing of the business to M.J. Canning in March, 1882, to accept a position as chief pharmacist for the C.&H. Mining company. He remained in this capacity for about five years finally resigning to enter upon newspaper work...

Mr. Isler was for several years the sole correspondent for the *Marquette Mining Journal* in the copper country, making daily visits to Calumet and the Portage Lake towns.

About 1900, he resigned his position with the *Mining Journal* to enter the employ of *The Copper Country Evening News* (now *The Calumet News*) in the capacity of city editor. He resigned in 1904 to become Calumet representative of the *Hancock Journal*, which position he held until 1908. He became connected with *The News* for a short period in that year and later was again associated with the *Hancock Journal*. Of late he had been giving his entire attention to his private business.

Mr. Isler was the possessor of one of the finest collections of historical photographs in the upper peninsula, including views taken many years ago and which could not now be duplicated. In the early days, he prepared and sensitized his own photograph plates, something that few photographers of the present day are able to do. A few years ago he supplied the C.&H. library with a complete collection of views.

JANUARY 31: Albert Webber, who arrived in this country from Croatia seven weeks ago, reached Calumet today to assume the editorship of the "Croatian Worker," a semi-weekly publication with offices on Sixth street.

FEBRUARY 1: Of interest to local baseball fans will be the announcement that John J. Halpin, a former professional ball player on the Calumet team, which he captained to victory in 1891, has been made chief of the detective force of Chicago.

FEBRUARY 12: A disastrous fire occurred in Red Jacket last night, when the Ryan estate building, corner of Fifth and Scott streets, was practically destroyed. The ground floor of the building was occupied by William Kehl as a saloon and the second floor by Arthur Landry as a cigar factory. A store room adjoining the saloon was used by the McRandle sisters as an art and book store.

FEBRUARY 16: Roch Mihelich, a local newsboy, has won the first prize offered by the *Saturday Evening Post* for the largest number of copies sold in a given time in Michigan.

FEBRUARY 17: Several new cars have been received for the Mineral Range train service between Calumet and Gay, which will be resumed on Monday morning, as announced yesterday. The cars, a combination baggage and smoker car and a first class coach, have formerly been on the run from Lake Linden to Hancock, but have been thoroughly overhauled.

FEBRUARY 19: It has been known for a long time that women have been frequenting saloons in Calumet. The majority of these are wives, daughters and other relatives of the saloonkeepers in question. However, the law is specific, and states emphatically that under no conditions are women allowed to frequent bar-rooms.

FEBRUARY 21: The Finnish-American Republican club of Calumet, is the name of a new organization launched at a well attended meeting at the Finnish hall on Eighth street last evening. The club will seek to promote citizenship on the part of the Finnish-American residents of Calumet and engage in politics.

FEBRUARY 29: The *Paivalehti*, the local Finnish daily newspaper, has just completed a three days' straw vote taken to ascertain the sentiment of its readers in the copper country in regard to presidential candidates, Republican and Democratic.

The fact that Roosevelt received so many votes and LaFollette ran second is proof that the Finnish-American voters are "Progressives."

The vote is as follows:

| | |
|---|---|
| Roosevelt | 486 |
| La Follette | 72 |
| Taft | 28 |
| Wilson | 4 |
| Harmon | 2 |
| Champ Clark | 2 |

MARCH 27: So successful was the effort of the Finnish Dramatic Club in its portrayal of "Uncle Tom's Cabin" Sunday night in the Calumet theater, that the ability of the

club has become known in all parts of the copper and iron countries, and demands for the club's services have arisen from both quarters.

The club make its headquarters in Laurium, where the initial rehearsals for the recent production were held.

Physical Director Applegate is making arrangements for a girls' game of basket ball to be played Saturday evening at the Y.M.C.A. between a team composed of Hancock high school girls and a local team.

MARCH 28: Red Jacket, as well as Laurium, is to have a carnival company the week of July Fourth.

Here are a few of the attractions that will be seen during the week of the carnival:—

Princess Maxine.

The Educated Mule, known as the fire-fighting mule.

Dyer's big animal show.

Turkey Trot. A mechanical show, on lines similar to the Katzenjammers.

The Tickler—Another mechanical show.

Mutt and Jeff.

The Great Galveston Flood. A mechanical and electrical show, which depicts the flood, the carrying away of buildings by the onrush of water, etc.

Up and Down Broadway, a musical show.

Farley's Midgets.

Richards' Animal and Jungle show.

Dandy Dixie Minstrels.

Doc Turner's side shows.

Evans' side shows.

Dante's Inferno.

The Human Roulette Wheel.

The Ocean Wave.

The Ferris wheel, diameter 96 feet.

APRIL 4: The honor of representing the copper country in the upper peninsula declamatory contest to be held soon, was awarded last evening to Miss Priscilla Hicks of the Calumet high school, whose "John Brown" declamation was accorded first place by the judges at the sub-district contest held in the Kerredge theater in Hancock.

The women of Calumet and Laurium do not intend to let the opportunity to win the right of the ballot slip by without a struggle, when the question of woman suffrage is submitted to the voters of Michigan at the November election. They are already organizing a campaign to be conducted in behalf of "woman's rights" in Houghton and Keweenaw counties and will begin work immediately.

APRIL 8: Alex Jarvinen, known as "The Slippery Finn," claimant of the Finnish wrestling championship, and Zbyszko, claimant of the World's championship in the catch-as-catch-can style, whose work on the mat has been witnessed in Calumet on two other occasions when he met Karl Lehto at the Palestra, have been matched to wrestle at the Palestra, the evening of Saturday, April 20.

Copies of a circular letter, issued by railroads throughout the country in an endeavor to put a stop to the practice of carrying dynamite and other explosives on passenger trains, have been received here.

APRIL 10: Houghton county, as usual, led all others in the number of births occurring during the month, its total being 170, and Marquette county had 107.

The name of the attraction which will hold the board at the Calumet theater April 15 is "Mutt and Jeff" and is founded on the famous cartoons by Bud Fisher.

APRIL 11: Physical Director Applegate has completed the list of attractions for the big circus entertainment to be given under the auspices of the Y.M.C.A. the evenings of April 25 and 26.

The famous chariot race is to be one of the special features and Convict Chain breaker, No. 999, has been specially engaged for the occasion. "The Mid-Air" artist, in dare-devil stunts, "The Roller Skating Bears," and "The Hoboes" in sight-seeing sketches, are other entertainers on the program.

In addition the Suffragette Baseball game, sharp shooting at targets, an animal show, pyramid work, "The Midgets," in their battle royal, club swinging, drills, broadswords and fencing, and a minstrel show will interest all who attend.

APRIL 16:          **1,350 ARE LOST**

ONLY 868 SOULS ARE SAVED FROM THE TITANIC

GRIEF OF RELATIVES OF DEAD IS DISTRESSING

These facts concerning the world's greatest steamship disaster—the sinking of the Titanic, off the Banks of Newfoundland—stood out prominently today as sifted from the wireless reports.

The Red Jacket council held one of the most important meetings in the history of the village last evening, when it met in an adjourned special session and acted on the applications of liquor dealers.

A total of 83 applications were received of which 46 were granted and 37 refused.

The following brewing companies also made application for licenses which were acted on favorably: Calumet Brewing Co., Joseph Schlitz Brewing Co. and Scheurmann Brewing Co., a branch of the Bosch Brewing Co.

The following is the official list of saloonmen granted licenses:

George Adda, Oscar Bayard, Maurice Bandettini, Felix Barsanti, Narcissi R. Bianchi, Ben Blum, Anton Comadero, Angelo J. Curto, Jacob Decker, Edward J. Dunn, John G. Ervasti, Martin Gasparovich, Matt Grahek, Elias Haanpa, John B. Hoffman, William Jones, John Karvala, Fred W. Kramer, Michael Klobuchar, John Knivel, Nathan Lurie, Mike Lucas, Peter Martinac,

G. Martini & Co., Martin G. Messner, Sam Michaelson, Joseph Mihelchich, Sam Mihelchich, James Ormsby, Steve Pytlewski, Joseph Roch, Frank Stepech, Paul Shaltz, Louis G. Sewnig, Frank Scheringer, John H. Schenk, Joseph Stefanac, Marcus Sterk, Joseph Stukel, M.J. Sullivan, Joseph F. Schroeder, John Tambellini, Armido Tambellini, John Tamulewicz, Dominic Vairo and William Yauch.

APRIL 17: A mass meeting of the local Croatians was held in the Italian hall Sunday afternoon to enter a formal protest against the action of the Hungarian government in declaring against the constitution of the Croatian province, the taking away of that province's right of home government, and the action of Hungary in forcing upon Croatia the Hungarian language and introducing it in the Croatian public schools.

Word was received this morning that 54 Finns, bound for the copper and iron countries, were on board the White Star liner Titanic, when she struck an iceberg off the coast of Newfoundland, and grave fears are entertained for their safety.

Four other passengers on the Titanic were bound for Calumet, William Cavines, Joseph Nicholls, Steven Jenkins and William J. Berryman, all of whom left Cornwall, England, to join friends and relatives here.

APRIL 18: The official announcement made today by the Calumet & Hecla Mining company of a voluntary ten per cent increase in wages for the men employed by the Calumet & Hecla and subsidiary companies, affecting over 8,000 men, was well received in Calumet. The increase is in line with the well established policy of the C.&H. of permitting the men to share in the profits derived from higher prices for copper metal, and may also be taken as an indication that the Calumet & Hecla management has confidence in the stability of the present copper metal market.

APRIL 25: A penny is made from almost chemically pure copper, which is obtained by the new electric method. While the "electrolytic" is the purest known copper, the "lake" copper brings a slightly higher price in the market. This is because there is a small amount of silver in all the copper from the Lake Superior regions. It is so small that it cannot be separated at a profit. Silver, however, is a better conductor of electricity than copper, and therefore, for commercial purposes, the "lake" copper is in such demand that it brings a better price.

Chas. Wirkkunen, a miner, committed suicide in a horrible manner in No. 6 shaft, north Kearsarge branch of the Osceola Consolidated, last night, when he laid on two sticks of dynamite, lighted a fuse and awaited certain death. His head was blown off and the upper part of the trunk badly shattered.

APRIL 27: Frank McGee and Michael Doyle of Cumberland, England, arrived in Calumet yesterday and are at the home of Mr. and Mrs. James Doyle, 135 Calumet avenue. They were passengers on the steamer "Lake Erie," which travelled along the northern steamship route from Liverpool to St. Johns, having passed close to the place where the Titanic sunk, and where they saw a number of large icebergs, one of which must have sunk the monster White Star liner.

Calumet high school students received the announcement of the result of the oratorical and declamation contest for the upper peninsula district, which was held last evening at Marquette, with great rejoicing. Ernest Warne of Calumet, speaking on the subject, "Universal Peace," won first place in the oratorical event and Miss Priscilla Hicks of Calumet, declaiming on, "John Brown" was accorded second place in declamation.

MAY 7: One of the best amateur productions ever seen in Calumet will be staged Friday evening in the Calumet theater and Saturday matinee, when "Mother Goose Up to Date" will be produced under the auspices of the Calumet Woman's club.

MAY 15: Car No. 10 left the Red Jacket terminal at 6:16 p.m. When it reached Pine street, it stopped to pick up a passenger. The car started up and had proceeded only a short distance at moderate speed when the little Frederickson girl was seen to run in front of the car, across the tracks, and then run back again, in front of the oncoming car. The child was caught beneath the wheels, however, which passed over her body, inflicting such severe injuries that death must have been almost instantaneous.

MAY 20: Active preparations for the entertainment of the eighteenth national convention of the Finnish Ladies Suffrage league in Calumet on June 24 will be commenced this evening…

Miss Maggie Walz will doubtless be able to give the local committee some valuable suggestions on the manner of entertaining the national gathering, she having attended a number of the conventions. She will be present at the meeting this evening.

MAY 22: The annual May party to be given under the auspices of the clerks of the Vertin Bros. department store at the Calumet Light Guard armory Friday evening probably will prove one of the big social successes of the season.

JUNE 3: G.E. Bromley, a negro porter employed on one of the South Shore trains entering Calumet, was arrested by Marshal Trudell in the Central Hotel early Sunday morning, charged with burglary.

JUNE 4: Matt Mehelich, a trammer, aged 32, was instantly killed about 8:20 o'clock last night. He was struck on the head by a piece of falling rock, while engaged in filling a tram car at the 16th level, south side of No. 3 shaft, North Tamarack branch of the Tamarack Mining company.

The deceased returned to this country from Croatia only a week ago after an all-winter's visit with his wife and three young children.

JUNE 8: Can a man break into a room by passing through an open transom? This interesting legal question probably will be decided in a case now on trial in Calumet.

All of the witnesses testified that Bromley had entered the room, and that he had apparently done so by climbing over the transom.

JUNE 13: The body of an unknown man found at 1 o'clock yesterday afternoon between the Tamarack and C.&H. waterworks on the lake shore, by A.C. Barclay, has been identified as that of Alex Seppola, a single man, aged 34.

The clothing worn by the man was positively identified by Mrs. John Huoki, with whose family he resided at Section 16. Seppola was a farm hand making the Huoki home his headquarters. He was able to do only light farm work, working only a day or two at a time. He was injured at the North Tamarack mine about nineteen years ago, and never recovered sufficiently to enable him to do heavy work. He had been despondent for some time past, and the suicide theory is the only solution. That he blew himself up with a stick of dynamite seems to have been proved beyond question.

JUNE 14: In an announcement of the courses and instructors of the Calumet High school issued for the coming school year, it is stated that the Calumet high school offers six courses of study to its students. Three of these courses prepare for college, and three are practical courses which prepare the student in a general way to take up readily and learn some special line of work after leaving school.

JUNE 21: "I have found nothing radically wrong with the fire protection afforded here, although there is room for improvement," said Edwin R. Townsend, engineer for insurance companies in the middle west, when seen by a *News* representative yesterday afternoon, just previous to his leaving Calumet…

Mr. Townsend praised the C.&H. mining company, especially for its generous supply of water at all fires, given without charge.

JUNE 24: In the issue of Wednesday's *Mining Gazette*, June 19, there appeared a challenge from James Cruse, candidate for sheriff of Houghton county on the Republican ticket, to run H.E. Lean, the well known Red Jacket business man, a foot race. This morning, Mr. Lean handed the following communication to *The News*:

"At present I am not in condition to run a foot race. Later on, if fit, I will run James Cruse or any corpulent man in Houghton county, my age and weight, 100 to 150 yards at one dollar per yard, daylight and Eighth street wood pavement preferred."

JUNE 25: Houghton county's Chinese residents, forty-six in number, have requested and have been granted permission to join in Red Jacket's celebration of the Fourth, thus celebrating jointly America's Independence day and the overthrow of the Manchu dynasty and the establishments of the Chinese Republic.

The forty-six Celestials have expressed a desire to fly the new flag of the Republic alongside of the stars and stripes and have been told that they may do so. They will also have entire charge of the fireworks display, having secured direct from China an assortment of fireworks worth about $600, probably the finest that has ever been shown in this section. Several novel figures have been arranged for, including a giant pyramid of firecrackers, fifteen feet high, and containing about 130,000 crackers, which will be set off simultaneously during the day.

JUNE 28: On Sunday, Rev. D.D. Stalker will complete his twentieth year as pastor of the First Presbyterian church of Calumet, establishing a record for long service which has never been equalled in the upper peninsula and only once before in the entire state.

Dr. Stalker came to Calumet on July 1, 1892, six months after the formal organization of the First Presbyterian church was completed. At that time there were no other Presbyterian churches in the copper country and the Sunday services were held in the Calumet I.O.O.F. hall.

JULY 1: The Wortham-Allen carnival company arrived in Red Jacket last evening, the shows being transported here from Negaunee and Ishpeming on twenty special cars. The sound of the hammer and saw resounded through the streets this morning as various stands were being erected and the tents set up.

The large traction engine of the Wortham-Allen shows, which was unloaded last evening, was mired this morning in the vacant lot adjoining the Red Jacket school. The soft ground and weight of the engine caused it to sink through the sod for about a foot into the earth. Much difficulty was experienced in extricating it.

Red Jacket business men have already completed their decorations and the town presents a gala appearance. The street lights which were turned on Saturday evening for the first time presented a very excellent appearance. They will be lighted again this evening and throughout the entire week, converting Fifth, Pine, Oak and Elm streets into a veritable "Great White Way."

JULY 5: Red Jacket's Fourth of July was a big success. Favored with magnificent weather, thousands of visitors thronged the streets all day long. Included in the parade were the C.&H. band; Company A. Engineers, ninety strong, with Capt. Jesse D. Meads on horseback; the Spanish-American and Civil War vets in autos and carriages; the Red Jacket band, officers of the day and speakers in autos and carriages, members of the village council, township and other officials; the Red Jacket fire department and hose truck, profusely decorated; the Finnish Humu band, and several business men's floats.

"Big" Lydia also was in the parade, and was the exposure of all eyes.

JULY 10: The old fire hall located on Fifth street, just south of Elm, which housed the Red Jacket department during the early days of the village's history, has outlived its usefulness and must give way to the march of progress.

The old fire hall has an interesting history, being one of the oldest structures in the city. It is situated on the only lot in Calumet that carries with it what is known as the "fee of the land," or the right of ownership for any distance beneath the surface. All other property held by private owners in Calumet gives the holder only surface rights.

The old fire hall was erected in 1875, the year in which the village was incorporated.

JULY 12: The Ringling Brothers' circus arrived from Hancock over the South Shore in four sections comprising eighty-six cars of circus material and sixteen sleeping cars for the circus people.

In annexing itself to Laurium the moving municipality of Ringlingville brought a Babel-like population of 1,200 people, 680 horses, forty camels, thirty elephants, and enough wild beasts to start any latter day Noah in the ark business.

JULY 18: According to the reports presented at the recent annual meeting of the Lake View cemetery association, there were a total of 408 interments made in the cemetery from June 1, 1911, to May 31, 1912. This number brings the grand total of persons now resting in the city of the dead up to 7,575.

The Lake View cemetery association was organized in 1894 and the first interments were made in October of that year. Since this cemetery was organized, the old Schoolcraft and the Hecla cemeteries, which had been used prior to 1894 were practically abandoned, except by those whose friends are buried there.

JULY 22: The attendance at Electric park during the Chautauqua assembly last week was very large. The place was declared by all the outsiders, as well as local people, one of the best summer resorts in the entire upper country, not only for its location but for all the different kinds of amusement; devices such as a merry-go-round, three flying-Dutchman, one circle dying wing device, two trapeze, 65 rope swings, 35 basket swings for children, eight boat-lovers swings, and six easy rocker swings.

The company rents the pavilion to any society and for private parties, for dancing or meeting for the small sum of $5.

JULY 25: Calumet and surrounding territory will furnish the stage and stage settings for a series of photo plays and moving pictures to be produced by the Essanay company.

Permission has been obtained to take pictures at the Wolverine, both above and below surface. It is also possible that events of local interest occurring during the next month in this locality may be filmed.

JULY 26: Fresh fish are reported to be a luxury in Calumet today and the big demand which always comes on Friday had to go unsupplied. This applies to white fish, lake trout, herring and all other deep water species.

AUGUST 1: Calumet is to have its first golf tournament next Saturday afternoon on the Swedetown links.

Golfing enthusiasm was permitted to wane in Calumet for several years, until this year, but it appears the tide has now turned. There are five other towns in the upper peninsula represented by strong golf clubs and that Calumet, the largest city in the peninsula, should be without a strong club, has long been a source of deep regret to the devotees of the game here. The links at Swedetown are fully as good as those in the other towns of the upper peninsula and the feeling exists that the game should be featured and promoted in every possible manner.

AUGUST 6: Eli Kuusisto, a miner in the employ of the Tamarack Mining company, residing at the Tamarack dam, was murderously assaulted by an unknown man about midnight last night, and is lying at the Tamarack hospital in a critical condition. His skull is fractured and he has knife cuts about the face and head.

AUGUST 10:
C.&H. TO OPERATE UNDER THE COMPENSATION ACT
MINERS TODAY ARE INFORMED OF GOOD NEWS
A.E. PETERMANN IN ADDRESS AT ANNUAL PICNIC
ALSO STATES AID FUND WILL BE USED FOR SICK EMPLOYEES
PAYS TRIBUTE TO OLD COPPER COUNTRY MINERS
AS THE RESULT OF THEIR INFLUENCE A SPIRIT OF HARMONY AND COOPERATION PREVAILS
RAIN MARS THE MEN'S OUTING

After weeks of preparation, rain today made several of the big features planned for the Calumet & Hecla miners' annual charity picnic impossible of fulfillment.

In the absence of General Manager James MacNaughton, Capt. John Knox presided as chairman and expressed regret that the weather had so interfered with the annual outing. He expressed his appreciation and the appreciation of his company for the loyalty of the men and said he was confident that the good feeling now existing between the company and its employees would continue for all time.

AUGUST 12: George Kasun, aged about 45 years and a well known resident of Calumet, died at the C.&H. hospital yesterday morning at 4:45 as a result of injuries received in falling down a flight of about ten steps into the basement of the Martin Gasparovich saloon on Scott street about 10:45, Saturday evening.

It is stated that Kasun entered the saloon about 10:45 and went directly to what he thought was the toilet. By mistake he opened the door leading to the basement, which was adjoining the other, and plunged to the bottom of the stairs, striking his head against the stone wall and suffering a fractured skull.

AUGUST 15: Buffalo Bill himself, robust, strikingly handsome with gray mustache, goatee and long white hair, occupied by no means a minor place in the day's activities. The famous old scout never put on a better appearance and never sat more firmly in his saddle. Glass balls were hurled in the air and he shot them, rarely missing.

The big concourse of Indians, Arabs, Cossacks, cowboys, cowgirls, fox hunters, cavalry men, and others, peoples strange and people familiar, galloped and thundered through and about the arena, always with the colonel in the lead, or not remotely distant, directing their maneuvers. Except for his snowy locks, no one could ever have been brought to believe that Buffalo Bill was drawing close to his three-score and ten.

AUGUST 22 : Hitting like major leaguers and running the bases like world's champions, the Red Wings, under the captaincy of Thomas Soddy, won the much heralded old-timers' baseball game from the White Wings under Capt. John MacNaughton at the Laurium Driving park yesterday afternoon by the score of 19-7.

AUGUST 26: The announcement today that the mines of the copper country would not be shut down tomorrow to permit the employees to vote in the primary election, came as a surprise and probably will mean a big reduction in the total vote cast.

SEPTEMBER 6: Mrs. Marie Gillet of Scott street, widow of the late Alex Gillet, will leave Monday for Ronchamp, near Paris, France, where she will spend her remaining days. She also hopes that on reaching her destination, which is her birthplace, she may recover at least a portion of a fortune bequeathed to her when a child, but which was stolen from her. Were it not for this hope, it is improbable she would make the trip.

SEPTEMBER 9: The board of education for Calumet township is working out a plan to provide a free night school for the men and youths of this community who work in the shops, mines or stores. It is probable that classes will be organized in elementary arithmetic, covering the four operations, addition, subtraction, multiplication and division, also classes in commercial arithmetic, algebra, geometry, trigonometry, mechanical drawing, elementary and advanced English, letter writing and elementary and advanced bookkeeping.

SEPTEMBER 14: John Watkins, of Calumet, a prominent member of the Michigan Audubon society, a great lover and student of birds and outdoor life, has presented the society with eighty acres of land near Hessel, Mich., to be used as a bird reserve.

"The greater portion of the funds for carrying on our work came from Henry Ford…"

SEPTEMBER 18: The meeting held in the Red Jacket townhall last evening in the interests of equal rights for women was very largely attended.

The Progressives of the copper country will formally launch their fall campaign in Calumet this evening with a big rally in the Calumet theater.

OCTOBER 1: Although overwhelmed Saturday by the Hancock high school eleven the members of the Calumet high school football team are not discouraged. The team will never be in poorer shape than it was last Saturday and when several of the real war horses join the squad, things will look different in the percentage column.

George Gipp may also be seen in the Calumet line up. With Gipp behind the line the punting and forward passes will be well taken care of. Gipp can become eligible by making up a few hours work and the school is waiting to see him in action.

OCTOBER 4: The Greeks of the copper country, of whom there are about ninety, are uncertain as yet as to how the call for reservists issued yesterday by the Grecian consul general, stationed in New York, will affect them. There are many reserves in the copper country and some of them probably will answer the call and go to Greece to fight the battles of their mother country.

OCTOBER 10: Calumet and Laurium and the surrounding towns last evening greeted Col. Theodore Roosevelt, ex-president of the United States and candidate of the Progressive party for another term in the White House.

Despite the fact that notification that Roosevelt would come to Calumet was not received until after 3:30 o'clock yesterday afternoon and that the meeting could not be held until 10 o'clock in the evening, several thousand people gathered at the Palestra and waited, even though they shivered as they waited to see and hear the man who for seven and one-half years wielded "the big stick" in the White House and who aspires to hold that honor for four more years.

Roosevelt's audience, while courteous and interested, was not overly enthusiastic. Many in the far end of the Palestra, beyond the range of his voice, left after they had seen him, but for the most part his auditors gave him the closest attention. His voice is beginning to show signs of rebelling against the strain he is placing upon it, and at times, it was very husky, but notwithstanding the fact that acoustic properties of the Palestra are not the best, most of those present were able to hear him.

"The first plank of the Progressive platform is the right of the people to rule themselves. You men of the mines and great woods—you and each of us asks the right to rule our own individual lives…

"The Progressive movement is a movement for the overthrow of the boss and conditions that lead to bossism in our political life…Most of you know that in any reform movement, we have got to look out for the cranks. We have kept clear of quacks and so have established a platform to the support of which we can ask all to come…"

OCTOBER 14: About eighty-seven copper country Bulgarians met in the Italian hall on Seventh street yesterday afternoon to hear the addresses of the distinguished Bulgarian visitors, and afterward making arrangements to organize a fighting force from among those present, and to contribute to the cost of the war. Other meetings will be held by the local Bulgarians, to discuss means of aiding their country and the other Balkan states in the proposed war with the Moslem army of Turkey.

OCTOBER 23: Ole Nelson met his Waterloo last night in the Italian hall, when he stacked up against Young Wittika, in what was to have been a ten-round exhibition. Nelson lost the match in the eighth round, taking the count of ten.

John Philip Sousa and his band gave two soul-satisfying concerts at the Calumet theater yesterday.

Greatly to the delight of the Finnish music lovers present, and at their special request, the band rendered Jean Silbelius' "Finland" and "Waitz Tristen," as the opening numbers of the second part of the program, having substituted them for "Jewels of Madonna" by Wolf-Ferrari.

OCTOBER 25: Justice Fisher's court room was the scene of an interesting exhibit of copper samples and specimens this morning, a box containing from 200 to 300 pounds, principally conglomerate mass copper, having been entered as evidence in the case of the People vs. Isaac Bletcher, complaint having been issued on the charge of receiving stolen goods.

OCTOBER 26: Yesterday afternoon's public meeting of the Calumet Woman's club was devoted to "Woman's Suffrage." It was held in the Y.M.C.A. assembly room, and was very largely attended by the ladies. A reporter for *The News* happened to be the only man present, but this was due to a desire on his part to earn his salary, as well as to please the ladies. *The News*, by the way, always covers the news.

OCTOBER 28: Socialism was given a severe jolt at the hands of David Goldstein, lecturer at the Calumet theater yesterday afternoon, when before an audience of more than 1,200 persons of both sexes he delivered a stinging rebuke to Socialism as defined today, and its relation to religion.

"Socialism is based upon the materialistic interpretation of history," said Mr. Goldstein, which was the keynote of his lecture.

NOVEMBER 9: The heavy sleet storm of yesterday and last evening did considerable damage in Calumet. The Red Jacket circuit of the Houghton County Electric Light company was thrown out of commission and for about two hours last evening the town was in darkness. The weight of the sleet accumulated on a heavy cable of the Michigan State Telephone company at North Sixth street caused the line to sag until it came in contact with two lines of the Electric Light company, forming a short circuit, which caused both electric light wires to burn through and drop to the ground.

NOVEMBER 20: Already the Calumet youngster has begun to conserve his appetite for the occasion, which is aggravated daily by the appetizing odor of mince and pumpkin pies which mother, sister or grandmother manage to secret in unheard of hiding places until the big day rolls around.

NOVEMBER 23: Moving pictures and vaudeville shows were the subjects under discussion at the regular weekly meeting of the Calumet Woman's Club yesterday afternoon.

DECEMBER 4: Red Jacket is rapidly becoming an electric city. The installation of attractive electric signs throughout the business section has transformed Fifth street into a veritable "white way" and contracts already provided for call for the installation of other similar signs.

Thomas Tunem, who, it was announced some time ago, had arranged for the appearance here this winter of Roald Amundsen, the discoverer of the South Pole, is daily awaiting a definite announcement of the date. The visit of Prof. Amundsen is eagerly awaited by Calumet Norwegians who take pardonable pride in the accomplishment of their countryman.

DECEMBER 11: The Calumet & Hecla and subsidiary mines will round up the year soon to end…The big mine's output will be somewhat lower than in 1911, while the Allouez, Isle Royale and Ahmeek will show an increase. This lessened production is due primarily to the scarcity of the labor desired, a situation that speaks well for conditions, meaning that there is employment for all.

DECEMBER 16: Composite statistics show that of the 328 deaths reported from Calumet, Laurium and Red Jacket in the year which is now rapidly drawing to a close, 36 were of a violent nature and 36 were due to tuberculosis in its various forms, principally tuberculosis of the lungs.

Thirteen of the violent deaths were due to suicide, one to an accidental shooting, one to the taking of poison by mistake, two to scalding, several to falls sustained on the surface and most of the remaining deaths to mine accidents.

DECEMBER 24: The Christmas spirit is abroad. It is everywhere, in the workshop, the store, and on the street, in fact, wherever people may be gathered together. Hundreds of Christmas trees have been delivered in Calumet homes during the past few days, and the majority of these have already been decorated and put in place, a thing of joy and beauty to the children, and a source of pleasure to the grown folks, derived from satisfaction in the knowledge that the younger ones are contented and happy.

DECEMBER 26: Christmas passed away quietly in Calumet, but was nevertheless thoroughly enjoyed. There were no arrests and no fires were reported in Calumet.

DECEMBER 28: The C.&H. public baths have just passed their first anniversary and during the year the bathing privileges which are public, were enjoyed by 41,190 people.

---

### Photos, pages 188-194

STRIKERS PARADE
CALUMET MICHIGAN
AUG. 10 1913

GUY MILLER X

MOTHER JONES X

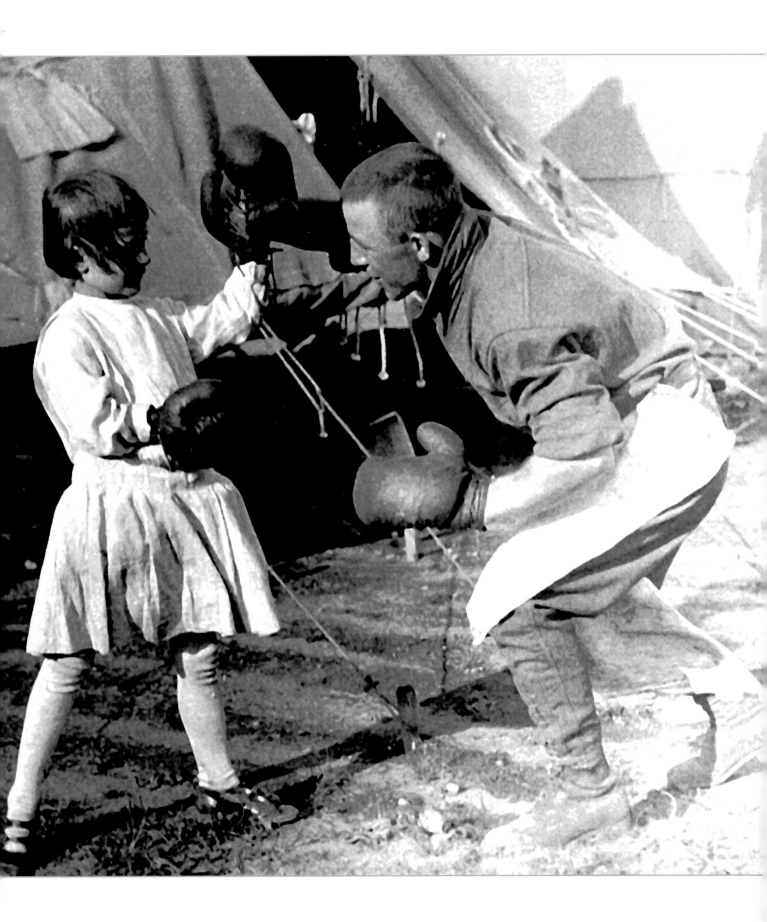

# Calumet **1913** News

*Women continued their activities on the South Range this morning, changing their point of attack from Painesdale to Trimountain. Armed with rocks, eggs and brooms dipped in filth, they waited the appearance of workmen and a shower of missiles followed in the wake of men going to work.*

JANUARY 3: Prosecuting Attorney Anthony Lucas stated today he is very much pleased with the effect of his warning against slot machines and that he is convinced most of the machines have been withdrawn from the saloons, pool rooms, candy stores and drug stores, where they were located.

After he has suppressed gambling in all of its forms, the prosecutor says he intends to go after the "blind pig" evil. Investigations for several weeks have convinced him that there are several unlicensed places in Red Jacket and other towns of the county, where it is possible to purchase intoxicating liquor, and if the proprietors of these places desire to avoid trouble, it would be best for them to close up at once.

JANUARY 8: According to Arthur Behner, the veteran traveling salesman for the American Candy company, Houghton county consumes a greater quantity of candy, in proportion to the number of people there, than any county that he knows of in the entire country.

JANUARY 15: "Water, water all around and not a drop to drink."

Ice and slush blown across the lake by a southwestern wind piled up on the western shore of the peninsula and covered an area of several miles directly over the C.&H. intake pipe early today. Then came almost a dead calm and the slush was drawn down into the intake, completely blocking it.

Because of the shortage of water, many of the public schools of Calumet were dismissed today.

JANUARY 16: The members of the class of 1902 of the Calumet high school recently presented the school with a beautiful picture to be added to the splendid art collection built up since the new school was erected several years ago.

FEBRUARY 11: Mrs. Oliver Richards, of North Kearsarge, aged 54, died at the family residence about 10 o'clock last evening from exposure to cold and heart trouble. She was the wife of the truant officer of School District No. 2.

The primary cause of death was exposure to the cold in last night's storm. The deceased attended the Kearsarge M.E. church, apparently in her usual health. She left the church at 9:30 o'clock to proceed to her home. A blizzard was raging and in the blinding snow and intense cold Mrs. Richards is supposed to have missed her way, as she was found about ten minutes later in a snow bank quite close to the church, exhausted and unable to extricate herself.

MARCH 7: Dan Cusick, who managed the recent dog race on Fifth street so successfully, is planning another event of almost equal importance, which likely will be conducted in the spring, as soon as the weather becomes warmer. Mr. Cusick proposes to conduct a pie-eating contest, open to every boy in the two countries.

MARCH 24: Wind velocity—Fifty miles per hour.
Snowfall—Twelve to fifteen inches.
Temperature—Ranging from twenty-six to seventeen above zero.

…After a heavy snowfall yesterday, turning to a heavy mist late last night, the storm swept upon the copper country from the northeast about midnight, freezing the wet snow on the tracks of the street railway and steam roads and effectually blocking traffic. On top of this came the new snowfall, which was driven by the fierce wind into huge and closely packed drifts.

MARCH 27: County officers are engaged in securing evidence in Sunday night's brawl in Raymbaultown in which no less than ten men escaped with serious and minor knife wounds.

A carload of Ford automobiles, 1913 models, was received today by J.F. Dupont who predicts an unusually active season in this line. Mr. Dupont has accepted the agency for the Detroiter and in addition will handle the Daytona motor cycle.

APRIL 3: Last night's sleet storm played havoc with the copper country's telephone service. It is estimated today that about one hundred Calumet phones, including those on the C.&H. board, are out of commission as a result of the storm

APRIL 15: Elias Kuusisto of No. 5 Beech street, Tamarack, was the victim of an atrocious murder early this morning. He was attacked, apparently with an axe, while he lay asleep in his bed. Mrs. Anna Kuusisto, wife of the deceased, is held at the county jail charged with the crime.

APRIL 18: The average unskilled workman is better off in Calumet than in Detroit, according to James L. Nankervis, former mineral statistician, who arrived here yesterday from Detroit, where he has been located for the last few months. Wages are no better, work is none too plentiful, rents are high and living expenses are greater in Detroit than in Calumet, according to Mr. Nankervis' summing up.

MAY 8: The mine rescue crew of five men being trained by the experts in charge of mine rescue car No. 8, of the bureau of mines, now in Calumet, is receiving very practical instruction.

MAY 9: Twenty-eight students of the Universities of Wisconsin, Minnesota and Chicago in the geology and mining classes, arrived in the copper country on a special car attached to the early morning train and spent the day here studying mine methods and the geology of the district.

MAY 12: Mothers' day was observed in Calumet yesterday. Sermons in several of the churches called attention to the purpose of the day and the white carnation was in evidence on the streets. Owing to the fact that Gov. Ferris designated May 18, next Sunday, as Mothers' day, it is probable the local observance will be even more general than that yesterday.

MAY 13: Next Sunday is the forty-third anniversary of the great Red Jacket fire, the conflagration which practically wiped out the little cluster of houses and business blocks in the original settlement.

JUNE 4: Announcement was made this afternoon that the Crestview park of the Keweenaw Central railroad will be opened to the public for the first time Sunday. The park and Casino have been placed in excellent condition for the coming season.

JUNE 9: The management of the C.&H. band announced the program of three free open air concerts to be given this week at the different mine locations. The first of the concerts will be given this evening, weather permitting, from the new band stand erected by the Osceola Mining company opposite the Osceola mine office, and on Wednesday evening, the band will give the same program at the Ahmeek mine location. On Friday evening an open air concert will be given from the C.&H. mine office lawn.

JUNE 12: The Armstrong-Thielman Lumber plant in Red Jacket suffered a fire loss estimated at $10,000 shortly after midnight.

JUNE 14: There will be a meeting of all C.&H. miners in the Red Jacket town hall at 3 o'clock this afternoon for the purpose of making arrangements for the annual picnic, which likely will be held in the C.&H. park the last of July.

JUNE 25: Complaints are being lodged with the village officers that autoists are disregarding the speed limit provided by the village ordinance and also that many of them fail to have rear lights. Eighth street, with its fine creosote pavement and light traffic, makes an ideal boulevard and the autoists are not slow to take advantage of this fact.

The work of preparing the grounds east of Fifth street and just south of Elm, which have been set apart for playground purposes, is progressing nicely.

JUNE 30: The enrollment in the summer school classes of the Calumet high school and manual training departments is bigger than the total normal enrollment of any other high school in the county. There are 120 students taking academic branches in the high school, seventy-five in the sewing classes and from 250 to 275 in the manual training department, making a total of about 460 in the summer school classes.

JULY 2: Excellent progress is being made with the work on the Calumet-Hancock road...It is expected the work will be completed in about two months and will provide the county with one of the finest highways in the state.

JULY 7: Historians who have attempted to relate the story of the discovery of the C.&H. mine and have described how the conglomerate outcroppings were discovered through the accidental rooting of a hog, invariably experienced difficulty in convincing the incredulous as to the veracity of this legend, but this, according to Paul P. Roehm, is due largely to the fact that they have failed to record the full details of the incident.

JULY 12: In the pay envelopes of employees of the C.&H. and subsidiary mining companies today is an announcement which will be gratifying to the men. It explains that on and after August 1, employees who are injured while working for any of these mining companies will receive benefits from the aid fund of that company, amounting to $1 per day and dating from the sixth working day after injury, payments to continue during the period of disability or until payment under the Employers' Liability and Workmen's compensation act begins.

JULY 16: The tennis courts of the Calumet Y.M.C.A. which are situated in the lot adjoining the Elks' temple to the south are proving very popular with the members of the tennis club and some spirited matches are held there each day.

JULY 17: Before the end of the week, streets in Red Jacket will assume a gay appearance in preparation for the reception of firemen of the upper peninsula who will gather here Wednesday for the annual tournament of the Upper Peninsula Firemen's association. Strings of incandescent lamps, exceeding 2,000 in number, are being strung on Fifth, Sixth, Scott, Elm, Oak and Pine streets and banners will bedeck each thoroughfare at intervals of twenty or thirty feet.

JULY 23: The first general strike in the history of the Lake Superior copper region, which has long been forecasted, became a realization today. Following a mass meeting of the miners, called by local officers of the Western Federation of Miners last evening, the strike was declared this morning, and underground operations have been suspended at practically every mine in the Lake Superior copper region. Local officials of the Western Federation of Miners give the following as the principal demands of the strikers:

Recognition of the union.
Shorter hours.
Increased Wages.
Two men to operate the one-man drilling machine.

JULY 24: Today the shutdown is complete. Every mine in the copper district, excepting one shaft of the Winona property, suspended operations today, this applying to the surface as well as underground work.

More acts of violence occurred in Calumet than in any other town in the district. Following the meeting of miners held in the Palestra yesterday afternoon, men marched to different shafts to see that they were closed and to dissuade all those who would work.

At the No. 2 shaft Calumet, Capt. Thomas Matthews was attacked as he was walking from the changing house to the captain's office and struck on the back of the head with a rock held beneath a handkerchief. He was rendered unconscious, but later recovered. Two aged "sprinklers" were attacked by the men and forced to beat a hasty retreat.

At the engine house, Capt. Henson, who feared the men would attempt to damage the machinery, warned them back and drew a revolver. He later turned the weapon over to Special Officer Beck. At the No. 5 shaft Calumet, several men who wanted to go to work were driven back with clubs and stones. One Austrian trammer, small of stature, was quite severely beaten.

Throughout the evening, up to midnight, the strikers marched from shaft to shaft and found no operations in progress. At the Red Jacket shaft, Nightwatchman Kenneth McLeod had his nose broken and received a cut on the face when he was hit by a rock. At the Hecla branch, Nightwatchman Alex McRae was struck in the shoulder by a rock and received a severe bruise. Other men were attacked by the strikers and more or less severely beaten.

Some of the miners and surface employees not in sympathy with the strike have been deputized and this morning they were stationed at different points to protect property. It is estimated fully 800 or 900 deputies were on duty today.

Near the No. 2 shaft of the Calumet branch of the mine, fresh disturbances broke out about 10 o'clock this morning. At this point a large number of deputies and strikers gathered and finally the deputies were attacked by the strikers who wielded heavy clubs, iron bars and hurled stones at the deputies as the latter retreated to points of greater safety. Several deputies found isolated from the others were attacked and beaten. George Unsworth was struck in the back of the head with a rock and received a bad scalp wound. Edwin Danbom was badly beaten and Simon Trestrall, who is about sixty years of age, was severely beaten. Most of these were removed to the C.&H. hospital for treatment.

From the No. 2 shaft Calumet, the strikers marched to the Hecla and South Hecla departments, closing all of the surface shops before them.

JULY 25: It was announced at the adjutant general's office this morning that practically every company of the Michigan National Guard was either on the way or would entrain for the copper country strike zone as soon as cars were available, in response to the governor's orders yesterday. It is expected more than two thousand militia men will be in the zone before tomorrow night…

Henry Sackerson, a union man employed at the Osceola mine was shot and quite seriously wounded last evening.

A corps of newspaper men arrived in Calumet this morning to "cover" the strike for their papers.

This morning eleven hundred strikers from the Ahmeek, Allouez, Wolverine, Mohawk and Centennial mines paraded to Calumet. It was a peaceable demonstration.

JULY 26: The annual picnic of the C.&H. miners, which was to have been held in the C.&H. park next Saturday, August 2, has been indefinitely postponed.

A statement of the position of the mining corporations was given to the press last evening. "The Calumet & Hecla or other companies under its management will never recognize the Western Federation of Miners. It will receive back in its employ any man not concerned in the violence of the past few days and not an enemy of the company.

"The impression is general that the Western Federation of Miners sent active gun men into the district with the avowed intention of creating trouble. Every leader in the strike is from outside this district.

"Until the Western Federation of Miners began its campaign for membership in this district this was a peaceable community. Twelve watchmen were all the Calumet & Hecla ever needed for the protection of its property and the preservation of life. Since the Calumet & Hecla was organized in 1866 it has had but two labor disturbances…

"Regarding the demands, it has always been the policy of the company to listen to any man in its employ. The demands for a conference that were presented came from men not employed by the company in the name of the Western Federation."

Vice President C.E. Mahoney of the Western Federation of Miners, who is here directing the strike for President Moyer, absent in Europe, this morning took exception to some of the statements made in the official statement of the mining companies.

"We have no gun men in the district," declared Mr. Mahoney. "Such a statement is absurd, and the same applies to the statement that outside men are the cause of the disturbances."

JULY 28: In addition to the moving picture records of important events in the miners' strike, press photographers from all parts of the country are busy in Calumet, as well as many local professional and amateur photographers. Pictures of any of the mines or miners in this district are in big demand.

The corps of newspaper writers who have been in the copper country "covering" the strike has been augmented during the last two days until now practically every large paper in the state and the leading press associations have special correspondents on the ground.

JULY 29: The big demonstration at the South Range mines yesterday afternoon was a picturesque affair and the biggest yet held in that district. The parade started at the village of South Range and proceeded to Painesdale, three miles distant, where a big open air mass meeting was held. At the head of the parade were a few mounted men, a band and Mrs. Nina Gioga, who carried a large American flag. She was followed by a large number of children of eight years of age and up and many women, a number of whom carried children too young to walk.

Unwilling to remain here in idleness until the present labor difficulties are adjusted, 800 residents of Calumet have during the last two days departed for other fields where they hope to find new homes…The tickets are for numerous destinations from Cobalt to California.

So far there has not been a single arrest as an outgrowth of the numerous assaults connected with the beginning of the strike.

JULY 30: Several clashes between men supposed to be strikers or strike sympathizers and the militia have occurred. Shots were fired early this morning at Isle Royale, last night at Isle Royale and in the Hecla & Torch Lake railroad yards at South Hecla, and at Superior yesterday afternoon.

The wife of a loyal miner who resides on Sixth street was badly frightened this morning when a large party of strikers gathered at her home and issued dire threats against both herself and her husband who is working. The poor woman reported the circumstances to the officers in an appeal for protection.

A conference of the mine managers, called at the request of General Abbey, in command of the state troops, was held in Houghton this morning to consider Governor Ferris' proposal for a conference between representatives of the mining companies and strikers.

The mine managers explained that under no circumstances would they take any action that even indirectly might be construed as recognition of the Western Federation of Miners; that the companies were willing to confer with their own employees, provided the men came to them as employees, and that under such circumstances they could not see the necessity of asking the men to send representatives all the way to the state capital.

At the meeting of the Calumet Union in the Red Jacket town hall last evening, addresses were given in English, Croatian, Finnish, Polish and Italian. Croatians were greatly in the majority while Finns and Italians were numerous. A few Englishmen were in attendance.

JULY 31: "The general situation in the strike zone is improving; more men are working and confidence is being reported," declared General P.L. Abbey today. "Some difficulty is being offered on the part of men who have adopted the step of intimidating women and chasing men into their houses. This is the most serious complication that has arisen in the past two or three days," continued the general. "If this continues, we will have to adopt some method to protect the people, possibly by securing a large building in which to protect the women and children during the night, at least."

During the night troops were on patrol in Red Jacket to guard against the carrying out of threats against women and children. This patrol will be continued.

"Mother Jones" is one of the best known strike workers in the country. She is affiliated now with the United Mine Workers, the coal miners' organization, but is active in behalf of other labor unions also. Although eighty years of age she is in good health and has an abundance of energy. She is "on the job" all the time.

Local strikers express their pleasure over the coming of "Mother Jones."

The copper strike has cost the state of Michigan to date, $68,000, according to figures prepared last evening by Major Walter G. Rogers, quartermaster-general. The expense, exclusive of transportation, is $7,500 a day.

AUGUST 1: Hot water, red pepper and various household utensils were used as a supplement to revolvers in a fight between deputy sheriffs and men and women inmates of an Hungarian boarding house at Wolverine mine last evening.

Outside a crowd of 200 mine workers had gathered and the fracas attracted also two squads of state troops. The crowd started to rush the posse and the militiamen drove them back at the point of their bayonets. Joseph Sufonia and Andrew Vince were arrested, charged with resisting the officers and with Sodder they were placed in an automobile and rushed to the Houghton jail.

That the strike is gradually drifting towards its second stage, a period of guerrilla warfare against loyal employees, and property damage by a few of the more desperate of the men, is demonstrated by the supposed attempted dynamiting at the Red Jacket shaft location last evening.

Last night's methods of the troops in keeping the streets clear brought vigorous protests from union headquarters this morning. The riot sticks used by the mounted patrols were especially condemned and in several authenticated instances citizens were struck while passing along the sidewalks and ordered into their houses while sitting on doorsteps.

This afternoon the strikers of the Calumet district held another big parade, going to the woods north of Calumet where a mass meeting was held, addressed by a number of speakers in different languages.

Merchants are fearful of seeing their business reduced to almost nothing if the strike continues very long. "This used to be God's country," said a man who conducts a big retail store, "but they are making a hell out of it with this strike."

AUGUST 2: In their reply to Governor Ferris' proposal for a conference between the mining companies and the Western Federation of Miners, the operators declare the history of the federation is one of lawlessness and bloodshed. Their reference to this is as follows:

"The history of the Western Federation of Miners is well known. That organization was directly responsible for the strike in the Coeur d'Alene district, the Homestake strike, the strike on the Mesaba range in 1907, the recent strike in the Porcupine district in Ontario, the strikes at Bingham and at El Paso, and others which may be recalled. Each of those strikes was accompanied by lawlessness, riots, assaults, violence, destruction of property and bloodshed...

"About the year 1907 this federation with such a record behind it, began to send their organizers from the west into this district."

Railroad officials today report that the exodus of copper country residents has practically come to an end. Up to yesterday it is estimated 1,500 people left Calumet and the north end of the county for points outside since the strike began.

AUGUST 4: Yesterday's mass meeting, attended by approximately 4,000 men, women and children, was practically a repetition of the meeting a week ago. The principal speakers were Vice President C.E. Mahoney, Claude O. Taylor and Homer R. Watterson, president and secretary, respectively, of the Michigan Federation of Labor; Janco Tersich and Guy Miller of the executive board of the Western Federation of Labor.

Vice President Mahoney took occasion to roast the press, local and metropolitan. "Stand firm and defy the insults and onslaughts of the employers through a kept press," he said.

Practically the entire strike zone in the copper country echoed to rifle and revolver shots last night. There were more than the usual number of "shadow shots" by sentries and an increased patrol force of armed deputies was blamed by troop commanders and union officials alike for an almost constant popping of revolvers that lasted from shortly after midnight until daylight.

The movement to bring about a better understanding and organization among the miners and other workers in this vicinity who desire to return to work took definite form at a meeting held this afternoon, attended by representatives of all nationalities who feel that their efforts may be useful in adjusting the labor difficulties and bringing the strike to an early settlement.

The meeting had progressed almost to its completion when Janco Tersich, at the head of a large party of strikers, visited the hall and succeeded in breaking up the meeting. Tersich mounted the platform and criticized the leaders selected by the men, also telling them that their only hope of gaining better working conditions than they have had rests with the Western Federation.

Yesterday was a great day for sightseers in Calumet. They came from all parts of the district, attracted here by the brigade camp with its several military branches, the infantry, cavalry and artillery. The streets in the vicinity of the camp were crowded all day. The battalion drill of Companies B. C. D. and H. of the First Regiment, in the afternoon in the field between the armory and Calumet avenue, which was reviewed by General Abbey and his staff, attracted a big crowd. The drill was almost perfect and it was much appreciated by the spectators.

AUGUST 5: A thousand strikers, hemmed in by a throng of twice that number of curious residents, greeted "Mother Jones" as she stepped from the Northwestern train this morning. At the office of the federation, she settled down in a comfortable rocking chair and talked to strike leaders and newspapermen.

"There is a lot of fun in this life, you don't have to take the sour," she said. "These strike movements are the greatest fun in the world." Union leaders told her the men wanted a speech to which she responded.

"I'm tired boys. Tell them I'm too tired to make a speech to them now, to come back later.

"If these danged working men had any sense, they wouldn't endure their wrongs over night," she said. "They'd vote right and put their own men into office. Then we'd have governors that wouldn't send militia to break strikes. Militia have no business in an industrial dispute; this is not a revolution.

"I'm going out and get the women lined up to keep up their nerve and I'm going to make some of these weak-kneed men buck up and fall into line. I'll take them back into the game instead of letting them sneak out into the grass.

"I'm a Socialist," she said in tones which teemed with pride. "Why shouldn't I be? That is the party that stands ready to help the working man."

"Where is Calumet?"

That is a simple question, apparently. Almost anybody will say it is a thriving city up in the country where they blow open the earth with dynamite and wrest copper there from which makes some people rich and others strike.

"It is a city of about 35,000 people, with lots of hills and some mighty fine roads around about; roads made of trap rock, which is hard to crush either by a crusher or traffic; hence wears well."

But the answer is not there. Calumet is a mirage city—it is here and it is not here. Calumet is the tomorrow of the country—it is always just ahead, yet it is not present. When you are in Calumet, you are in Red Jacket, but when you are in Red Jacket, you are not in Calumet. When you are in Calumet, you are in Laurium, but when you are in Laurium, you are not in Calumet.

A federal investigation of the strike will be made at the instigation of the Western Federation of Labor, a message to this effect having been sent from local headquarters to Secretary Wilson of the department of labor. The department has detailed Walter B. Palmer to investigate the strike and he is now en route to Calumet.

AUGUST 6: A parade, in which hundreds of strikers participated, and headed by "Mother Jones," was formed at union headquarters, and proceeded direct to the Palestra.

"Ferris will hear from 18,000 miners on election day."

"We demand an eight-hour working day and a minimum wage schedule."

"Richest mines but poorest miners."

"Good enough to work for mine operators but not good enough to talk to them."

Another banner, upon which was painted a one-man drill, bore the words, "The one-man machine, our agitator."

AUGUST 7: In her speech at the Palestra yesterday afternoon, "Mother" Jones counselled the strikers to avoid trouble and remain sober.

"I want you to use your brains, not your hands," the quaint appearing little speaker began. "Your masters want you to use your hands. I see they have the militia up here to take good care of you. The militia loves you dearly. You make the guns and the bayonets and they've got to be used on you. I've had experience with the militia. They're not bad fellows. All there is about it, they put on dress uniforms and let you know they'll clean hell out of you if you don't do as they tell you to. Washington and Lincoln didn't want the militia. We didn't have the militia in their days…We were Americans then.

"What's the matter with you fellows? Why don't you elect the right men to public offices? You elect these men and most of you take a glass of beer—scab beer—for your votes and let it sink into your groggy, scab brains. You did that and you elected a scab governor to bring out the militia and camp on company ground and take care of company property. This ground belongs to you.

"Don't carry a gun or pistol. Let the other fellow do that. If he goes after you use your fists and black his two eyes and then he can't see to shoot you…

"You don't need to have a fight here. Just be firm and be peaceful. They can't operate the mines without you… Just use your brains and wake up to the fact that you have the power.

"The capitalists are organized, the doctors are organized, the lawyers are organized and the corporations are organized to skin you. Everyone's been organized right along but you fellows…

"Militarism is becoming an atmosphere disease in America and you see the girls, the poor little things, talking and laughing with the soldiers who come to shoot their fathers…

"The stars and stripes shall float in Calumet and Michigan over free workingmen."

AUGUST 8: Many underground employees of the Calumet & Hecla Mining Co. are calling at the Washington school hall to enroll their names on the registration book opened yesterday afternoon to all those who wish to return to work under protection. It was estimated this afternoon that between 1,200 and 1,300 men have signed the lists…

AUGUST 11: By tomorrow night nearly forty per cent of the state troops, of 970 men, will have left the copper country. This will leave a force of about 1,500 which will remain in the strike zone until it is believed all danger of serious disorder is passed.

"Mother Jones" said that in all the strikes she has taken part in, she found judges, governors and others guarding the interests of the money classes...She advised the men to remain firm and to hold out until the operators grant every concession that is demanded by the Western Federation of Miners.

AUGUST 13: The first assault upon a guardsman in the strike zone occurred at South Kearsarge about 2:30 o'clock this morning when Private John Kelly of Co. E, Detroit, was waylaid about 75 feet from the picket lines.

Headed by the Humu band, playing the air made famous during the French revolution, the "Marseillaise," members of the Calumet local of the Western Federation of Miners today went to the Socialist park near the Natural Wall to participate in a "picnic."

The story of the copper country mine strike, that is the combined stories sent out by metropolitan and local newspaper men who have been "covering" this big news event, has already run into more than a million words. For three weeks, stories emanating from Calumet have been used under display headlines on the front pages of every important newspaper in the country as well as the metropolitan papers of foreign lands.

AUGUST 14: At the Calumet & Hecla mine some 1,800 men had resumed work last week and about 2,000 employees have signed a petition asking that the mines be again started, and they be given work, so it is likely that the present week will see the Calumet & Hecla again hoisting rock. (*Native Copper Times.*)

AUGUST 15: Two dead and three wounded is the toll of a clash between strikers and deputies at Seeberville, a location near the Champion mine, about 5:30 o'clock last night, following an attempt to make an arrest. One man was instantly killed and the second victim died today.
  The dead:
  Diozig Tazan, a striker, shot through hip, killed instantly.
  Steve Putrich, a striker, shot in stomach, died at 11:30 o'clock today.
  The injured:
  John Stimach, a striker, shot in stomach.
  Starka Stepoc, a striker, shot in back and left arm.
  Josh Cooper, a deputy sheriff, struck on head with a ten-pin.

AUGUST 18: Reports of intimidation were numerous and cases of threatening workmen by strikers were reported. Strikers are halting almost every man who carries a dinner pail, and railroad employees have been followed to their work and homes.
  Several women today acted as pickets for the striking miners at the various mine workings of Calumet and vicinity, supplementing the usual activities of the men. At the No. 5 shaft Calumet women intercepted men on their way to work and tried to dissuade them and the same course was followed in the vicinity of the machine shop and blacksmith shop.

The white hearse bearing the remains of young Tazan was followed by a number of girls dressed in white, one of whom, directly back of the hearse, was attired as a bride with long bridal veil. This is a custom at Croatian funerals of young unmarried men, signifying that the life of the departed was incomplete because he had not married. The girls carried flowers and many men in line had twigs of green or bouquets. The numerous American flags in the procession were draped with black. Several signs to the effect that the two victims were murdered by thugs were conspicuous. The Humu band lead the procession.

AUGUST 19: A shipment of 20 cars of rock this morning marked the beginning of shipments to the Calumet & Hecla mills, after a period of idleness of nearly a month.

To revel in fairyland, with its weirdness and daintiness made realistic by Maude Adams and her capable company, was the privilege enjoyed by Calumet theater goers last evening...Her realistic presentation of "Peter Pan" was one of the events in Calumet's theatrical history.

AUGUST 20: There is evidence that the men are beginning to realize what a continuance of the strike may mean to themselves, their wives and families, and this fact has resulted in daily addition to the "Back to Work" force, which has grown, so that today upwards of 3,000 of the employees of the Calumet & Hecla are either working, or have signified their readiness to do so, as soon as conditions underground will permit.
  The strikers, or at least many of them, are reported to be getting tired of waiting for the assistance promised by the agitators, and even if they should be given the one dollar a day, or $26 per month, that sum would look small, alongside what the average miner is capable of earning today.

AUGUST 21: As the officers neared the Calumet postoffice with their fourth prisoner women attempted to take the men from the officers and another small riot ensued. With the women beating and striking at the officers, the fight was carried along Sixth street to the jail. Another woman leaped into the fracas, struck a deputy in the face several times and would undoubtedly have been arrested had not another taken her from the officers. Hysterically, the woman screamed, injecting profanity into her wild ejaculations, and when a company of infantry arrived, she ran before the line, repeating her cries of "scab."

According to a story sent by the *Detroit Free Press* correspondent to his paper, James Waddell, strike breaker, employed by Sheriff Cruse, expects his New York attorney here to start libel suits against members of the Western Federation of Miners and "Työmies," a Socialist paper in Hancock. The basis of the suits will be the plainly spoken accusations of murder made directly against Waddell.

Sheriff Cruse, it is said, will also be a plaintiff in suits against federation orators for declaring that he was responsible for the killing of two strikers at Painesdale and that he deliberately permitted the escape of four Waddell detectives, for whom warrants were issued about or shortly after they disappeared.

AUGUST 22: The following is an editorial in the *Detroit News-Tribune*:

J.H. Walker, president of the Illinois Mine Workers, has sent to the national headquarters of the American Federation of Labor, thence to be distributed to the numerous local headquarters of the country, a statement in which he makes four charges against the character of the Michigan National Guard. The allegations are: (1) That the guardsmen rode down defenseless people on the sidewalks of Calumet; (2) that the guardsmen assailed and abused strikers and members of strikers' families; (3) that a guardsman shot a man in the back while the victim was peaceably on is way home on a country road; (4) that guardsmen mistreated young girls of Calumet.

These charges have roused the indignation of Brig. Gen. Abbey, commander of the brigade in the strike district.

The *News Tribune* knows fairly well the conduct of the guardsmen at Calumet. The fact is that the militiamen gave an excellent account of themselves, and made, many of them, lasting friends among the very strikers whom they were sent to hold in check.

A party of twelve strikers attempted to stop three workmen from going to work at South Hecla this morning. One of the non-union men drew a revolver and fired over the heads of the strikers who immediately dispersed.

The strikers arrived here shortly after 5 o'clock this morning and as the line swung on to Calumet avenue, a troop of cavalry and infantry met and accompanied them. The line of march proceeded to the neighborhood of the armory where the military forces were augmented with a mounted patrol of the signal corps and a troop of infantry. As the strikers marched through the militia, the cavalry fell into line in the rear and retained this position until the procession traversed through the location toward Keweenaw county.

AUGUST 23: John Mitchell, second vice president of the American Federation of Labor, arrived in Calumet this morning to address the copper mine strikers at the Palestra. This afternoon he will talk to strikers of the south end of the district at Houghton. Mr. Mitchell is one of the greatest labor leaders in the world.

"I take pleasure in announcing that the American Federation is heartily in accord and sympathy with the Western Federation in this fight," he continued. "If by chance you should fail, your failure will cause sadness and disappointment among the whole working class of America."

J.H. Walker, representative of the United Mine Workers, reiterated his charges against the militia in a speech at the Palestra this morning, scoring the guardsmen in no gentle terms. Walker admitted that he did not claim all the state militiamen did these things, saying "there are a number of good men among them, but I'm not going to throw bouquets to the enemy in a war like this."

Moving pictures showing the strikers and strike sympathizers in their monster parade from the Palestra in Laurium on Sunday, July 27, the first Sunday of the strike, as well as other views taken in Calumet at about that time will be shown at the Royal theater tomorrow.

AUGUST 25: With the resumption of mining work in five more shafts of copper country mines this morning, a total of seventeen shafts are now in operation. This is considered strong evidence that the strike is rapidly weakening.

Non-union men are prevailing upon strikers to return to their posts and the result of this action is productive. Men are continually leaving the union ranks. Sentiment even among the most radical is changing and the futility of the strike is everywhere apparent.

Strike pickets, both men and women, attempting to gain access to No. 15 shaft of the Calumet & Hecla this morning were halted by deputies and for a time trouble was imminent. A detail of guardsmen arrived and the strikers dispersed.

Three revolver shots were fired from an automobile containing a party of men at a guard near Tamarack No. 5 shaft Saturday night at 10 o'clock. None of the shots were effective but they struck rocks that showered the sentry. A sergeant of the guard was lying in wait for the return of the auto when he was struck by a rock thrown by someone in the rear and knocked unconscious. Members of the guard fired upon a man seen running over a rock pile.

AUGUST 26: The Calumet strikers marched out on the Centennial Heights road and met a delegation of women, children and strikers from the north end of the district, and joining forces they proceeded to Pine street, where they were met by General Abbey and staff, a big company of infantry, a troop of cavalry, the signal corps patrol and deputies. From that time on General Abbey and his staff in an automobile led the parade. Following the general were the infantry and cavalry and strikers, while the signal corps patrol and deputies brought up in the rear…

The strikers were not permitted to march to any of the shafts and few men with dinner pails were met throughout the parade. The demonstration had no effect as the loyal employees went to their work as usual. They were unafraid, having confidence in the strong combined force of troops and deputies to protect them should any attempt be made to reach the shafts.

AUGUST 28: Women strike sympathizers again came into prominence in the strike zone this morning when they pummeled workmen returning to their homes from the mines, took dinner pails from non-union men and otherwise made displays…

A non-union man at Osceola was beaten early this morning and only the timely arrival of deputies saved him from serious injury. Another workman was set upon by a band of women at Mine street and Red Jacket road and after taking his pail from him, he was struck several blows in the face.

Another workman, provoked by women who followed him several blocks toward Red Jacket, exchanged a few light blows with the leader. This angered the dozen or more women in the crowd and a free-for-all melee followed, in which the women were bested. This development is perplexing as the men are timid in resisting such attacks.

AUGUST 29: The reduction in the force of troops, which now number 1,000, to half the present strength, and the mounting of more men probably will occur early next week as the result of a meeting of the military board this afternoon. The action is made necessary by the excessive cost of maintaining troops in the district. The daily expense to the state for the present force is approximately $2,300 and it is intended to reduce this to $1,000.

AUGUST 30: Spitting in the faces of deputies and hurling curses and slurs upon the civil guards were the tactics resorted to by women strike sympathizers today, and a situation that is becoming more perplexing each day now faces the authorities.

Women continued their activities on the South Range this morning, changing their point of attack from Painesdale to Trimountain. Armed with rocks, eggs and brooms dipped in filth, they waited the appearance of workmen and a shower of missiles followed in the wake of men going to work.

SEPTEMBER 2: As a result of a clash between a force of eighteen deputies and a body of from 150 to 200 strikers, women and children, near the North Kearsarge mine yesterday morning between 6 and 7 o'clock, Margaret Fazekas, aged fifteen, lies at the point of death in the Calumet Public hospital, with a bullet wound in the head.

Nineteen hundred men, and about eight hundred women and children marched in the sweltering heat to the Palestra Sunday to hear the addresses of President Charles H. Moyer, of the Western Federation, Vice President C.E. Mahoney and William Davidson, a member of the executive council….

President Moyer in his address characterized the eight-hour day as the vital issue of the strike, but devoted practically all of his address to asserting the right of the miners to organize and demand recognition.

SEPTEMBER 3: Near riots were again frequent in Calumet today. Between 6 and 7 o'clock a large party of strikers and women sympathizers gathered on Oak street and hurled stones, tin cans, other missiles and filth at men on their way to work in the C.&H. mine and later at deputies and soldiers. Kate Rajacich and Annie Fabich were arrested as a result of the morning riot on Oak street…

On Scott street at the corner of Sixth and close to the Y.M.C.A. another small riot developed at about the same hour, strikers and women making attacks on non-union men with stones and cans.

Centennial Heights is reported to be a veritable hotbed of minor disorders by Maj. Britton, in command of the Signal corps who recommends that a force of militia be maintained in that location continually, day and night. Non-union men have been frequently assaulted with stones, gardens despoiled and a campaign of intimidation pursued, with the result that many men in the locality, willing and desirous to go to work have been brought to a state of destitution because they have been afraid to work.

It is said that women have been the ringleaders in terrorizing families of non-union men. It is comparatively common to see men on their way to work from that locality with their backs covered with filth thrown at them by the women.

SEPTEMBER 4: The streets of Red Jacket were patrolled both by mounted men and foot soldiers. Women strike sympathizers gathered as usual, intent on interfering with men going to work, but they were not permitted to do any damage, being held in check by the guards. One woman in particular insisted on starting trouble, but she was driven back each time.

SEPTEMBER 5: Clarence Darrow, of Chicago, the well known attorney for labor interests, and President Moyer of the Western Federation of Miners arrived in the copper country this morning. Mr. Moyer's return here had no special significance, but Attorney Darrow came for the express purpose of making an effort in the direction of a settlement of the strike.

Arbitration is the plan of Mr. Darrow. He would have the operators appoint two representatives, the men select a like number and the governor act as the odd member of the committee himself or appoint some other person suitable to both the operators and the men.

For two weeks, women strike sympathizers have been attacking men going to and from their work. Now the wives of workmen or other women of their families have come to the assistance of the men. They escort them to and from work and are prepared to mix matters with women sympathizers should the latter seek trouble.

SEPTEMBER 8: Women pickets continued their activity today, though the presence of civil and military authorities prevented possible disorder. A band of twenty or more women congregated near the Union building, and men, on their way to work, were jeered as they passed. One man was stopped, but deputies came up and he was allowed to proceed. The women continued to yell "scab" at him until he had gotten beyond earshot.

While the attention of the women was directed toward a man near the C.&H. foundry, a woman, about 60 years of age, passed with her husband, a non-union man, whom she was escorting to work. As soon as they saw her, the women strike sympathizers hurled jeers and insults at her. Fearing injury to her, the woman was taken to her home in an automobile by deputies.

Strikers, women and children to the number of 1,862 paraded yesterday in Calumet previous to holding mass meetings in three halls, the Italian, Dunn's and Red Jacket town hall.

James McNaughton, general manager of the Calumet & Hecla Mining company, and Governor Ferris discussed the upper peninsula mine strike situation at Big Rapids Saturday afternoon.

Fire early this morning caused a $2,500 loss at the Vienna Bakery, owned by Wickstrom & Keisu and located at the corner of Pine and Fourth streets.

SEPTEMBER 9: Miners employed at Red Jacket shaft were threatened last night by strike sympathizers and asked for a military escort to take them to their homes at Centennial Heights. Several privates and Capt. Blackman of Co. I, accompanied the men to their homes and as they were returning, a crowd of women accosted them.

Capt. Blackman urged the women to disperse and when the guard proceeded toward Red Jacket shaft, a shower of stones and clubs followed them. Private Woodward of Co. L was struck upon the head by a woman and slightly injured. Similar encounters at Centennial Heights have been numerous and soldiers have frequently been compelled to submit to aggravating treatment rather than use force in compelling the women to disperse.

Says a Big Rapids dispatch: "There is no sign of any change in the situation," declared Governor Ferris at the conclusion of his interview with general manager MacNaughton, of the C.&H. and A.E. Petermann.

"Mr. MacNaughton came voluntarily. I went at him from every angle I was able to conceive, and I am convinced that not only from what he said, but from the condition now prevailing that the companies will not change their attitude one iota. One thing that did encourage me was MacNaughton's declaration that he believed the operators would have to come sooner or later to the 8-hour day, and I gathered the impression that he was not particularly opposed to it."

SEPTEMBER 11: Capt. Bernard Goggia's (Goggin's) little band of women strike pickets, whose militant acts are believed by the officers to have been the fruitful cause of numerous early morning disorders in the Calumet district, came to grief this morning, when six of their number were arrested, two charged with assault and battery, and four with resisting and interfering with officers in the performance of their duty. With them two men, Goggia and one James Aggarto, were arrested, also charged with resisting and interfering with officers.

Wilbert Kissaneimi, an employ of Edward Ulseth, was the victim of this morning's attack. He has no connection with the strike and has been little interested up to this morning.

He was proceeding along Fifth street on his way to work today with a dinner pail under his arm, and alleges he was attacked, when near the Western Express office, by a large party of strikers and women. He charges that Annie Clements and Maggie Aggarto assaulted him.

Deputies saw the affray, which amounted to a small riot and hastened to the scene to arrest the women. The deputies in turn claim they were attacked by the four other women, Maggie Vranish, Kate Grentz, Mary Klobucher and Tres Kiriza and the two men, the six attempting to liberate the two women already arrested.

Edward Danbom and Frank Traven of Calumet, non-union workmen employed by the Calumet and Hecla, were given compensation by the industrial board this week for injuries received at the hands of the strikers during the strike troubles July 24. The men sustained injuries to their heads and other body bruises. This is the first instance of the state board granting compensation to workmen injured during labor troubles.

SEPTEMBER 12: About four hundred and fifty strikers and women sympathizers marched to Calumet from Kearsarge, Copper City, Ahmeek and Allouez about 5 o'clock this morning and contributed to the disorders which the officers have had to contend with every morning for several weeks. The visitors were in an ugly mood as was the disturbing element, among the local strikers and tense scenes followed one another in rapid succession.

SEPTEMBER 13: The American flag became a feature in the clashes between the strike pickets and soldiers this morning, when the former, impressed with the belief that the soldiers would not attempt to defend themselves in the face of the American flag, waved "Old Glory" in the faces of the cavalrymen and horses.

SEPTEMBER 15: Saturday, at a conference at Lansing, Clarence Darrow, representing the miners, practically agreed to forget the question of organization. He wanted the matter of arbitration put up to the operators without any organization tag to it. This move Governor Ferris agreed to.

SEPTEMBER 16: The strike investigating committee of the Copper Country Commercial club is progressing satisfactorily with its mission. That they might see for themselves what actual underground conditions are, the members of the committee went underground in the Calumet branch of the C.&H. mine this afternoon.

"Big Louie" Mollainen, the world's biggest man, died here this morning shortly after 6 o'clock, death following a convulsion. Big Louie was 7 feet 8 inches tall and was beyond all question the biggest man in the world. He traveled for two seasons a number of years ago with Ringling Bros.' circus, but he was naturally shy and he did not enjoy the life. He returned to his home and took up farming, his farm being located in Hancock township near the location of Salo.

SEPTEMBER 19: The calendar of cases to be tried next Wednesday in Justice Fisher's court is as follows:

Ben Goggia and James Aggarto, resisting an officer.

Annie Clements and Maggie Aggarto, assault and battery.

Yanko Terzich, creating a noise and disturbance. (Village ordinance.)

George and Veronica Beijan, (man and wife), intimidation.

John Kuchnich, resisting an officer.

Mary Staduhar, intimidation.

Carlo Denasich, resisting an officer.

Anton Severinski, intimidation.

Rokus Polian, resisting an officer.

Anton Minagetti, resisting an officer.

Peter Siankivich, intimidation.

John Bohte, intimidation.

John Severenski, Frank Tolenz, Mike Duganza, John Siotovich, Joseph Staduhar and Vasil Kruzensovich, assault with intent to do great bodily harm less than the crime of murder.

Alec Verish, carrying concealed weapons.

Peter Ostermann, creating a noise and disturbance. (Village ordinance.)

The investigating committee of the Copper Country Commercial club, composed of Edward Ulseth of Calumet, John T. Black of Houghton and Henry L. Baer of Hancock, held its first session today in offices in the Quello block.

SEPTEMBER 22: One of the most flagrant and uncalled for acts of violence in the copper strike occurred at Centennial early this morning, when Joseph Richards and son, William Richards, both residents of that location, were attacked and beaten by a body of strikers, while on their way to work.

The injunction issued by Circuit Judge P.H. O'Brien, on petition of the mining companies, prohibiting parading and picketing of strikers while men are going or coming from work in the mines, or interfering in any way with mine employees, was roundly scored by speakers at a meeting of strikers in the Italian hall yesterday afternoon. One of the speakers compared it with Russian methods and declared it would do credit to the czar.

SEPTEMBER 23: Legal advisors of the Western Federation of Miners today took their first steps to counteract the effect of the sweeping injunction granted Saturday afternoon by Judge P.H. O'Brien of the twelfth judicial circuit, restraining the strikers from molesting workingmen, interfering with the operation of the mines, holding parades during the hours when men are on their way to and from work, picketing and similar activities.

SEPTEMBER 26: Sheriff James Cruse and James A. Waddell will return tonight from Lansing, where they conferred this week with Governor Ferris on the strike situation. The sheriff informed the governor that he could control the situation and that infantry troops could be removed.

SEPTEMBER 27: "Mrs. Annie Clemenc, parader, grasped a flag from a parade flag-bearer and attempted to use it as a 'Talisman' to cause the soldiers to permit her to lead the parade forward into forbidden territory. On finding this 'Talisman' ineffective, she held the flag horizontal in front of her and refused to move back at command of soldiers and dared them to molest her 'through the folds of their own flag.'" Uncontradicted verbal testimony of Mrs. Annie Clemenc.

SEPTEMBER 29: After announcing the dissolution of the injunction Judge O'Brien declared formally that the court stands ready to protect the rights of persons who want to work, but at the same time he feels the strikers have a right to organize and to make an effort to persuade others, peaceably, to refrain from work for the purpose of strengthening the position of the strikers.

SEPTEMBER 30: Picketing prevailed in Red Jacket, Swedetown and other Calumet locations and rough tactics were employed by strikers and women sympathizers in their effort to prevent men from going to work.

Dinner pails were jerked from the hands of men by the women and the contents strewn about the pavements, while the strikers who stood in the rear jeered and shouted at the workmen. The arrest of two women and a man was the result of the fracas in Red Jacket.

About 5 o'clock, women and strikers congregated on Seventh street, between Oak and Portland, and the disturbance was centered in that block. A workman came into view, and a woman approached him and jerked his pail from his hands, pounding it on the pavement. He retaliated with a blow from a club and despite howls and hisses, he continued on his way.

Later two men, carrying dinner pails approached Seventh street from Portland and they were immediately surrounded by women and strikers. The pails were pulled from their hands, the irate women beating the receptacles on the walks.

General P.L. Abbey and staff officers arrived on the scene and Annie Clemenc, one of the leaders, was arrested. As she was being taken to the Red Jacket jail in an automobile, strikers hurled jeers and hisses at the military officers. She was arraigned before Justice William Fisher, charged with intimidation.

It is alleged she incited women and strikers to attack a man on his way to work on Seventh street this morning and that the man was badly beaten and his dinner pail smashed. She demanded an examination which was set for Monday, and was released on bonds of $300. She protested her innocence of any crime and stated she would be on the picket line again tomorrow morning, starting at 4 o'clock.

OCTOBER 1: Ten arrests, nine in Newtown and Swedetown and one in Laurium, are the tangible evidence of this morning's strike disorders in the Calumet district.

One of the most serious of this morning's disturbances occurred near Swedetown. Annie Clemenc, the central figure in yesterday morning's disturbances, it is said, is alleged to have spit in the face of a man on his way to work this morning, and was promptly placed under arrest by a deputy.

OCTOBER 2: With the apparent intention of compelling the cessation of operations at Allouez, strikers from Ahmeek, Mohawk and Copper City directed their intention to that location this morning. A crowd of about 1,500 strikers and women collected on a road leading to the mine and attempted to prevent miners from going to work.

Not including the cases of those arrested today, there have been 191 arrests since the copper strike was declared on July 23. Of these there have been only six convictions, while forty-eight cases have been dismissed, one found not guilty and 136 are pending.

OCTOBER 3: Parading and picketing at the mines marked today's activities of strikers. Disturbances were eliminated generally and the only arrest was made at Red Jacket where a crowd of about 300 strikers and women refused to move when ordered to do so by military and civil officers.

The band congregated on Pine street between Seventh and Eighth, with the apparent intention of intercepting men on their way to work at Red Jacket shaft.

Deputy Walter Rost, while in the act of forcing a striker to move, was assailed with an awl and before he could defend himself, the instrument was thrust into his scalp three times. Rost recovered and retaliated with a riot-stick.

OCTOBER 6: The sympathetic strike of school children in Keweenaw assumed large proportions this morning when nearly 500 pupils of the Ahmeek, New Allouez and Mohawk schools remained at home. About 9 o'clock they formed a parade, marching about Ahmeek, yelling and employing tactics similar to those of their parents in a federation demonstration.

OCTOBER 9: The action of the state supreme court yesterday in continuing in force the injunction granted by Circuit Judge O'Brien on Sept. 20 prohibiting picketing and violence, had a good effect this morning, and except for a disturbance in Keweenaw county, the strike zone was free from disorder.

Strikers numbering several hundred formed several parades in Red Jacket about 6 o'clock, and each division, headed by American flags, traversed the streets for two hours. Other Federation men were conspicuous on the corners in anticipation of the non-union demonstration which was planned for this morning. Fearing a serious clash, Mrs. John Kocjan, the leader of non-federation forces, was prevailed upon to abandon the plan and she consented. Notwithstanding this, nearly a hundred women who had been mustered to take part in the procession, appeared on the streets. No attempt was made to form a parade.

OCTOBER 14: An eight-hour working day will be in operation in every mine in the district by next January. No minimum wage scale can be established in justice to all of the mines. The one-man drill has come to stay. A system for hearing grievances and complaints will be arranged, the mine managers agreeing to set aside a day or half day each week for that stated purpose, agreeing also to investigate and adjust every legitimate grievance with all possible speed.

…A table in the report shows the dividends and assessments on 70 mines that have operated in the district from 1849 to 1910. During this period, only 14 mines have paid back more money than was invested.

The committee has also investigated thoroughly the question as to whether or not there existed in the Copper District of Michigan a "blacklist" of any kind and whether discharge from one company would affect the possibility of obtaining re-employment with some other company. On this point the committee finds that, beyond any question, there has never existed, in recent years at least, any agreement of any kind between the various companies, nor has there existed any blacklist of employees.

President C.H. Moyer returned to Calumet today, bringing assurance that aid is forthcoming from unions in the east and west. In the face of this, however, strikers are soliciting food, clothing and cash of local business men.

Children attacked the home of a non-union man at Centennial Heights last night and several windows were broken.

OCTOBER 15: The copper mining companies of the Michigan copper district have uniformly pursued the policy of attempting to look after the welfare of their employees along certain well defined lines. All of the companies operating undertake to provide medical attendance and hospital service for the employees and their families. The company had built a substantial library building and equipped it with some thirty-five thousand volumes. The company built at a cost of fifteen thousand dollars, a modern bath house, containing tubs, showers and a swimming pool twenty-six feet by forty feet.

In 1904 the Calumet & Hecla Mining company started a pension fund.

OCTOBER 18: The most desperate of the numerous acts of violence in connection with the copper strike was an attempt to wreck the Keweenaw Central train with dynamite at Copper City at 10 o'clock this morning. The dastardly attack was directed against a detail of mine guards, forty-two in number, who were en route to Mohawk, from a New York agency.

OCTOBER 22: Thwarted in their attempt to prevent men from working, strikers continue parading or gathering in groups in the mine locations, where they gaze upon lines of men returning to their posts. The mood of the federation men indicates that they are satisfied that the strike is a failure, and to add to this realization is the gradual departure of agitators and leaders for other parts. Four of the so-called leaders left the zone this week.

While the strikers admit there is nothing to be gained by parading, it has become known that leaders insist upon a daily demonstration. According to the strikers the alternative of refusing to parade is the levying of a fine, and it requires only a few fines to exceed the small amount paid in the form of "strike" benefits. These parades which formerly occurred in the business sections are now extended to the resident districts.

A meeting of strikers was held yesterday afternoon in the Italian hall at which leaders are said to have urged the men to greater activity. The influx of outside workmen was also called to the federation members' attention by agitators who urged their auditors to be more alert. However, no mention of strike benefits was made at the meeting.

Workmen are arriving in the copper country in such great numbers that the places of strikers, who have not already gone back to work will be filled shortly. While many of the federation men who have been conspicuous in the conduct of the strike, or who have resorted to violence, will eventually be forced from the district, others who have been less active may be given positions.

Annie Clemenc, charged with assault and battery is being tried by jury this afternoon in the court of Justice William Fisher. It is alleged she spit in the face of a man on his way to work.

OCTOBER 23: A parade, headed by "Big" Annie Clemenc, traversed in this section and two of the strikers are said to have left the ranks to pummel the officers. Hirsch was pounded over the head with a club and was taken to the hospital.

OCTOBER 25: The South Shore train, due to arrive in Calumet at 8:50 last night, was the object of an attack by armed men, supposed to be strikers, just as it began to climb the Quincy hill, and several volleys of shots were fired at two coaches bearing outside workmen to the C.&H. mine. The shooting continued for a distance of three-quarters of a mile, and passengers aboard the train claim that scores of shots were fired.

OCTOBER 31: Strong pressure is being brought to bear by the non-Socialistic class of Finns in the copper country on the Finnish strikers to return to their work and break away from the influence of the Finns that are identified in any way with the Socialistic element.

NOVEMBER 3: Instead of calling a mass meeting to take a vote of the Finnish strikers as to whether they were in favor of withdrawing from the Western Federation of Miners and returning to work, as originally proposed, it has been decided by a committee of prominent leaders of the Finnish nationality to conduct a "buttonhole" campaign, in which Finnish workmen may be reached individually instead of collectively. A conference of leaders was held Sunday morning when this plan was adopted.

NOVEMBER 6: The shipment of three carloads of meat to the district yesterday marked the arrival of the first consignment of food to the strikers that was promised by imported agitators at the inception of the strike…Merchants, who have been accepting federation orders, are much concerned over the reported establishment of the Hennessy "cost" stores. Some of these business men have been making a concession of five per cent to the union, and in this manner they have financially assisted the strike. Many of these merchants have also been recognized as leaders among various nationalities and the effect upon them is obvious.

NOVEMBER 8: Cavalrymen stationed in Calumet this morning arrested ninety-nine strikers and sympathizers on a blanket charge of violating the injunction. The arrests were made on Calumet avenue near the M.E. church, between 6 and 7 o'clock. A parade, headed by "Big Annie" Clemenc, proceeded north from Red Jacket road, and when a number of workmen passed the marchers yelled and cursed them, it is alleged. It is also charged that the strikers attempted to go into the colony of imported workmen for the purpose of intimidating them.

NOVEMBER 10: Resolving that the organization of the Western Federation of Miners must be eliminated from this district, thousands of citizens of the copper country are signing their names to the membership lists of the Citizens' Alliance, an organization which will pledge itself to assist in ending the strike of the underground employees of the copper mining companies.

Mrs. Annie Clemenc, the Calumet woman strike leader, who rejoices in the sobriquet "Big Annie," was convicted in the circuit court this morning of a charge of assault and battery, preferred by Wilfred Kesaniemi.

Mrs. Clemenc had taken an inconspicuous position in the rear of the court room but her height and the red hood she wore made her prominent. All eyes were turned on her when the verdict was read. At the announcement "guilty" "Big Annie's" head dropped as though it had received a blow. But she gave no other sign.

NOVEMBER 11: The Red Jacket fire department was called out at about 12:30 o'clock last night to quench a small blaze in a porch attached to the third floor of the Maggie Walz building on Pine street. As far as can be ascertained the fire was caused by a single piece of cordwood which ignited the floor beneath it, causing a blaze which scorched the woodwork, and had it not been for its prompt discovery, might have caused a much bigger fire.

NOVEMBER 26: Phillip Mihelcich, aged 21, a striker, lies near death in the Calumet Public hospital as a result of an encounter this morning between strikers and mounted police in the employ of the Calumet & Hecla Mining company. Mihelcich is suffering from a bullet wound alleged to have been inflicted by Lloyd Lyman of Ypsilanti, a former member of the signal corps. The shooting occurred in a hall at the bottom of a stairway leading to the Union headquarters on Sixth street. According to Lyman, two shots were fired as a call for help after he had been assaulted and beaten with clubs.

DECEMBER 1: Today marked the introduction of the eight-hour shift in the mines of the copper district, and with it, a general rumor of a movement of federation members for their old positions is prevalent. It is believed that more men would desert the federation ranks but for fear that bodily injury might be done by the more erratic members.

The old fashioned paynight, which frequently ended in a dozen or more justice court cases, came pretty near being re-enacted in Calumet Saturday. Bad feeling growing out of the strike and the spirit of hilarity mingled together on the streets. There were several clashes between union men and non-union men, but hardly any of them ended disastrously. Several shots were reported from different parts of the town but no one was injured and as far as can be ascertained, only two arrests have been made.

There were several clashes Saturday night and yesterday between strikers and the wearers of the little white and red buttons, "Citizen's Alliance," but so far no arrests have been made.

DECEMBER 6: Plans are being prepared for a big celebration in honor of the completion of the new Colosseum skating rink. It is recognized that the Colosseum, as it stands, represents a much greater outlay than the actual expenditures of the Central Storage company, its builders. The work was done by the C.&H. Mining company at cost and in this manner, a big saving was made possible.

DECEMBER 9: The parade of Calumet, Keweenaw and Torch Lake citizens who have allied themselves on the side of law and order, which it is claimed will include at least 10,000 marchers, will leave the Calumet Light Guard armory at 1 o'clock tomorrow afternoon, prior to instead of after the big mass meeting.

The enthusiasm which marked the mass meeting in the Armory Sunday still prevails throughout the county and the campaign to rid the district of agitators is on in earnest. The wave of indignation is apparent in every direction. Business men, fraternal organizations and other bodies of men met yesterday or last night to formally take a stand against the agitators, and all of these will attend the meetings tomorrow at the Armory or at the Amphidrome in Houghton.

Business houses and saloons will be closed tomorrow afternoon and every opportunity will be given the populace of the county to attend the mass meetings. Not a wheel will turn from noon until 6 o'clock and the greatest demonstrations ever witnessed in the copper country will be the result.

The good women of this community who always have been on the side of law and order are asked by the leaders of the women's societies of the different churches to engage in silent prayer in their homes from 10 to 10:30 a.m. tomorrow. The women of Calumet have also been asked to meet at the Calumet Congregational church from 1:30 to 2:15 tomorrow afternoon to engage in a similar prayer service.

Citizens of Red Jacket will do their utmost to make tomorrow afternoon's mass meeting in the Calumet light guard armory a success. Practically every business house in the village, including the saloons, will be closed from 12 o'clock noon tomorrow for the remainder of the day, so that the proprietors and employees may join in the big demonstration for law and order.

DECEMBER 10: Officials of the American Federation of Labor advised President Wilson today that they have been informed an attempt is about to be made to banish labor organizers from outside states from the copper fields of Michigan.

The information transmitted to the president came in this telegram from Charles H. Moyer, president of the Western Federation of Miners, sent from Calumet, Michigan:

"Mine operators and Citizens' Alliance have announced that Wednesday they will give all representatives of organized labor from outside the state twenty-four hours to leave. If they fail to do so they will be sent out of the district in a manner most convenient and effective. We urge you to give this the fullest publicity and bring it to the attention of the president of the United States immediately so the constitutional right of the labor representatives may be protected."

Judge P.H. O'Brien this afternoon granted a writ of injunction, to attorneys of the Western Federation of Miners, restraining members of the Citizens' Alliance from interfering with or molesting, by threats or intimidation, any of its members, organizers or officers of the federation.

Aroused to a high pitch of enthusiasm over the overt acts committed in the county, through Socialistic teachings of outside agitators, nearly a thousand Torch Lake citizens went to Calumet today to attend the mass meeting which formally protested against the presence of trouble breeders in this district. The contingent was headed by the Lake Linden band. A special Copper Range train and extra cars were chartered and the towns were practically deserted. Business houses and the mills and smelters were closed to give employees an opportunity to attend the meeting.

DECEMBER 11: "If you expect blood and thunder to come out of this meeting, forget it. Come clean in this strike. We can't take a chance of coming out of it with foul hands," declared A.E. Petermann, in his address at yesterday's Citizens' Alliance meeting in the Colosseum. "We can't get down to the same class as these hirelings of the Western Federation of Miners. Stop and think…You can't afford to have any blood on your hands."

"Six months ago people of the copper country of Michigan would have been proud to say in the outside world, I am from the copper country of Michigan. We had a happy community. There were no murders, no disorders, no lawlessness. See what has happened in four months. It has been brought about by whom? By men who have been hired to come here and spread their poisonous slime."

DECEMBER 15: The grand jury investigation of acts of lawlessness and violence that have characterized the strike since its inception, July 23, formally began today in the circuit court.

C.H. Moyer, president of the federation, was the first to be summoned before the grand jury…It is the intention to summon every officer, agitator and organizer of the federation now in the district, so sweeping will be the probe.

DECEMBER 18: The number of men still striking in the copper country is estimated at from 2,500 to 3,000. To enlighten these men show them the folly of their lost cause and encourage them in resuming their old positions before they are given to outside men, is the aim of the business men. To do this business men propose to hold a series of mass meetings in different localities of the copper country, Calumet, Red Jacket, Laurium, Wolverine, Kearsarge, Ahmeek, Allouez, Mohawk and towns in other parts of the county.

Speakers will address the men of different nationalities in their own tongues, will advise them that unless they return to work between now and January 1, their old positions will be gone. The strike will be over and they will merely be men out of work, with no money to go elsewhere to seek employment.

General Manager James MacNaughton of the Calumet & Hecla Mining company, this morning agreed at the solicitation of a committee representing business men in the northern part of the copper country district to extend the time limit until January 1 for former employees who are willing to return to work.

DECEMBER 20: Many of the strikers are beginning to realize that the five months of strife, hardships and poverty, in many instances, have come to naught. Goaded on by fiery speakers, they have continued the struggle, vainly but untiringly to do as they were bid by oily-tongued orators who have but recently left the district.

Businessmen have come to their aid, and wise counsel is prevailing. By coming in personal contact with the strikers, by inspiring them with the truth of the situation and by convincing them that nothing can be gained by adhering to the oath of the federation, conservative citizens are playing a major part toward bringing the struggle to an end.

DECEMBER 23: While Calumet has hitherto been known as the most cosmopolitan mining camp in the United States, the influx of men from all parts of the country will tend to make it the home of subjects from practically every country in the world. To the thirty-odd nationalities that were represented in the underground department, twelve have been added through the strike.

The new comers are Bohemians, Welsh, Swiss, Dutch, Greeks, Armenians, Roumanians, Malteze, Brazilians, Turks, Lithuanians and Belgians. For a greater part, they represent the 1,500 men who have been imported to Calumet in the past ninety days.

DECEMBER 24: A holocaust unparalleled in the history of Michigan and ranking with the Iroquois theater fire and such catastrophies as the sinking of the Titanic in its frightful import, occurred about five o'clock this afternoon in the Italian hall on north Seventh street when approximately eighty lives, mostly children, were lost.

An alarm of fire from box forty-five contributed to the confusion which existed in the building at the time. There was, however, no fire in the Italian Hall building.

During a Christmas entertainment arranged for by the Ladies Auxiliary of the Western Federation of Miners, a man, who has not been apprehended, called "fire."

Instantly there was a rush for the narrow exits and at the bottom of the stairway, the little children were jammed into one solid mass, from which none could emerge.

All efforts of those at hand to stop the onrush of the hundreds in the room were futile, and one by one the little lives were snuffed out. More than seventy-five dead have been accounted for, and it is estimated there are from six to eight others who were removed to their homes by parents and friends before the authorities arrived on the scene.

Practically every death was caused by suffocation, physicians assert. Although many of the bodies were mangled, none were so badly disfigured that identification would be impossible.

There were approximately 600 persons, about ninety-five per cent of whom were children, in the hall during the Christmas entertainment, which was arranged for by the women. Some estimates place the number at 700. Two versions of the accident are given by those in the hall.

Mrs. Annie Clemenc, president of the Auxiliary, stated immediately after the accident that she was on the stage together with some of the other ladies, who crowded toward the front of the building, really pushing to the platform. Those in charge of the distribution were doing their utmost to restrain the crowd and restore order when some man appeared at the door and called "fire."

Instantly there was a rush for the door. Efforts to stem the tide was ineffectual and the onrushing crowd poured through the door, into the narrow hallway and down the stairs, many of them to their deaths. The jam in the rear of the hall was almost as bad as in the stairway and as the excitement grew the children, many of them mere infants of less than five years of age, fought and struggled to gain the street.

At the bottom of the stairs the little ones were literally buried beneath a mass of humanity, a living tomb.

Mrs. Caesar, of 421 Kearsarge street, Laurium, states that she was in the hall and close to the man who called "fire." She identifies him as a large man, with a heavy beard.

When the cry was first heard, she realized its danger instantly and reached up and grasped him by the shoulders in an effort to make him sit down. He escaped her grasp, however, and soon the cry of fire was taken up by others. The rush of the excited children towards the door was frightful to behold, Mrs. Caesar asserts. She herself succeeded in getting her little daughter out of the building to safety after semblance of order was restored.

Another woman who was in the building asserts the man who called "fire" spoke in two languages, first in English and then in Austrian. She asserts she heard the cry distinctly both times.

Others who were in the building assert that the call was heard from the stage as well as from the doorway, after the alarm first came.

Words are inadequate to describe the terrible scene in the Italian hall immediately afterwards. The dead lay on every side, old men, women and little boys and girls, their bodies huddled up into heaps and strewn out along the chairs on the floor, on the stage, in a little office adjoining the main hall and in a kitchen at the front of the hall and beneath the stage.

Hurried calls were sent out and soon every physician in town was on the scene. The living were separated from the dead and many that were thought to be dead, recovered from the first shock and were taken to the C.&H. hospital.

The parents and relatives of the dead surged into the building and many of them took charge of the bodies of their loved ones before the authorities could take charge of the situation. The moaning of the injured mingled with the sobs of bereaved parents, brothers, sisters and friends. Palled by the horror of the calamity, the officers quietly circulated here and there, helping where they could.

After the injured were cared for, the dead were gathered together and removed to the Red Jacket town hall where temporary provision was made to keep them until identification was made.

At the rear of the building, there is a narrow fire escape, but few were aware of its presence, and those who did seek to escape from the rear part of the building did so by jumping from the windows of the kitchen. Perhaps a dozen reached points of safety in this manner, the distance being so short that few were seriously injured.

Several hundred of the children escaped from the building over the fire escape, better order having apparently been maintained there than in the front part of the building.

A large proportion of the victims were of the Finnish and Slovenian nationalities.

Of the dead, John P. Wessalo, probably is the best known. He held the office of secretary of the Finnish Mutual Insurance company and had important business interests here.

The Italian hall is a comparatively new building, having been erected about five years ago. It was supposed to be well prepared for emergencies of this kind.

The front stairway is about eight feet wide and leads up from an entrance perhaps ten feet from the doorway. At the top of the stairway is a small landing, perhaps eight feet wide by six long. Leading off from this is the main doorway. There is a room a little larger than the landing at the top of the stairway and connected with it by a narrow doorway. Here occurred almost as heavy a loss of life as at the foot of the stairway and in the stairway.

At the end of the building furthest from the street is a spacious stage, elevated from the main floorway about three feet. It was here that the distribution of Christmas presents, clothing, shoes, etc. was being made. Beneath this stage and considerably lower than the main floor is the kitchen, rather spacious in size. There were several deaths in this portion of the building, but not as many as elsewhere.

In the face of the appalling calamity that has befallen the community, the strike which has occupied the attention so completely for months has been completely forgotten in Calumet. Residents of the entire district have been touched to the depths by the horror of the situation and are a unit in their desire to extend the quickest possible relief to the sufferers.

DECEMBER 27: In deporting Charles H. Moyer from the copper strike district last night, the president of the Western Federation of Miners says he was shot, beaten and dragged through the streets of Hancock, and guarded on the train until 2 o'clock this morning when the train reached Channing, Mich.

"I was assaulted in the Hotel Scott, Hancock, by members of the Citizens' Alliance and a Waddell-Mahon gunman," Moyer said. "I was terribly beaten, shot in the dark and dragged more than a mile through the streets, threatened with death and hanging and finally placed aboard a train about 8:50 last night."

---

## Photos, pages 212-215

Page 212: Citizens' Alliance, Fifth Street, Red Jacket, looking north. *Finlandia*

Page 213: Top: Italian Hall, December 25, 1913. *MTU-Copper Country Historical Collections*

        Bottom: Italian Hall victims. *Houghton County Historical Society*

Page 214: Top: Funeral for Italian Hall victims at Finnish Lutheran church, Pine Street. *Houghton County Historical Society*

        Bottom: Funeral for Italian Hall victims. *Voelker*

Page 215: Top: Italian Hall burials at Lakeview Cemetery. *Voelker*

        Bottom: Mass grave, Italian Hall victims at Lakeview Cemetery. *Houghton County Historical Society.*

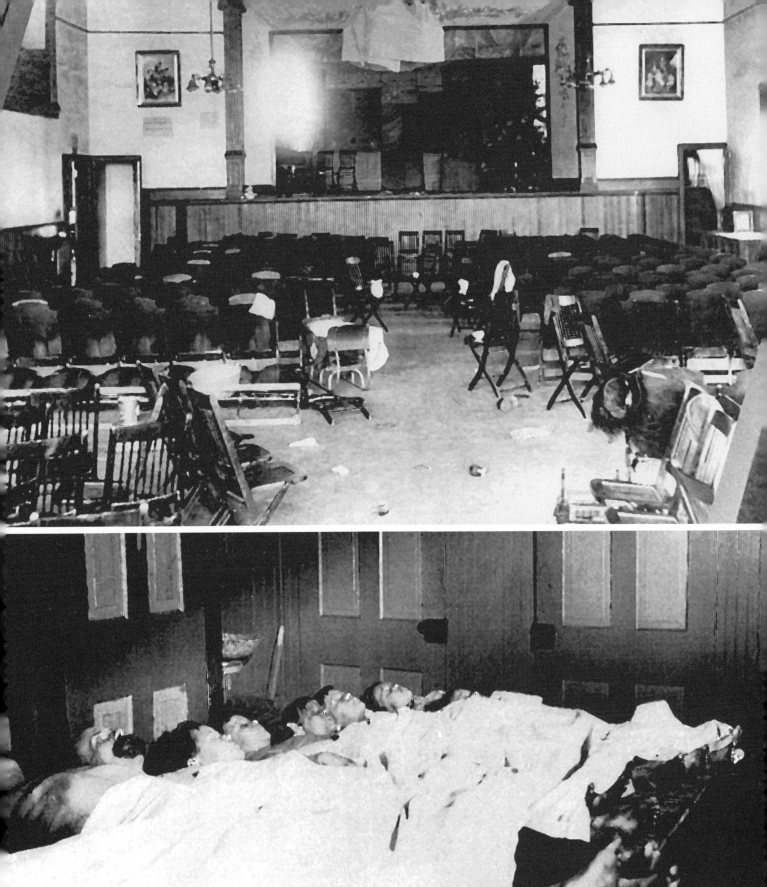

## Acknowledgments

Anne Agnich, Thomas Baker, Tony Bausano, Brad Beaudette, Dave Bezotte, Calumet Theater, Copper Country Historical Collections (Michigan Technical University Archives), Coppertown USA, Jack Deo, Debra Ebert, Donna Effinger, Kathy Engel, Finlandia University Archives, Frank Fiala, Col. Jack Foster, Graphic Communications Center, Paul Grathoff, Greenlee Printing Co., Cathy Greer, Carol Griffin, Kaye Hiebel, Brian Hoduski, Houghton County Historical Society, Weikko Jarvi, Brian Juntikka, Big Kahuna, Michael Karni, Donald Kelman, M.D., Keweenaw National Historic Park, James Kurtti, Robert Langseth, Larry Lankton, Gene La Rochelle, Don Litzer, Kelly Lucas, Bill Luokkanen, Dave Maki, Peter Manzini, Hugh Mechesney, McMillan Memorial Library, Phil Meyers, Marquette County Historical Society, Michigan House, Joe Mihal, Clarence Monette, Kevin Musser, Erik Nordberg, Randy's, Olaf Rankinen, Maggie Robinson, John Ryan, Shute's, *t.kilgore splake*, Superior View Photography, Wisconsin Historical Society, Arthur W. Thurner, Charles Voelker, Watertown Public Library, Wrangler

## Selected Bibliography

Avery Color Studios. *Copper Country—God's Country*. Au Train, Mich.: Avery Color Studios, 1973.

Benedict, Harry. *Red Metal: the Calumet and Hecla Story*. Ann Arbor, Mich.: University of Michigan Press, 1952.

*Calumet News* and *Calumet Evening News, 1908-1913*. Available complete at MTU Archives and in part at other archives, including the Wisconsin Historical Society.

Courter, Ellis W. *Michigan's Copper Country*. Lansing, Mich. Michigan Department of Natural Resources, 1994.

Drier, Roy W. *Copper Country Tales*. Calumet, Mich., 1967.

Dodge, R.L. *Michigan Ghost Towns Of The Upper Peninsula*. Glendon Publishing, 1973. Reprint 1996.

Frimodig, David Mac. *Keweenaw Character: The Foundation of Michigan's Copper Country*. Lake Linden, Mich., Forster, 1990.

Holmio, Armas K.E. Translated by Ellen M. Ryynanen. *History of the Finns In Michigan*. Detroit: Wayne State University Press, 2001.

Lankton, Larry D. *Cradle to Grave: Life, Work, and Death at the Lake Superior Copper Mines*. New York: Oxford University Press, 1991.

Lankton, Larry D., and Hyde, Charles K. *Old Reliable: An Illustrated History of the Quincy Mining Company*. Hancock, Mich.: Quincy Mine Hoist Association, 1982.

Monette, Clarence J. Lake Linden, Mich. (55-plus books of Keweenaw history, including Calumet)

Murdoch, Angus. *Boom Copper: The Story of the First U.S. Mining Boom*. New York: Macmillan, 1943.

Thurner, Arthur W. *Calumet Copper and People*. Hancock, Mich.: 1974.

　*Rebels on the Range: The Michigan Copper Miners' Strike of 1913-1914*. Lake Linden, Mich.: Forster, 1984.

Voelker, Charles. *Copper Country Reflections* at www.pasty.com.

Back page: Strike leader, "Big Annie" Klobuchar Clemenc, 1913

(Heroine) Big Annie Clements
of the Michigan Copper Country Strike - 1913
Calumet, Michigan